Paul Revere – Artisan, Businessman, and Patriot

The Man Behind the Myth

The Paul Revere
Memorial Association
Boston, Massachusetts

The exhibition and catalogue were funded in part by a grant from the
National Endowment for the Humanities, a federal agency, with additional
support from the Massachusetts Society of the Cincinnati, Paul Revere
Chapter of the Daughters of the American Revolution, Eugene F. Fay
Trust and an anonymous donation.

The Exhibition
17 April 1988—19 March 1989
Museum of Our National Heritage,
Lexington, Massachusetts

Contributing Authors

Patrick M. Leehey
Coordinator of Education and Research
Paul Revere Memorial Association

Janine E. Skerry
Assistant Curator
Historic Deerfield

Deborah A. Federhen
Curator
Society for the Preservation
of Long Island Antiquities

Edgard Moreno
Silver Consultant

Edith J. Steblecki
Coordinator of Collections,
Research and Programs
Paul Revere Memorial Association

This book was designed by
Deborah Kehoe, and
assisted by Martha
Podren. The text was set
at Dix Type Inc., in
Bodoni Book, and printed
by Meridian Printing on
Mohawk Superfine.

Copyright © 1988
Paul Revere Memorial
Association
All rights reserved
Printed in the United
States of America

Distributed by the AASLH
Library in association with
University Publishing
Associates
4720 Boston Way
Lanham, Maryland 20706
3 Henrietta Street
London WC2E 8LU
England

ISBN 0-9619999-0-X
(Cloth)
ISBN 0-9619999-1-8
(Paper)

Library of Congress
Catalog Card Number
88-4460

Photography Credits:
© Herbert K. Barnett
Fig. 42, Cat. Nos.
105 + 134
David Bohl
Figs. 3, 35, 49, 50
Cat. Nos. 101, 103, 104,
155
John Miller Documents
Figs. 5, 6, 22, 26, 38, 39,
40, 43, 44, 46, 47, 48
Cat. Nos. 13, 15, 24–25,
26, 29, 32, 46, 81–82, 118,
122, 131, 137, 165, 172,
203, 221 + 234
Mark Sexton
Cat. Nos. 96 + 219

Contents

Foreword and Acknowledgments

Eighty years ago, on 18 April 1908, the Paul Revere House opened to the public as a house museum. Though the immediate agenda of the Paul Revere Memorial Association had been to save the house from continued deterioration and threatened destruction, their actual objectives proved to be much broader. The Association's original statement of purpose set the following goals:

> the pursuit of historical interests, with particular attention to the life of Paul Revere, to the end that an understanding of our heritage may be actively fostered; the preservation of the house known as Paul Revere's as a historical and architectural landmark; and the education of the public hereto.

This exhibition and catalogue, produced to honor the eightieth anniversary of the opening of the museum, though beyond the scope of what was imagined at the time, are consistent with, and are, in fact, logical extensions of the Association's original intentions.

Beginning with its choice of noted architect Joseph E. Chandler to restore the house, the Association has continued to solicit the advice of prominent scholars to inform its decisions and direct its research. In the mid-1970s, this commitment and the need for improved management resulted in the hiring of a professional staff. This particular project provides evidence of how far this active collaboration has taken the Association.

In the last ten years, a primary focus for the Association has been research and the development of new interpretations of Paul Revere, his life and work, and his place in eighteenth- and early nineteenth-century Boston. As is so often the case with historical figures elevated to the status of "romantic hero," the most widely held image of the person, though initially appealing, is ultimately limited and unsatisfying. In Revere's case, the desire to place him among the pantheon of American patriots in the struggle for independence has obscured his vital role in the economic and social life of Boston and America during the late colonial and early national periods.

This exhibition and catalogue go beyond the myths to present a balanced and more complete picture of Revere, placing his family, business, and public life in proper perspective and examining them within the context of the social, political, and economic climate of Revere's own time. Through this reinterpretation Revere becomes an example of important trends in eighteenth- and nineteenth-century life which are imbedded in larger themes from social, economic, and political history. These themes include assessments of the significance of Revere's rise from artisan to entrepreneur and its effect on his political and economic status in the Boston community; his development as a businessman and the effect of the Revolution and the policies of the new nation on that development; aspects of eighteenth-century urban family life; and Revere's social and political affiliations and their influence on his business decisions and on his life and family.

The final impetus for the development of this particular exhibition and catalogue was a growing awareness on the part of the Association staff that while we have been successful in expanding our interpretation at the House, it continues to be frustrating and difficult to try to force a complete interpretation into the neat package that visitors are able to assimilate in the context of a single visit to a small house museum. The opportunity to collaborate with the Museum of Our National Heritage provided the perfect avenue for developing a project of a size and type not feasible at our own site and presenting a broader and more complete interpretation of Paul Revere while examining themes that provide new insight into the study of life and work in Revolutionary and Federal Boston.

Clearly a project of this magnitude requires the insights and energies of a great many people over a number of years. At the top of this list are former Association directors, Frank Rigg and Patricia Sullivan. As the first professional director, Frank Rigg set the stage by renewing the Association's commitment to scholarship and introducing careful interpretation. Patricia Sullivan initiated this project and guided the Association through the initial planning phases. Without their direction and enthusiasm, and the encouragement and support of the officers and members of the Association, there would be no exhibition or catalogue.

Certainly no show is possible without the cooperation of the lenders. We are truly grateful to all who generously agreed to share their collections with the public through this exhibition. For institutional lenders participation requires the work of many hands in many departments. To all the directors, curators, registrars, and their assistants who attended committee meetings, signed forms, supplied information, mailed photographs, and wrapped and shipped objects; your understanding, attention to detail, and professionalism are genuinely appreciated.

As the major repositories of Revere materials, the Massachusetts Historical Society and the Museum of Fine Arts, Boston, must be singled out for their enormous and significant contributions to this project. From the outset, both institutions have extended to us every courtesy. Their collections were essential to our work in both the research and display phases. In particular, special thanks to Jonathan Fairbanks, Pat Loiko and Ned Cooke from the MFA, and Louis L. Tucker, Ross Urquhart and Peter Drummey from the MHS for your advice, expertise, and support.

Throughout this entire project, we have had the invaluable assistance of Dr. William M. Fowler, Jr., Edgard Moreno, and Janine Skerry who served as special consultants. As an experienced publisher and historian, Bill Fowler provided sage counsel during the planning and implementation phases for both the exhibition and catalogue. Ed Moreno and Janine Skerry ably guided us through the very specialized field of Revere silver by selecting and interpreting pieces that were appropriate for use in the exhibition.

Additionally, we are indebted to those authors whose work on Revere preceded ours. In particular, we acknowledge the contributions of Elbridge Goss, Esther Forbes, Clarence Brigham and Kathryn Buhler.

This catalogue was also a collaborative venture. It reflects the scholarship and skill of all who contributed to it, particularly the authors—Patrick M. Leehey, Edith J. Steblecki, Edgard Moreno, Janine E. Skerry, Jonathan Fairbanks, and Deborah Federhen. The massive job of editing fell to Jonathan Sisk who handled the task with diligence, patience, and sensitivity. Deborah Kehoe's considerable talents as a designer are clearly obvious. Thanks to John Miller for doing his usual masterful job photographing our collection. Special thanks also to Dagmar von Schwerin and Elizabeth Safford.

My personal thanks to the staff members of both the Paul Revere Memorial Association and the Museum of Our National Heritage. For us at the Association it was often difficult to maintain a balance between the demands of our own site and the demands of a major off-site exhibition and catalogue. Thanks to my staff at the PRMA, Mike McBride, Heather Smith, and Sybil Johnson for consistently going the extra mile and above all to co-curators Pat Leehey and Edith Steblecki for your determination, insights, scholarship, enthusiasm, and all the hours. To the staff at the Museum of Our National Heritage, Laura Roberts, Millie Rahn, Jackie Oak, Addis Osborne, and John Hamilton, the exhibition clearly bears the mark of your collective experience and professionalism. Special thanks to Clem Silvestro for supporting the idea of a joint venture and to Barbara Franco for somehow managing to keep it all under control.

Finally, the Association wishes to thank the National Endowment for the Humanities and all our sponsors for their generous support.

Nina Zannieri
Project Director
Director, Paul Revere Memorial Association
1 November 1987

Lenders to The Exhibition

American Antiquarian Society

Anonymous

The Boston Athenaeum

The Boston Public Library

The Bostonian Society

John Carter Brown Library, Brown University

Sterling and Francine Clark Art Institute

William L. Clements Library, University of Michigan

Commonwealth of Massachusetts, Archives Division

The Connecticut Historical Society

Dedham Historical Society

Essex Institute

Grand Lodge of Masons in Massachusetts

Harvard University Art Museums, Fogg Art Museum

Historic Deerfield, Inc.

Lodge of Saint Andrew

Massachusetts Charitable Mechanic Association

Massachusetts Historical Society

Massachusetts Medical Society

The Metropolitan Museum of Art

Morristown National Historical Park

Museum of Art, Rhode Island School of Design

Museum of Fine Arts, Boston

Museum of Our National Heritage

New England Historic Genealogical Society

Old North Church

Old Sturbridge Village

Paul Revere Memorial Association

Saint Stephen's Church

Washington Lodge

The Henry du Pont Winterthur Museum

Worcester Art Museum

Worcester Historical Museum

Yale University Art Gallery

Introduction

Boston was 105 years old when Apollos Rivoire, the Huguenot immigrant, and his wife had their first son. When Rivoire married Deborah Hitchborn in the year 1729, he married into an old Boston family. Their baby was christened with the father's Anglicized name, Paul Revere, and that young child is the subject of this catalogue and exhibition. The elder Revere had learned the mysteries and art of his goldsmith work from Boston's finest worker in silver, John Coney (1655/6–1722). Coney died before Revere completed his apprenticeship, but not before endowing the newcomer with great skill and a superb sense of design. Revere passed this knowledge on to his son, who later became one of America's best-known patriots. In 1754 the elder Revere died. Through his widow's right to continue his shop, the elder Revere's business remained in the family and his son and namesake was left at age nineteen to carry on the family work. With the exception of military service, Revere worked as a silversmith for nearly half a century. He was phenomenally productive. Numerous pieces of silver from his shop grace not only the silver galleries in the Museum of Fine Arts, Boston, but also are owned in many other collections, both public and private, throughout the nation. Revere personally described the main occupation, by which he supported his family, as "my Goldsmith's business." Yet he also engaged in an amazing range of other enterprises. These included merchandising, dentistry, copperplate engraving, cannon and bell founding. During his mature years, he developed a major copper rolling industry in Canton, Massachusetts, which successfully competed with imported British copper at a time when the young nation needed to assert its independence.

As the new nation emerged from its colonial or provincial status, Revere the individual and his works matured and expanded in scope and enterprise. Starting with a small shop and ending with an industry, which was large in scale for its day, Revere's work evolved from craftsmanship in Boston's North End to, finally, in his mature years, entrepreneurship and a gentleman's country seat in Canton. Parallels between the emergent nation and Revere's own personal development must have given the craftsman/entrepreneur an acute sense of his place in history.

Without his participation in both continuity and change in America, it would be hard to explain why Revere posed for the three life-size portraits that are extant today. They represent different phases in his life: youth, maturity, and old age. No other colonial or Federal craftsman in this country is as well documented by portraits. Revere's portraits reflect the purpose often cited for early portraiture—to record important men of honor and thereby inspire future generations to noble deeds.

The earliest image of Revere is John Singleton Copley's justly famous half-length oil made in the mid-1760s when both the painter and silversmith were in their thirties. Revere is depicted wearing a vest and shirt seated behind a table, facing the viewer almost directly. Copley painted the craftsman as he contemplates his work, holding a teapot in his left hand, and his chin in his right. Revere, it seems, may be planning to engrave the teapot. A large leather covered sandbag, used for maneuvering the teapot during the engraving process, supports the foot of the teapot. Two burins and a needle used for engraving are on the highly polished table. This painting is an example of the hard-edged, candid provincial portrait tradition which matured over four generations in America. In Copley's hands it came to full flower, just as Revere and his works in silver represent the penultimate colonial mastery that had evolved over the same span of time.

The second portrait of Revere was made in Philadelphia in 1800 by profile artist Charles Balthazar Julien Fevret de Saint-Memin. Revere is pictured at age sixty-five in a classical, almost cameo-like pose. He is dressed in a fashionable high-collar coat, befitting a respected foundryman, honored mason, and successful businessman, just as he was entering his life's most ambitious endeavor, the production of rolled copper. Revere's face is unlined, and his hair, combed forward at the forehead where it is cut short like that of a noble Roman senator, is his own, not a wig. In the period, the plumpness of his face would have been regarded as a sign of prosperity.

The third portrait shows Revere at age seventy-seven, with snow white hair. It was painted by Gilbert Stuart in 1813, five years before the silversmith's death. Though Revere's face shows signs of age, the clear, intense brown eyes reflect a still vital personality. The painting was conceived as a pendant to Stuart's portrait of Revere's wife, Rachel Walker Revere, which was finished only weeks before her death in 1813. The couple's eldest surviving son, Joseph Warren Revere (1777-1868), was probably instrumental in commissioning the paintings.

Taken as a group, the portraits of Revere offer a range of styles which were almost exactly paralleled in Revere's own work in silver and in the expanding complexity, ambition, and successes of his enterprises. This pictorial record is no accident. Its preservation reveals that Revere and his descendants were aware of their importance in the mainstream of history. Revere's own career reflects in many ways—and was influenced or aided by—the nation's coming of age. As this catalogue documents, Revere was a man of action, profoundly moved by the necessity and opportunity of the nation to find manufacturing, material, and economic freedom. That he was conscious of his part in helping to shape the destiny of the country is documented by his deposition made to the corresponding secretary of the Massachusetts Historical Society, Dr. Jeremy Belknap, in 1798, which recalls his historic ride in April of 1775.

Revere in his day was known to be "cool in thought and ardent in action." His contemporaries described him as bold—a concise profile which defines an essential trait of a successful craftsman or entrepreneur. It is instructive to watch an excellent craftsman at work. The best artisans perceive the meaning of patterns in what they do. They comment upon and improve the material order of society. In the process, the craftsman shapes himself as well as his products or environment. Revere had the additional ability to shape the opinions and actions of others through political cartoons. More importantly, he successfully managed an industry which depended on the coordinated energies and skills of many workmen.

Few American craftsmen stand out as clearly as Paul Revere in the national memory. Undoubtedly, this is due partly to the success of Henry Wadsworth Longfellow's *Paul Revere's Ride*, printed in a variety of publications and recited for generations. But also sustaining the memory of

Revere is his home in Boston's North End, visited by hundreds of thousands of Americans, who search for tangible evidence of history. The house is a unique survivor from seventeenth-century urban Boston. Other than gravestones, precious little remains out of doors in Boston from this earliest period of colonial settlement.

So much has been written about Paul Revere, his life and times, that the reader might wonder what new insight could be offered. As a matter of fact, the exhibition and catalogue bring to light a great deal of new information and fresh analyses. In addition to new discoveries and insights pertaining to his silver, the catalogue contains a systematic study of Revere's New England kinship and French ancestry. His involvement with civic responsibilities, fraternal organizations, and voluntary associations is lucidly articulated in context with the era of enlightenment. Success and management of the copper mills at Canton are analyzed in detail, revealing how extraordinarily complex that enterprise was, how embryonic the support technology was, and how marginal was the chance of success. Revere the silversmith, founder, and entrepreneur discovered resources to make the mills a success, providing copper sheathing for the Massachusetts State House dome, for coppering the hulls of United States naval vessels, such as *U.S.S. Constitution*, and making plates for Robert Fulton's steam boilers in New York. Such achievements helped build the material substance of the fledgling nation.

Jonathan L. Fairbanks
Katharine Lane Weems Curator of American
Decorative Arts and Sculpture
Museum of Fine Arts, Boston
1 November 1987

Figures 1 + 2

Bookplates presumed to
have been engraved by
Paul Revere Sr. in the
1720s and by his son Paul
Revere ca. 1758 for their
own use. The coat of arms
on each plate resembles
the coat of arms of the De
Rivoire family of eastern
France though no connec-
tion between the families
has ever been established.
(Cat. Nos. 2 and 4.) Courtesy, American Antiquar-
ian Society.

Reconstructing Paul Revere

An Overview of His Ancestry, Life, and Work

Patrick M. Leehey

For nearly half a century after his death, the name of Paul Revere lapsed into relative obscurity (except in the metals trade where "Paul Revere and Son" continued to be a respected firm). That began to change, however, in 1861 when Henry Wadsworth Longfellow published a popular lyrical poem entitled "Paul Revere's Ride." Within a few years, and particularly following the centennial of his famed midnight journey to Lexington and Concord, Revere had come to symbolize the American patriotic spirit. His part in early American history was soon publicized in articles, books, and popular songs.

In many ways, history has been kind to Paul Revere, allowing him to represent the quintessence of American patriotism and craftsmanship. In the process of endowing his life with these mythic qualities, however, we have lost sight of the diverse influences and activities that shaped his life. As many as one-third of the settlers in British North America claimed, like Revere, non-English ancestors. His father, born Apollos Rivoire but known throughout his adult life as Paul Revere, was a descendant of French Huguenots from the Bordeaux region in southwestern France. The first of his family to emigrate to the New World, Paul Revere Sr., as he will be known in this volume, traveled to Boston in his early teens where he entered an apprenticeship with a prominent goldsmith. Paul Revere's mother, on the other hand, had descended from several families with roots already well planted in New England's soil. Though Revere maintained a keen interest in his father's French background, as evidenced by his extended correspondence with two Old World relatives, his mother's New England relatives exerted far more influence on his career, providing indispensable financial assistance and business opportunities.

While family was the primary force in Revere's life, other associations affected him as well. In addition to his many business relationships, Revere was also a prominent Freemason, a lifelong member of the Seventh Congregational ("New Brick") Church, a member of numerous political clubs in the years prior to the Revolutionary War, and a prominent member of many civic and voluntary organizations after the war. From these organizations, as well as family and neighbors, he drew many of the customers who patronized his businesses.

Revere has often been seen as either a well-to-do colonial dignitary or quintessential workingman and proletarian hero. In reality he was neither. A craftsman by birth and training, he owned his own shop and was a member of the economic class referred to as "mechanicks"—shopowners, manufacturers, and lesser merchants—who made up the bulk of the population in an urban port such as Boston. Socially superior to the "lesser sort"—journeymen, laborers, sailors, and servants—mechanics were nonetheless inferior to the "better sort," a small group of merchants, shopowners, lawyers, and clerics who were the leaders of colonial society. Although Revere achieved much throughout his life and became quite wealthy, he failed to ascend completely into the highest ranks of Federal

Paul Revere's Paternal Ancestors — The Rivoires

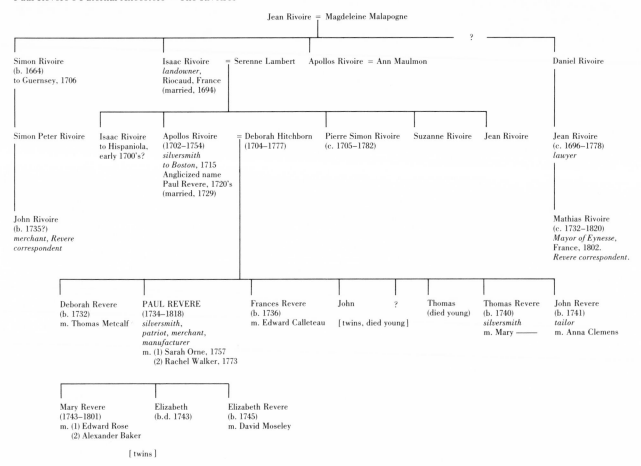

society—the existing social barriers ultimately proved insurmountable for the son of a French immigrant goldsmith.

This, in brief, is the outline of Paul Revere's life. This essay, and those that follow, are intended to continue the process of re-establishing a balanced view of his life, a process begun with considerable success in Esther Forbes's Pulitzer-prize-winning biography, *Paul Revere and the World He Lived In* (1942). Still, we have much to learn about the different aspects of Revere's experience, particularly his ancestry and the vital role family played in his life, his involvement in philanthropic and other voluntary associations, his business activities (especially his increasingly diverse interests in the post-Revolutionary War years), and his contributions to the early years of the American Industrial Revolution. As we weave these aspects of his experience into the fabric of his reputation as a historical figure, Paul Revere becomes a multifaceted individual who was able to take advantage of the opportunities one century offered the son of a French immigrant artisan while helping to lead the way into the next.

The Rivoires of Ste. Foye la Grande
The story of Paul Revere's French ancestry can be traced to southwestern France and to the increasing repression of its Protestant community in the seventeenth century. Jean Rivoire, Revere's great-grandfather and earliest-known French ancestor, married Magdeleine Malapogne in the mid-1600s (Chart 1). Although it is not known exactly where Jean and Magdeleine were born, their descendants could be found in a number of small villages and hamlets centered around the town of Ste. Foye la Grande, on the lower Dordogne River, about forty miles east of Bordeaux

Figure 3

A New and Accurate Map of France with it's Aquisitions. Drawn by Eman! Bowen, ca. 1747. Locations relating to the Rivoire family are indicated: Ste. Foye, Vienne, and the Island of Guernsey. Courtesy, Massachusetts Historical Society.

(Fig. 3). Revere's grandparents lived in Riocaud, a small village located a few miles south of Ste. Foye; several of Revere's cousins and contemporaries owned land in Martet, a hamlet of the village of Eynesse several miles away.[1] Since the sixteenth century, southwestern France had been a center of the French Huguenot (Calvinist) faith. After years of civil war, Huguenots were granted limited political and religious autonomy in 1598 when King Henry IV, himself a former Protestant, issued the Edict of Nantes. Although they lost most of their political rights in the early seventeenth century, the Huguenots maintained their religious liberties until the early years of the reign of King Louis XIV, when systematic persecution began. In 1685 Louis XIV revoked the Edict of Nantes, outlawing protestantism in France and driving thousands of Huguenots into exile or hiding.[2]

Although it cannot be known for certain in the case of Paul Revere's direct ancestors (due to gaps in existing records), most of the descendants of Jean and Magdeleine Rivoire were Protestant.[3] Most remained in the Ste. Foye la Grande area; of those, a number may have become *nouveaux convertis* (new converts), as former Protestants who converted to catholicism to keep their property and other civil and political rights were known. The state authorities were suspicious of *nouveax convertis*, however, and watched them constantly for signs of reversion.[4]

Jean and Magdeleine Malapogne Rivoire had three sons: Simon, Isaac, and Apollos. Simon, the eldest (born 1664), was one of the few Rivoires to leave France at the time of the Revocation. According to information in letters later exchanged between Paul Revere and his European relatives, "in the time of persecution" Simon fled with his master, a surgeon, to Holland, and later (1706) settled in Guernsey, one of the two principal Channel Islands. Simon married and was the father of two sons, Simon Peter and William. Simon Peter in turn was the father of John and William Rivoire, contemporaries of Paul Revere. Paul Revere corresponded extensively with his cousin John in the years surrounding the American War of Independence and these letters are an important source for recovering Revere's French ancestry.[5]

By the 1780s John Rivoire, a bachelor, had by his own account been appointed harbormaster of St. Peter's Port (the principal town of Guernsey) as well as receiver-general of the Estates of Guernsey, receiver of funds for the Royal Hospital at Greenwich, and captain of the local militia.[6] As he described in some detail, John Rivoire had previously been involved with his brother, William, shipping wine and wheat between Barcelona and Quebec. After William was lost at sea in November 1771, John discovered to his chagrin that his brother had concealed many of his activities, and left him with a debt of near £2000. John Rivoire stated that he had been able to pay off this debt, but only with difficulty, and at the expense of his business activities.[7] In several letters written in the early 1780s (prior to the signing of the Treaty of Paris), John tried to convince his American cousin that the American-French alliance was a mistake, and that if the English and the Americans would only patch up their differences, together they might "laugh at the world."[8] John also frequently advised his cousin concerning prices that might be had for various New England goods in Guernsey and asked for consignments. In particular he was interested in "St. Croix and St. Kitts rum" selling at 2 shillings 6 pence per gallon local measure, as well as New England rum, oak pipe staves, hogsheads, pitch, planks, and other lumber goods. In return he wished to ship Bohea tea, wine, brandy, and other "India goods."[9] John repeatedly stressed the advantages of shipping goods to or from Guernsey, where they would be "free of all duties."[10] The only remaining male Rivoire in Guernsey, John mentioned several times that he intended to marry. As of the early 1780s, however, he had not. He offered his hospitality to his American cousin, but regretted that although in the past he might have been able to travel to the New World for a visit, to do so at that time would mean giving up his many advantageous appointments in Guernsey.[11]

In the years following the Revocation, Simon Rivoire's younger brothers, Isaac and Apollos, remained in the Ste. Foye la Grande area. Little is known about Apollos, other than that he and his wife, Ann Maulmon, were recorded as godparents to Isaac's son, Apollos (Paul Revere's father).[12] Isaac Rivoire of Riocaud (a village located a few miles south of Ste. Foye la Grande) married Serenne Lambert in 1694. Isaac Rivoire seems to have been a man of some substance in his locality: he was listed second (as Isaac Rivoire, *Bourgeois*) on the Capitation Tax Roll for Riocaud in 1720. His tax was 7 livres, 17 sous for that year, and he is listed as having one tenant (*metayer*, or sharecropper).[13] The fact that Isaac and Serenne were relatively well-to-do, at least by 1720, may explain why they did not emigrate to the New World, and suggests that they may have become *nouveax convertis*.

Isaac and Serenne Lambert Rivoire had five children: Isaac, Apollos, Pierre Simon, Suzanne, and Jean. Isaac, the oldest, emigrated to Hispaniola, where he became a planter. Pierre Simon (1705-1782) remained in France and was referred to several times in Paul's correspondence with Mathias as the possible source of a considerable estate (most of which seems to have gone to another nephew, Simon Merveilhaud). Suzanne Rivoire married Pierre Merveilhaud, Simon Merveilhaud's father. Jean, the youngest son, married Marie Guibert; their son Jean married Magdelaine Merveilhaud, Simon Merveilhaud's sister. By the 1780s both Simon and his widowed sister owned land in Riocaud, as did Pierre Simon—all three of these estates were probably portions of land originally owned by Paul Revere's grandfather, Isaac.[14]

Paul learned of Mathias in Ste. Foye la Grande through his correspondence with his cousin John in Guernsey. Mathias Rivoire was a slightly more distant cousin of Revere's than John. He was the son of Jean and Marie Constant Rivoire, and was born about 1732 in Martet, a hamlet of the village of Eynesse located a few miles downstream from Ste. Foye la Grande. Following his father's death in 1778, Mathias inherited the family estate, including a house which is still standing in Martet. Mathias Rivoire married twice, and was the father of five children. In 1802 he served as mayor of Eynesse. He died in 1820.[15]

Paul's correspondence with Mathias was hindered by the fact that Mathias knew only French, while Revere wrote only in English. In an early letter, Mathias requested that Paul have his letters translated prior to sending them, "for without a person who is the only one here who knows English I could not understand your letters."[16] In this same letter, Mathias referred to several members of the Rivoire family in Ste. Foye and the surrounding villages, and answered Paul's questions about his ancestry as best as he was able. Mathias claimed he was Revere's second cousin, but listed his father, grandfather, and great-grandfather as Jean, Daniel, and Daniel, respectively, making him Paul's fourth cousin at best. Mathias informed Revere that he had asked John Rivoire for a copy of the family "coat of arms" but had never received it. He repeated this request of Revere, who stated in a later letter that he had a seal with the coat of arms sent, along with an engraving of George Washington. Mathias acknowledged receipt of the seal and engraving, but could not enlighten Revere as to the source of the coat of arms.[17] John wrote to Revere on the same subject, stating that his grandfather Simon had brought the coat of arms with him when he settled in Guernsey. Revere's father probably acquired a copy when he stopped in Guernsey in 1715, prior to his departure for Boston. Both Paul Sr. and Paul engraved bookplates showing the coat of arms as their family insignia (Figs. 1 and 2).[18]

In a March 1782 letter, Mathias included an extract from a private family record that is the only known source for the birth and early life of Paul Revere's father. Following the Revocation of the Edict of Nantes, Huguenot baptisms, marriages, and burials were not recognized or recorded by the state. Private records were kept by local Huguenot pastors or by the families themselves. These records, however, were often lost or destroyed. The "Records of the Children of Jean Rivoire" from which Mathias stated he copied his extract were probably just such a private account. According to Mathias, these family records were in the possession of his relative, Simon Merveilhaud, at the time he examined them. We must accept Mathias's word that he copied the records accurately, or even that they existed at all, as the original document has never been found. The portion referring to Apollos read in part:

Apollos Rivoire our son was born on the thirtieth of November, 1702 about ten o'clock at night, was baptized at Riaucaud [Riocaud]. Apollos my brother was his godfather, Ann Maulmon my sister-in-law his godmother. He set out for Guernsey the 21st of November, 1715.[19]

That Apollos Rivoire traveled alone to the New World was not unusual at the time. Protestant families that chose to remain in France after the Revocation often sent their children abroad, to prevent their being taken from them by the state (a real possibility if the authorities suspected that the children were being raised secretly as Protestants). At age thirteen, Paul Sr. was sent by his parents to his uncle Simon in Guernsey, who arranged for his passage to Boston, and for his apprenticeship there as a

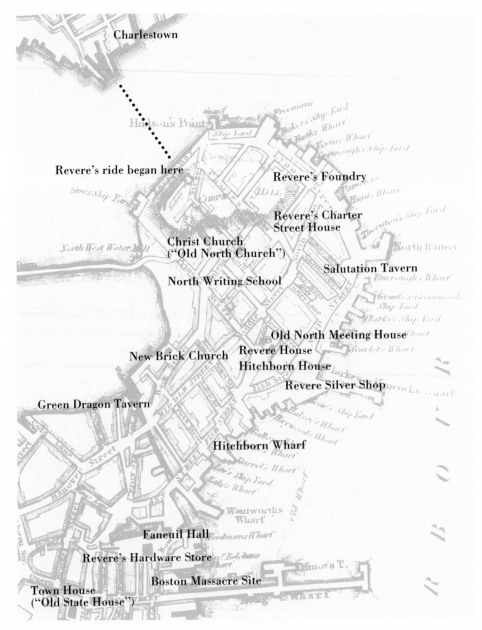

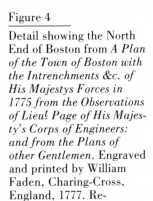

Figure 4

Detail showing the North End of Boston from *A Plan of the Town of Boston with the Intrenchments &c. of His Majestys Forces in 1775 from the Observations of Lieu! Page of His Majesty's Corps of Engineers: and from the Plans of other Gentlemen*. Engraved and printed by William Faden, Charing-Cross, England, 1777. Re-engraved in 1849. Courtesy, Bostonian Society.

goldsmith.[20] He arrived in Boston in early 1716, and was apprenticed to the English-speaking goldsmith John Coney, one of the most prominent in his day. Coney died in 1722, at which time Paul Sr. had three years remaining on his indenture, valued at £30 on Coney's estate inventory. A notation on the inventory records that "Paul Rivoire," as he now called himself, was able to purchase the remaining three years of his indenture for £40 ("Cash received for Paul Rivoires Time, more than it was prized at £10").[21] Sometime in the 1720s, possibly after working as a journeyman, Paul Sr. established his own goldsmithing shop in the vicinity of Dock Square in the center of Boston.[22] Unlike many Huguenot refugees in Boston, who joined Anglican churches in addition to their own French church on School Street, Paul Sr. (and, later, his children) joined the Congregational New Brick ("Cockerel") Church, located on Middle (today's Hanover) Street in the North End. There is no evidence that Paul Sr. ever joined the French Church, which by the 1720s was rapidly being transformed into an aristocratic, essentially memorial, congregation (Paul Sr. may have felt more comfortable in the more plebeian North End Church).[23] His surname is recorded in various spellings in the 1720s (Rivoire, Reviere, Revear); after settling on Paul Rivoire for a time, he finally adopted the name Paul Revere sometime prior to his marriage. On 19 June 1729, Paul Sr. married Deborah Hitchborn, daughter of a local artisan and wharfowner; soon afterwards he moved his home and business from the vicinity of the Town Dock into the North End.[24] At the time that Paul Revere was born late in 1734, the Revere house and shop was probably located at or near the corner of Love Lane (now Tileston Street) and Middle Street, a few doors away from the New Brick Church (Fig. 4).[25]

The Hitchborns: Paul Revere's New England Heritage

Deborah Hitchborn Revere was the descendant of a number of New England families, most of whom were already established in the New World well before 1660 (Chart 2). Her great-grandfather, David Hitchborn, sailed from Boston, England, to Massachusetts in 1641, along with his wife, Catherine, and their one-year-old son, Thomas. David Hitchborn appears in public records only once, when sentenced to wear an iron collar for an unknown offense.[26] David and Catherine's son Thomas was described by Revere biographer Esther Forbes as a "lively, picturesque fellow," who once went outside the law to settle a debt by confiscating shoes from Grimstone Bowd.[27] In an entry in his diary, Samuel Sewell described Thomas Hitchborn leading a procession advertising a "Challenge" (duel) to be fought a few days later:

> *Another Challenge goes with his naked sword through the Street with Hitchborn, drummer, and a person carrying a quarterstaff.*[28]

Thomas and Ruth Hitchborn's son, Thomas II (1673-1731), a joiner, was the first in the family to own a small wharf at Ann and Cross Streets in the North End, usually referred to as Hitchborn's Wharf, which included a "mansion house" and other buildings. That the Hitchborn wharf was small is shown by the fact that it does not appear on any period maps.[29] According to an entry in his diary dated 10 September 1747, Benjamin Bangs of Eastham, Massachusetts, docked at "Hitchbon's" wharf to sell wood and unload mackerel; four days later he moved to the "yard" to "grave" his vessel.[30] In addition to repairing boats and unloading cargo, Thomas probably constructed boats. He received a license to sell liquor at his wharf as well.[31]

In 1703, Thomas Hitchborn II married Frances Pattishall (1676–1749). She was the daughter of Captain Richard Pattishall, who had emigrated to the New World with his parents in the mid-1600s. Captain Pattishall acquired large amounts of land in Maine, as well as a house and wharf in Boston. He was killed by Indians while aboard his sloop off Pemaquid, Maine, in 1689. As a boy, Paul Revere would visit his great-aunt, Anne Pattishall Thomas, another daughter of Captain Pattishall, to hear how his ancestor had been butchered.[32] Captain Pattishall's second wife, Martha Woody (Frances's mother), was the descendant of both Captain Richard Woody (soap-boiler and saltpetre manufacturer) of Roxbury, and Thomas Dexter, a large landowner and "promoter" of the Saugus Iron Works. The Woody family was well known in both Roxbury and Boston—in 1673 the entire family was dismissed from the Third Church of Boston.[33]

Thomas II and Frances Pattishall Hitchborn had six children (three girls, three boys), two of whom, Nathaniel and Richard, died young. Thomas Hitchborn III, the only surviving son, inherited the bulk of his mother's estate, including Hitchborn Wharf. As noted previously, Deborah (1704–1777), the oldest daughter, married Paul Revere Sr. in 1729.

Paul Revere's Maternal Ancestors—The Hitchborns

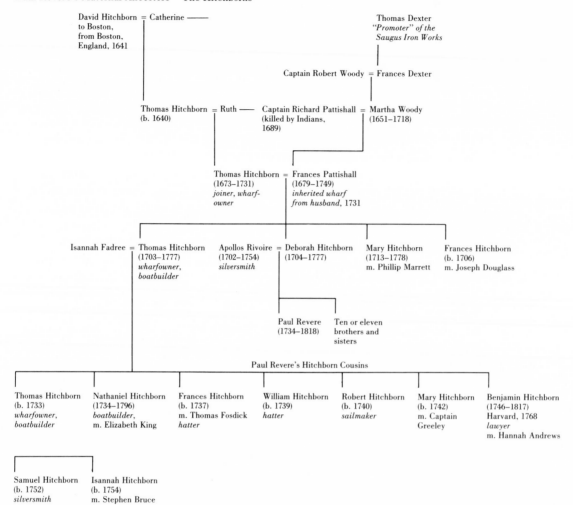

Mary (1713–1778) married Captain Phillip Marrett while Frances married first John Montgomery, and then Joseph Douglass. (Phillip Marrett, son of Phillip and Mary Hitchborn Marrett, served under his cousin Paul Revere at Castle Island in Boston Harbor during the Revolutionary War.)[34]

Following her husband's death in 1731, Frances Pattishall Hitchborn continued to operate the wharf in her own name and inherited her husband's liquor license.[35] In the early 1740s, Paul's family appears to have rented living quarters from Deborah's mother. According to Frances Pattishall Hitchborn's will, after bequeathing the bulk of her estate (including a Negro boy) to her son, Thomas III, she left "To my daughter Reveer, named Deborah, 1½ years rent for her house she now lives in."[36] In February 1743, Deborah, along with her sisters, Mary and Frances, sold their shares in the family wharf to their brother, Thomas III. After leaving Hitchborn wharf, the Revere family probably moved directly to Clark's wharf, where Paul Sr. rented a house and shop, and where his son Paul began his apprenticeship.[37]

Thomas Hitchborn III married Isannah Fadree, with whom he had ten children: Thomas IV, Nathaniel, William, Samuel, Robert, Benjamin,

Phillip, Frances, Mary, and Isannah. Thomas III seems to have done reasonably well as a wharfowner and boatbuilder. His sons (with possibly one exception) apprenticed well; his second youngest, Benjamin, attended Harvard. Thomas IV, the oldest (born 1733), eventually inherited the family wharf; Nathaniel (born 1734) became a boatbuilder, and his younger brother Robert (born in 1740) a sailmaker. Both Nathaniel and Robert probably worked for their father and then their brother at Hitchborn Wharf.[38] On 12 July 1781, Nathaniel purchased a three-story brick house on North Square, two doors away from the house of his cousin Paul Revere.[39] Nathaniel Hitchborn married Elizabeth King; their son Samuel Hitchborn, Jr., a sailmaker, inherited part of his uncle's house after his death in 1797.[40] Robert Hitchborn seems to have had financial difficulties at times and was forced to borrow money from his cousin Paul to pay for his son's education. William Hitchborn (born 1739) became a hatter, and his younger brother Samuel (born 1752) a goldsmith. As a young man, Samuel may have apprenticed with his older cousin Paul Revere.[41] Both Samuel and his older brother Benjamin assisted Revere at the time he was establishing his foundry business in the North End, lending him money and paying some of his bills.[42]

Thomas IV and Isannah's three daughters married and seem to have lived comfortably. Frances (born 1737) married Thomas Fosdick, a hatter, in 1756 (Thomas's brother, Nathaniel Fosdick, was a lifelong customer of Revere's). Frances's second husband was General John Glover of Marblehead. Mary Hitchborn (born 1742) married a Captain Greeley, and Isannah (born 1744) married Stephen Bruce.[43] The death of Phillip Hitchborn (born 1744), the only one of Thomas IV and Isannah's children who died young, was described in a contemporary document: "hearing the cry of Fire [Phillip] ran out of his master's shop (a taylor) which so chilled his blood that he fell into a Lethargy and expired soon after."[44]

Benjamin (1746–1817), the second youngest son of Thomas and Isannah Fadree Hitchborn, was the best known of the Hitchborn family in his time, and probably better known to his contemporaries than his cousin Paul Revere. Although both were sons of artisans, only Benjamin managed to ascend completely into the upper class of Boston society, an achievement that probably reflected no more than that his paternal ancestors had settled in New England several generations before Revere's father, and had acquired modest property. Paul Revere was frequently associated with his younger cousin, but seemed to maintain a respectful distance, as would be appropriate in relation to a person of a somewhat higher station.

In colonial artisan families, one particularly gifted son was often designated to receive a higher education; the rest of the family were then expected to sacrifice to accumulate the necessary funds. Benjamin Hitchborn apparently took advantage of just such an opportunity. He attended Harvard College (Class of 1768), received an M.A., and then read law with Samuel Fitch. In rapid succession he was admitted to the Suffolk Bar (1771) and qualified to practice before the Inferior Courts (1772) and Massachusetts Superior Courts (1774). Benjamin became a successful attorney with an upper class clientele. In the 1780s and 1790s, the Suffolk

Bar was accustomed to meet at "Brother Hitchborn's office" where many of the best young lawyers in Boston received their initial training.[45]

Soon after the outbreak of the Revolutionary War, Benjamin and fellow patriot Perez Morton organized the Boston Independent Corps, an elite group of militia. The Independents, as they were known, took part in the first Fourth of July Celebration in Boston in 1777 (along with a detachment of militia from Paul Revere's command at Castle Island) and participated in both unsuccessful expeditions to dislodge the British at Newport, Rhode Island, after which both Hitchborn and Morton resigned their commissions. Paul Revere also took part in both Rhode Island expeditions, as an officer of artillery, and he occasionally referred to his cousin Hitchborn in his orderly book.[46]

Not long after he resigned his commission, Benjamin was involved in the incident that came to be known as the "Hitchborn Murder." While visiting his friend Benjamin Andrews at his home in Boston, Hitchborn handed Andrews a pistol he had been cleaning; the weapon discharged, mortally wounding Andrews in the head. Slightly more than one year later Benjamin married Andrews's widow, Hannah, provoking scandalous rumors that persisted for years. The couple lived in a house on Brattle Street and later purchased a house in Dorchester.[47]

Like his cousin Paul, Benjamin Hitchborn served on a number of public committees both during and after the Revolutionary War, and was a founder or member of several civic and voluntary associations. He was a member of the Committee of Inspection, Correspondence, and Safety (1777), and later served on the committee to obtain the incorporation of Boston as a city. He was one of the founders of the Massachusetts Fire Insurance Company, of which Paul Revere and his son Joseph Warren were also members. As a member of Boston's upper class, Benjamin possessed the necessary prerequisites to run for public office. In the 1790s he served as representative to the Massachusetts House from Boston and Dorchester; in 1801 he was elected state senator from Norfolk. Benjamin Hitchborn was a personal friend of Presidents Jefferson and Monroe. He died on 15 September 1817, just eight days after President Monroe visited him at his brother Samuel's home in Boston.[48]

The Hitchborn family has sometimes been perceived as Paul Revere's "poor cousins," and their influence on his life overlooked in favor of his more exotic French ancestry. In reality, several of the Hitchborns were reasonably well-to-do, and their influence on the early life of Paul Revere was probably greater than that of his father's French heritage. Paul Sr. arrived in Boston alone at age thirteen and apprenticed with an English-speaking master; he had little, if any, contact with the small French Protestant community in Boston at the time; his surviving silver pieces are thoroughly English in style; when he married Deborah Hitchborn he was certainly allying himself with a family of his equals, and may have been consciously "marrying up" into a large, well-established landowning New England family. Though their influence has often been overlooked, the Hitchborn family clearly played a leading role in Paul Revere's life.

An Artisan Family

Paul Revere Sr. and Deborah Hitchborn had eleven or possibly twelve children, seven of whom survived to adulthood (Chart 1). Paul was the oldest surviving son (and, incidentally, the only Revere child to receive a non-Hitchborn first name).[49] The baptisms of Paul Sr. and Deborah's surviving children were recorded in the records of the New Brick Church.[50]

Deborah, Paul's older sister, was born in 1732 and married Thomas Metcalf in 1759. Frances, the next youngest sister (born 1736), married Edward Calleteau, whose name suggests a Huguenot origin. Thomas (born 1740) probably apprenticed in his father's shop along with his older brother Paul, and may have been the "Mr. Rivoire" referred to in a letter dated 12 January 1775, written by John Rivoire to his cousin Paul in Boston:

> *Our Cousin Mathias Rivoire of Martel [Martet] near Ste. Foye . . .*
> *writes me there is a Mr. Rivoire of New England now in France, un-*
> *doubtedly he must be one of your brothers or your son . . . I should be*
> *very glad to see this Rivoire in Guernsey.*

Several pieces of silver fashioned by Thomas have survived to the present day.[51] Paul and Thomas's younger brother John (born 1741) married Ann Clemens and apparently became a tailor. Mary Revere (born 1743) married twice, first to Edward Rose, with whom she had several children, and then to Alexander Baker. She died in December 1801 and was buried at Copp's Hill Burying Ground in the North End. The youngest child, Elizabeth (born January 1745), married David Moseley. It is not known where or when she died.[52]

Paul Sr. was sufficiently prosperous to help support the *two* ministers of the New Brick Church in the 1740s; his name was included on a subscription list drawn up on 28 January 1747, as "Paul Revere . . . £0/4/0."[53] The elder Paul Revere died on 22 July 1754 and was buried near his Hitchborn relatives in the Granary Burying Ground. According to one of Paul's letters to his cousin Mathias, Paul Revere Sr. "left no estate, but he left a good name and seven children, three sons and four daughters." Deborah Hitchborn Revere outlived her husband by twenty-three years, and died at the home of her son Paul in May 1777.[54]

Paul Revere, patriot, goldsmith, and early American industrialist, was born in December 1734, "New Style," and baptized on 1 January 1735 (22 December 1734 "Old Style" as actually recorded in the New Brick Church records).[55] He attended the North Writing School on Love Lane, and then apprenticed with his father. In the 1740s he was hired, along with several other boys, as a bellringer at Christ Church, known today as the "Old North Church," where the signal lanterns were hung the night of his famous express ride to Lexington in April 1775. When his father died, Paul, nineteen, was too young, by law, to inherit his father's goldsmith shop. It

Paul Revere's Family

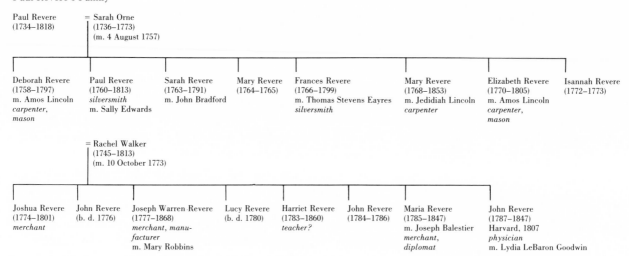

is likely that his mother, or possibly an unknown journeyman, became the formal proprietor while Paul and his younger brother Thomas probably carried on the family business.[56] Early in 1756, the year that marked the beginning of what would become known as the "Seven Years War" in Europe and the third year of the "New French and Indian War" in North America, Paul was commissioned a second lieutenant of artillery in the Massachusetts expedition sent to capture the French fort at Crown Point, in what is now New York. "French and Indian" warfare was endemic in North America in the colonial era, and only became more intense whenever formal war was declared in Europe. In this war, the French were eventually driven out of both Canada and India. The Crown Point expedition was a failure, however, and Revere returned to Boston, where he assumed responsibility for his father's goldsmith shop.[57] Soon afterwards, on 17 August 1757, he married Sarah Orne (1736–1773) from a predominantly artisan family of Salem and Boston.[58] Paul Revere joined the St. Andrew's Lodge in 1760, beginning an association with Freemasonry that would last most of his working life and provide him with numerous personal and business contacts. Members of St. Andrew's Lodge, primarily artisans, met most often at the Green Dragon Tavern (owned by the lodge) on Union Street, near the Mill Creek not far from Dock Square. Also known as "Freemason's Arms," the Green Dragon would later be one of the meeting places of the North End Caucus, a patriot group that included many St. Andrew's masons.[59]

Paul and Sarah Orne Revere had eight children, two of whom died young (Chart 3). Their oldest daughter, Deborah (1758–1797), married Amos Lincoln, who later served under his father-in-law during the Revolutionary War. Amos and Deborah had eight children. Paul and Sarah's oldest son, Paul Jr. (1760-1813), apprenticed with his father, but his training was disrupted by the political agitation and economic instability that preceded the Revolutionary War, and he never achieved the technical ability of his father (judging by his few surviving pieces of silver and gold work). In the 1780s Paul Jr. assumed formal control of the family silver shop, as his father became increasingly involved in other enterprises. Paul Jr. married Sally Edwards (1761–1808) with whom he had twelve children and today their descendants are particularly numerous. Paul and Sarah's second daughter, Sarah (1762–1791), married John Bradford; their third daughter, Frances (1766–1799), married Thomas Stevens Eayres, a promising young goldsmith who later went insane. Eayres probably apprenticed with his father-in-law, and then attempted to establish his own shop. After he became incapacitated, Eayres was partially supported by his father-in-law Paul. Eayres's son, Thomas Stevens Eayres, Jr., later joined with two other Revere descendants (Joseph Warren Revere, Paul's son by his second wife, Rachel Walker, and Paul Revere III, oldest surviving son of Paul Jr. and Sally Edwards Revere) to assume legal ownership of the Revere family businesses when Paul retired in 1811. Paul and Sarah's fourth surviving daughter, Mary (1768–1853), married Amos Lincoln's brother, Jedidiah, in 1797, less than one month after her younger sister Elizabeth (1770–1805) married the recently widowed Amos. Jedidiah and Mary Revere Lincoln had seven children; Amos and Elizabeth Revere Lincoln had five. The lives and marriages of Paul and Sarah Orne Revere's daughters illustrate several important aspects of family life in colonial America. Families were large, and often interrelated in ways that seem unusual by today's standards (the Revere-Lincoln marriages); and mortality was high, especially among women who married and had children. Elizabeth Revere Lincoln, Frances Revere Eayres, and Sarah Revere Bradford died at the ages of thirty-five, thirty-three, and twenty-nine respectively. Their mother, Sarah, died at the age of thirty-nine (in 1773), not long after the birth of her eighth child.[60]

A Prominent Craftsman and Political Agitator

Paul Revere is considered to have been one of colonial America's most competent goldsmiths, whose work is valued as much for its artistic as for its historic value. It is now known that Revere was also one of Boston's most prominent craftsmen, the proprietor of a large shop with apprentices (including his sons and relatives) and probably journeymen employees, and with a network of associated and subsidiary craftsmen. As a leading Boston artisan-manufacturer, Revere used his family, neighborhood, masonic, and political contacts to secure customers and acquire orders. Revere's extensive business records reveal that many of his customers belonged to St. Andrew's Lodge, the North End Caucus, and other organizations to which he belonged.[61]

In addition to fashioning silver and gold pieces for wealthy and lesser customers, Revere cut numerous copperplate engravings, including such everyday items as trade cards, bookplates, mastheads, and illustrations for broadsides and magazines (Fig. 6), as well as more specialized works, such as a complete set of plates for a volume of music.[62] Revere also practiced dentistry, to the extent that his skill allowed. He sold dentifrice, cleaned teeth, and wired in false teeth. (However, he never made a set of dentures for George Washington, as is sometimes believed; such a task was beyond his ability.[63]) Revere's business activities were disrupted repeatedly by the political unrest of the years 1760–1775. He was a member of the loosely organized "Sons of Liberty" Whig Club as well as the North End Caucus, of which he was a founder. Revere also produced numerous satirical engravings, including his famous "Boston Massacre" print. The North End Caucus met variously at the Salutation Inn, on Salutation Street near the North Battery in the North End, and the Green Dragon

Figure 6

The Gerbua or Yerboa.
Line engraving by Paul
Revere for the *Royal
American Magazine*, I
(XVI) November 1774.
Taken from an engraving
that appeared in *Gentle-
man's Magazine*, London,
April 1768. (Cat. No. 102.)
Courtesy, Paul Revere
Memorial Association.

Figure 7

Gold wedding ring be-
lieved to have been made
by Paul Revere in 1773 for
his second wife, Rachel
Walker Revere (Cat. No.
10). Courtesy, Museum of
Fine Arts Boston. Gift of
Mrs. Henry B. Chapin and
Edward H. R. Revere
(56.585).

Tavern. Patriot leaders from outside the North End (particularly Samuel
and John Adams) often attended these meetings. According to tradition,
the "Boston Tea Party" incident was planned at the Green Dragon in late
November and early December 1773; Revere, along with many of his artisan neighbors and fellow masons, may have taken part in the actual destruction of the tea.[64]

In February 1770, Paul purchased the seventeenth-century wooden
house on North Square, in the North End, which still stands.[65] On 3 May
1773, Revere's wife, Sarah, died. On 10 October 1773, he married Rachel
Walker (1745–1813), daughter of Richard Walker and Rachel Carlile of
Boston (Fig. 7). Paul and Rachel Walker Revere had eight children, three
of whom died young (Chart 3). Joshua, Paul and Rachel's oldest son, was
born in 1774 and died in 1801, at the age of twenty-seven. Joshua was
probably involved in his father's postwar businesses. The "pain in his
chest" which he referred to in a letter written to his father while on a
business trip to Portland, Maine, probably led to an illness that caused his
early death.[66] Their second son, Joseph Warren Revere (1777–1868),
named after Revere's friend and fellow patriot Dr. Joseph Warren, was
involved in all of his father's postwar businesses. In 1805 he undertook an
extended trip to several European countries to obtain the latest technical
information about metallurgy. In 1811, Joseph combined with his nephews
Paul Revere III and Thomas Eayres, Jr. to assume control of the Revere
family businesses. Joseph married Mary Robbins, with whom he had eight
children.[67]

Harriet (1782–1860), Paul and Rachel's oldest surviving daughter,
never married and died at the age of seventy-eight at the family's home in
Canton, Massachusetts. Maria (1785–1847), her younger sister, married
Joseph Balestier, businessman and diplomat, and accompanied him to
Singapore in the 1830s. John (1787–1847), Paul and Rachel's youngest
child, attended Harvard and then completed his education at the Univer-

sity of Edinburgh. John later taught at Jefferson College in Philadelphia, conducted innovative scientific experiments, and became a professor at New York University. He married Lydia LeBaron Goodwin (1785–1854) with whom he had four children, one of whom, General Joseph Warren Revere, traveled to France in the 1870s in search of his grandfather's French ancestors.[68]

In the 1770s, the Massachusetts government employed Paul Revere as a courier to carry messages, news, and legislative enactments as far as New York and Philadelphia. On the night of 18 April 1775, he was detailed to ride from Boston to Lexington to warn Samuel Adams and John Hancock that British regular troops were marching to arrest them. As he "alarumed" the countryside, "minutemen," the local militia, gathered and confronted the troops at Lexington Common, where the first skirmish of the Revolutionary War took place. Although bills exist for many of Revere's other rides, none has ever been found for this most famous mission indicating that he may have considered his journey to Lexington to be in the nature of a volunteer effort.[69] For almost a year after this confrontation, British troops occupied Boston. During this time, Revere continued to aid the Revolutionary cause by printing bills both to raise funds and pay the militia.[70] On 10 April 1776, following the British withdrawal from Boston, Revere was commissioned a major in the Massachusetts Militia, but was soon transferred to the Massachusetts State's Train of Artillery, where he became a lieutenant colonel in November 1776. The State's Train was headquartered in Boston, but Revere was stationed most often at "The Castle," one of the forts guarding the entrance to Boston Harbor. As the British never attempted to reoccupy Boston, Revere's command quickly degenerated into keeping his men from deserting and presiding over numerous "courts-martial" dealing with minor disciplinary problems. In the spring of 1777, an artillery detachment commanded by Revere marched to Worcester to collect British prisoners captured at the Battle of Bennington. Later in the same year, and then again in the summer of 1778, Revere and the State's Train of Artillery took part in the unsuccessful expeditions to dislodge the British in Newport, Rhode Island.[71] Soon after his second return from Rhode Island, Revere was placed in command of the artillery on the ill-fated Massachusetts expedition to capture a British fort at Castine, Maine, near the mouth of the Penobscot River. Lack of cooperation among the American commanders was rendered irrelevant by panic at the arrival of a small British squadron. The leaderless American forces made their way back to Boston as best as they could; Revere was accused of failure to follow orders, and although he was formally cleared a few years later (1782), these charges ended his military career in 1779.[72]

Manufacturer and Public Servant

Following his dismissal Revere resumed his business career, but was restricted at first by the suspension of trade with England pending the signing of the Treaty of Paris in 1783, and the economic disruption brought on by six years of war. Writing to Mathias in 1781, Revere revealed that he did "intend to have gone wholly into trade, but the principle part of my interest I lent to government, which I have not been able to draw out, so I must content myself until I can do better." (In the same letter, he adds that he was "in middling circumstances, and very well off for a tradesman."[73])

Figures 8 + 9

Portraits of Paul and
Rachel Revere, painted by
Gilbert Stuart, 1813. Commissioned by the Revere's
son, Joseph Warren Re-
vere, the portraits were
completed only a few

weeks before Rachel's
death (Cat. Nos. 20 and
21). Courtesy, Museum of
Fine Arts, Boston. Gifts of
Joseph W., William B.,
and Edward H. R. Revere
(30.782 and 783).

As was often the case with successful artisans, Revere wished to advance into the ranks of the merchant class. For a number of years in the
1780s and 1790s, he operated a "Hardware Store" at various locations in
central Boston, where he sold locally made and imported goods as well as
items fashioned at the family goldsmith shop (by then under the formal
proprietorship of Paul Jr.).[74] Following the formal conclusion of the war in
1783, Revere was able to order the large quantities of English merchandise he needed to stock his store, but he experienced considerable difficulty paying for his early shipments and obtaining credit with London
wholesalers. In June 1783, Revere wrote to Frederick Geyer in London,
ordering merchandise and asking for the "longest customary credit," explaining that he should be able to pay on time "as my dependence for a
living will chiefly depend on the Goldsmith's business, which will be carried on by my son, under my inspection." Later in the same year, Revere
explained to Geyer that his money was still tied up in government securi-
ties, and asked that his credit be extended further, and more merchandise
sent. He informed Geyer that partial payment would arrive through a Captain Byfield Laide, consisting of "three hundred and forty Spanish Milled
Dollars besides four ingots of silver," one of which was a "composition of
mettals the sweep of a Goldsmith's shop" and another "gold lace burned
and melted."[75] Geyer eventually refused to ship any more merchandise,
and Revere was forced to turn to other London wholesalers, with whom he
had many of the same difficulties.

Revere eventually abandoned the hardware business to concentrate on his newly established foundry (or foundries), the earliest of which was in operation in 1788.[76] By the 1790s, he was supplying North End shipyards with large quantities of bolts, spikes, and nails (as well as cannon) from his foundry on Lynn and Foster Streets, opposite the Hartt shipyard. Revere supplied the bulk of the brass fittings for *U.S.S. Constitution*, built at the Hartt yard in the 1790s; he also crafted a silver tea service for the Hartt family.[77] In addition to shipfittings and cannon, Revere also cast bells, many of which can be found today in New England churches.[78] In 1800, Revere purchased the site of an old gunpowder mill in Canton, Massachusetts, which he converted into one of the first successful mills for rolling sheet copper in the United States. In the early 1800s, possibly after his Boston foundry had been damaged in a storm, Revere transferred his casting operations to Canton. He continued, however, to sell his products in Boston, either from his newly purchased home on Charter Street or from a separate office.[79]

Although Paul Revere concentrated most of his energies after the Revolutionary War on his business affairs, he did serve as an appointed public official on several occasions, including terms as county coroner and president of the board of health.[80] He also helped found a number of civic and voluntary associations.[81] Revere enjoyed unusual popularity as one of the recognized leaders of the "Mechanick" or artisan class in Boston. In spite of its name, this group consisted primarily of shopowners and manufacturers, who on several occasions organized to further their own interests, usually in association with Boston's merchant and commercial classes. In 1785, Revere was probably involved in artisan agitation in favor of increased tariffs on imported goods.[82] Three years later he presided over a large meeting of "Tradesmen and Manufacturers" at the Green Dragon, where resolutions in favor of the proposed United States Constitution were adopted; these resolutions were then carried in procession to the Massachusetts Ratifying Convention.[83] In the 1790s, Revere was one of the first members and perhaps one of the founders, of the Massachusetts Charitable Mechanic Association, organized to further the economic interests of Boston's tradesmen and to provide relief for distressed members.[84]

Although Revere never ran for a national or state elective office, he did aspire to be appointed the first director of the United States Mint or, failing that, to be appointed to the Custom's Service. He received neither appointment for reasons referred to obliquely in letters from Massachusetts representative Fisher Ames.[85] Revere opposed many of the policies of the Jefferson and Madison administrations, as reflected in several letters and in at least one attempt at satiric poetry. Revere's copper business also kept him involved in national issues, particularly with respect to tariffs on imported raw and manufactured goods.[86]

Paul Revere's sheet copper rolling mill established on the site of an old gunpowder mill in Canton, south of Boston, proved to be his last and most lucrative business, making him a wealthy man by the time he retired in 1811. After some initial difficulties Revere was able to manufacture copper sheets in sufficient quantities to supply customers both famous and ordinary. Although *U.S.S. Constitution* was plated with English copper when it was constructed in the 1790s, Revere supplied the sheets when it was recoppered in the early 1800s. Revere copper sheets were used to plate the dome of the "New State House" on Beacon Hill (since covered with gold leaf) and the dome of New North Church (now St. Stephen's Church) in the North End, and to construct boilers for several of Robert

Fulton's Hudson River steamboats. Revere also continued to cast bells for a variety of customers.

English copper provided Revere's chief competition in many of the markets in which he dealt. This was particularly true in New York, where there was a large demand for "brazier" copper—lightweight sheets used by coppersmiths to fashion cookware, utensils, and similar items—as well as the heavier sheets suitable for plating ships. Revere wished to acquire a larger share of the New York market, but felt that he was unfairly discriminated against by the existing laws setting tariffs on manufactured and scrap copper. Beginning in 1806 he attempted for almost a decade to have these laws revised to his advantage.[87] He first petitioned Treasury Secretary Albert Gallatin directly in April 1806, explaining in detail why he felt the duty charged on imported scrap copper sheets (Revere's primary raw material) was contrary to existing regulations:

> By the Act of Congress, Copper in _Plates_, _Pigs_, and _Barrs_ are free; but Copper Manufactures are charged with a duty of seventeen and one-half percent. We are at a loss to account why the Collectors take no duty on New Sheet Copper . . . calling them plates; when under the Article of Pewter (tho old pewter is free) yet _Plates_ are charged with a duty of 4 cents pr. pound. We have never heard that Copper, with which ships bottoms are covered, called by the name of plates, but sheets . . . but tho a large proportion of the Old Copper which is imported here, is what is ripped off ships bottoms, and is in sheets, yet they take a duty.[88]

Unable to convince the secretary that scrap copper sheets were not liable for a duty, Revere next formally petitioned the United States Congress (1807) to remove the duty on scrap copper and place a duty on imported English sheets. Revere felt that these sheets were in fact a manufactured product, usable as received, and not "plates" (flattened pigs of irregular thickness and shape) under which term they were being imported.[89] The Revere petition was referred to the Committee of Commerce and Manufactures, which after considering it, as well as counterpetitions presented by New York and Philadelphia coppersmiths, came to the following two conclusions:

> Resolved, _That so much of the petition as prays for the imposition of seventeen and an half per centum ad valorem as a duty on copper manufactured into sheets, is unreasonable, and ought not be granted._
> Resolved, _That so much of the petition as prays that old copper may be considered as a raw material, and that the importation thereof into the United States may be free from duty, is reasonable, and ought to be granted._

In his petition, Revere stressed that were English copper excluded from New York, his copper works had the capacity to supply the New York braziers and coppersmiths. This in particular the committee did not believe, which was their primary reason for not recommending that a duty be placed on imported copper sheets.[90]

Although the duty on scrap copper was removed, Revere was not satisfied. In 1810 he applied again, unsuccessfully, to Gabriel Duval, comptroller of the Treasury Department, for a duty to be placed on imported sheet copper. Later in the same year, Revere again petitioned Congress (this time conceding that "brazier" copper should not be liable for a duty), but was unsuccessful. Even as late as 1815, Revere was writing to Soloman Isaacs, his former agent in the New York City area, about the possibility of obtaining a duty on English copper.[91]

Paul Revere "retired" from his various businesses in 1811, transferring ownership of "Paul Revere and Son" to his son Joseph Warren and his grandsons Paul Revere III and Thomas Stevens Eayres, Jr. in a series of transactions, all of which were dated 1 March 1811.[92] Although no longer the formal proprietor of the family business, Revere remained actively involved until just before his death. In 1813, both his son Paul Jr., and Paul's second wife, Rachel, died. Paul Revere died at his home on Charter Street, in the North End, on 10 May 1818 and was laid to rest in the Granary Burying Ground on Tremont Street near the Boston Common. The *Boston Intelligencer* of 16 May 1818 carried his obituary, which read in part:

> *Such was Col. Revere. Cool in thought, ardent in action, he was well adapted to form plans, and to carry them into successful execution, —both for the benefit of himself & the service of others. In the early scenes of our revolutionary drama, which were laid in this metropolis, as well as at a later period of its progress, his country found him one of her most zealous and active sons. His ample property, which his industry and perseverance had enabled him to amass, was always at the service of indigent worth, and open to the solicitations of friendship, or the claims of more intimate connections. His opinions upon the events and vicissitudes of life, were always sound and formed upon an accurate observation of nature and an extensive experience. His advice was therefore as valuable as it was readily proffered to misfortune. A long life, free from the frequent afflictions of diseases, was the consequence of constant bodily exercise, & regular habits,—and he has died in a good old age & all which generally attends it.*

One of his biographers, E. H. Goss, quotes several individuals who had known Revere personally including Rowland Ellis, then of Newton Center, Massachusetts, whose description of Revere as "a thick set, round faced, not very tall person, who always wore small-clothes" is decidedly less dignified. Another person, whom Goss does not identify, described Revere as:

> *A Prosperous North End Mechanic, quietly but energetically, pushing his business interests. He had an organizing brain, great judgement and courage, a determined will, unfailing energy, and remarkable executive ability. He was a born leader of the people, and his influence was pervading, especially among the mechanics and workingmen of Boston, with whom his popularity was immense.*[93]

Paul Revere's contemporaries knew him as an innovative craftsman, enterprising businessman, public-spirited citizen, and responsible family man. The passage of time, a romantic poem, and the need for national symbols have transformed him into a disembodied figure on a horse crying an alarm in the dark.

Notes

1.
Although Ste. Foye la Grande today is a substantial town, the village of Riocaud and the hamlet of Martet cannot be found on any generally available modern map of France. Andre J. Labatut, "Paul Revere, hero of the American Revolution (1735–1818) and his cousins of Ste. Foye en Agenais in France" (Unpublished manuscript, New England Historic and Genealogical Society, Boston [NEHGS], and Paul Revere Memorial Association, Paul Revere House, Boston [PRMA]) has included a photocopy of a portion of a map from a 1772 French atlas which shows Riocaud and the surrounding villages and hamlets. Esther Forbes, *Paul Revere and the World He Lived In* (Boston, 1942) and others' characterization of Ste. Foye la Grande, Riocaud, and Martet as a "triple village" or something similar, is entirely fanciful (and misleading) and was the result of the unavailability of maps of sufficient detail. Labatut also notes the correct spelling of locations and names associated with Revere's ancestry: For example, Riocaud instead of Riancaud, Martet instead of Martel, Magdeleine Malapogne instead of Madelaine Malaperge.
2.
Altogether between one hundred thousand and two hundred thousand Huguenots left France as a result of the Revocation; of these, only a few thousand emigrated to British North America, and perhaps two hundred overall to New England prior to 1700. The bulk of the Huguenot refugees left in the years 1680–1690; later Huguenot immigrants (as well as those leaving prior to 1680) often had little to do with the "Revocation" exiles in the countries where they settled. Paul Revere's father, who arrived in Boston in the early 1700s, was a typical example of a later Huguenot immigrant.

Information about the Huguenot immigration to the New World can be found in Jon Butler, *The Huguenots in America: A Refugee People in New World Society* (Cambridge, 1983), and Charles W. Baird, *History of the Huguenot Emigration to America*, 2 vols. (1885; reprint, Baltimore, 1966). A brief treatment of the Huguenot experience in France from the sixteenth century to the present can be found in Nancy L. Roelker, *The French Huguenots: An Embattled Minority* (St. Louis, 1977).

3.
Labatut, 1, 2 (note 4).
4.
Butler, chapter 1, *passim*; Roelker, 8–9.
5.
Most of what is known about Paul Revere's ancestors in France can be found in letters written to Revere by his cousins John Rivoire in Guernsey and Mathias Rivoire in France. The series of letters, unfortunately incomplete, are in the Revere Family Papers in the Massachusetts Historical Society, Boston, Massachusetts. All quotations are by permission. The letters are in the loose manuscripts, and were also copied into a letterbook by an unknown person at some later date. When examining the Revere-Rivoire correspondence, it is important to note that the letterbook copies differ at times from the loose manuscript originals. (In one instance there are three copies, all of which differ slightly: A first rough translation into English of a letter from Mathias to Paul dated March 1782; a second copy, probably in Revere's hand, with some of the original text obviously deleted or rearranged; and the letterbook copy.) The quotation referring to John Rivoire's ancestors is from a letter written by John Rivoire to his cousin Paul, dated 23 September 1784. Unless otherwise stated, all letters to or from John Rivoire or Mathias Rivoire are from the Revere Family Papers, and will be cited by the initials of the sender and recipient, followed by a date.

Further genealogical information about Revere's French ancestors can be found in Herbert Eugene Revere and Robert Rodgers, "A Record of Ancestors and Descendants of Paul Revere," no date, unpublished manuscript available at NEHGS and PRMA. See also Elbridge Henry Goss, *The Life of Colonel Paul Revere* (Boston, 1899), 6; and Forbes, 5, 488-89.

For information on the Huguenot immigration to the Channel Islands, see David T. Koenig, "A New Look at the Essex 'French': Ethnic Frictions in Seventeenth Century Essex County, Massachusetts," *Essex Institute Historical Collections*, 110 (July 1974): 167–80. (Many of the Essex "French" were from Jersey, the second of the two principal English Channel Islands.)

6.
Most available information on John Rivoire appears in his letters to Paul Revere. John Rivoire describes his various government posts in JR to PR, 28 January 1781. J.H. Lenfestey, Island Archivist of the States of Guernsey, has to date been unable to confirm any of John Rivoire's official appointments, although he is continuing his search. (He has discovered that a "Jean Rivoire" held a very minor judicial appointment in the 1760s.) John may have been exaggerating the importance of his situation to impress his American cousin.

7.
JR to PR, 12 January 1775; 23 September 1784, RFP.

8.
JR to PR, 28 January 1781 [1782?]; 9 September 1782; and 15 October 1782, RFP.

9.
JR to PR, 12 January 1775; 15 October 1782; 4 March 1783; and 9 March 1786, RFP.

10.
JR to PR, 12 January 1775; and 15 October 1782, RFP.

11.
JR to PR, 4 March 1783; and 23 September 1784, RFP.

12.
MR to PR, March 1782, RFP.

13.
Labatut, 11.

14.
JR to PR, 9 March 1786, RFP; Labatut, 4–8, *passim*, and genealogical table, 12. See also Revere and Rodgers, 3–4.

15.
Labatut, 6.

16.
MR to PR, 8 April 1781, RFP.

17.
MR to PR, March 1782, RFP.

18.
JR to PR, 23 September 1784, RFP. The origin of the Revere coat of arms is obscure at best. In the 1880s, General Joseph Warren Revere, a grandson of Paul Revere, traveled to France in search of his family's ancestry. Near Vienne, in the province of Dauphiny in southeastern France, he discovered a De Rivoire family whose coat of arms was similar to that used by Paul Revere and his father. He collected a considerable amount of information about the De Rivoires. Although he could establish no direct connection, General Revere assumed that his ancestors were related to one of the five branches of the De Rivoires he identified. General Revere's research notes are in the Revere Family Papers, at the MHS. In 1923, Paul Cadman of the State Street Bank and Trust Company of Boston, traveled to France to confirm or refute General Revere's conclusions. Mr. Cadman was able to confirm much of the genealogical information in the Revere-Rivoire correspondence, but he could discover no evidence linking Revere's ancestors with the De Rivoires (other than the coat of arms). See Paul Cadman, *Boston and Some Noted Emigres* (Boston, 1938), 25–37. See Clarence Brigham, *Paul Revere's Engravings* (New York, 1969), 158-66 for a discussion of the coat of arms bookplates used by Paul Revere and his father (facsimiles - plates 52 and 53). See also Goss, 629–33 (which includes a facsimile of the De Rivoire coat of arms). See also Forbes, 467, note 1.

19.
MR to PR, March 1782, RFP. The fact that Mathias refers to the origin of his information as a private record strongly suggests that Isaac and Serenne Rivoire were underground Protestants, even if formally they were Catholics (New Converts).

20.
JR to PR, 12 January 1775, RFP: "My father Simon Rivoire, who defrayed all expenses and sent your father (whom they called Apollos) to Boston to learn the Goldsmith's trade."

21.
John Coney, estate inventory, Suffolk County Probate Records, 15 October 1722 (on microfilm in the Boston Public Library).

22.
Apollos's career as a journeyman is entirely conjectural. Evidence for his shop at the Town Dock is derived from his later advertisement in the *Boston News-Letter* (21 May 1730), where he announced he was moving his shop to the North End.

23.
Forbes, 13; Goss, 11. The New Brick Church ("Cockerel" or 7th Congregational Church) was founded in 1722 as an offshoot of the New North Church on Middle Street in the North End. The Records of the New Brick Church (1722–1779) consisted of three lists: 1) Admission of Members, 2) Owners of the Covenant, and 3) Baptisms. These lists were combined and categorized by surname in Thomas B. Wyman, Jr., "New Brick Church, Boston, List of Persons Connected Therewith from 1722 to 1775. Compiled from the Records," *NEHGR* 18 (1864), 237–40, 337–44; 19 (1865), 230–35, 320–24. A handwritten copy of the records, also categorized by surname, can be found in the Boston City Archives, City Hall, Boston. The original three lists have not been located. The baptisms of nine of Paul Revere Sr.'s children, and five of Paul Revere's first eight children are recorded in the New Brick Church records, along with the baptisms of many other North End families, including the Hitchborns.

Information about the Huguenot Church in Boston can be found in Butler, 65–90; and Baird, 2:220–45.

24.
Goss, 10; Forbes, 13.
25.
Goss, 11.
26.
Forbes, 13, 489. David Hitchborn was sentenced to wear an iron collar "till the court please and serve his master." See also Ed Gordon, "Pierce-Hitchborn House Owners and Occupants 1781–1951," PRMA (unpublished research report), 1.
27.
Forbes, 13–14.
28.
M. Halsey Thomas, ed., *The Diary of Samuel Sewell 1674–1729* (New York, 1973), 138. Thomas Hitchborn may also have been the drummer for a procession the previous Friday, which Sewell described in more colorful terms (137).
29.
Forbes, 13, 488; Gordon, 2.
30.
Benjamin Bangs, Diary, 10 September 1747, MHS. Quoted in Forbes, 469, (Fn. 8).
31.
Gordon, 2; Forbes, 14.
32.
Forbes, 15–16, 468 (Fn. 4), 489.
33.
Ibid., 15, 320, 489–90.
34.
Ibid., 488–89.
35.
Ibid., 17.
36.
Frances Pattishall Hitchborn, Will, Suffolk County Probate Records, 26 December 1749.
37.
Forbes, 29.
38.
Forbes, 68–69; Gordon, 3.
39.
Both Revere's house, at 19–21 North Square, and the Pierce-Hitchborn House, at 29–31 North Square, are standing today and are operated as museums by the Paul Revere Memorial Association. The Pierce-Hitchborn House, built in 1711 for Moses Pierce, a Boston glazier, is a fine example of early Georgian architecture, and was acquired by the PRMA in 1970.
40.
Gordon, 3; Ed Zimmer, "Early History of the Pierce-Hitchborn House and Residents." PRMA (unpublished research report), 7.

41.
Forbes, 68, 403, 480 (Fn. 45).
42.
The Rising States Lodge Record Book, kept by Revere and now in the possession of the Massachusetts Grand Lodge of Masons, Boston, includes numerous entries in the back concerning Revere's early foundry operations, including the following items:
(1787) Dec. 5 - By Cash for Sam¹ Hitchborn to pay Mr Wllm Little's bill £ 10/0/0
(1788) Aug. 12 - By Cash from Col. Benjamin Hitchborn £ -/12/0
Oct. 10 - By Cash (of Sam¹ Hitchborn) for 50 bricks £ 1/6/6
43.
Forbes, 69–70; Gordon, 3.
44.
Quoted in Forbes, 39 (Source uncited).
45.
Forbes, 68; Gordon, 3; Clifford K. Shipton, "Benjamin Hitchborn," *Sibley's Harvard Graduates* (Boston, 1975), 17:36–41.
46.
Forbes, 280, 325–26, 332–33,342; Shipton, 37–39; see also below, note 71.
47.
Forbes, 347–48, 370; Shipton, 39.
48.
Shipton, 40–44.
49.
Forbes, 17, 488; Goss, 11; Revere and Rodgers, 5–6. Revere and Rodgers are the only authorities to list a John Revere (born and died, 1730) as *older* than Paul Revere. They also list twin boys, who also died young. Forbes (p. 16) makes the observation about the Hitchborn origin of the Revere children's names.
50.
Wyman, 19:235.
51.
Kathryn C. Buhler, *American Silver 1655–1825 in the Museum of Fine Arts, Boston,* 2 vols. (Greenwich, CT, 1972), 2:479.
52.
Forbes, 40, 488; Revere and Rodgers, 10-12.
53.
Forbes, 31; Goss, 12–13.
54.
PR to MR, 6 October 1781, RFP.
55.
Wyman, 19:235. Paul Revere was number 347 on the original list of baptisms. The "New Style" Calendar, adopted in the fifteenth century to compensate for the slight inaccuracy in the standard "leap year" calendar, was not generally accepted in the British Empire until 1752. On Revere's date of birth, see also Forbes, 17 and Goss, 11.

56.
Forbes, 21–34; Goss, 14–18.

57.
Paul Revere's commission as second lieutenant of artillery, under the command of Richard Gridley, and the general command of John Winslow, is in the possession of Morristown National Historic Park, Morristown, New Jersey. See also Forbes, 41–47; Goss, 18–22.

58.
Forbes, 58; Goss, 25; Revere and Rodgers, 7. The Worcester Art Museum, Worcester, MA has several silver pieces made by Revere for Dr. William Paine at the time of his marriage to Lois Orne, daughter of Timothy Orne of Salem (1773). These pieces were engraved with the Orne coat of arms and included a coffeepot, teapot, tankard, pair of canns, and other smaller items.

59.
Edith J. Steblecki, *Paul Revere and Free-masonry* (Boston, 1985), 11–27; Forbes, 60–61; Goss, 465–66.

60.
Revere and Rodgers, 23–164; Wyman, 19: 235 (only Paul Jr., Sarah, Mary, Frances, and Isannah were baptised at the New Brick Church). See also Forbes and Goss for some details about Revere's children and other descendants. Letters concerning the affairs of Thomas Stevens Eayres can be found in the Revere Family Papers. On Eayres, see also Forbes, 399–407.

61.
A large number of Paul Revere's business records have survived (wastebooks, letterbooks, memoranda books, cash and stock books, etc.), most of which are in the Revere Family Papers. For a survey of Revere's various business enterprises based partly on his business records, see Ruth L. Friedman, "Artisan to Entrepreneur: The Business Life of Paul Revere," unpublished research paper, on file in the PRMA Library.

62.
For a complete discussion of Paul Revere's career as an engraver, with numerous plates as well as many of the English and American originals from which he often worked, see Brigham, *passim*.

63.
For information on Paul Revere's career as a dentist, see Forbes, 128–33; Goss, 439–47; and Robert I. Goler, *The Healing Arts in Early America* (New York, n.d.).

64.
Forbes, 91–168, *passim*; Goss, 53–175, *passim*; and Appendix C. (635-44), "Proceedings of the North End Caucus."

65.
Paul Revere purchased his now famous home on North Square for £213/6/8 from Captain John Erving, merchant and real estate speculator. The house had been built in 1680 for the merchant Robert Howard. The Revere House is the only remaining seventeenth-century residential structure in the downtown area of a major city in the United States.

66.
Joshua Revere to PR, 9 July 1795, RFP.

67.
For Joseph Warren Revere's trip to Europe, see letters and documents for the year 1805 in RFP. For the formal transfer of ownership of the firm of "Paul Revere and Son" to Paul Revere Jr., Joseph Warren Revere, and Thomas Stevens Eayres, Jr., see documents dated 1 March 1811 in the Revere Family Papers.

Two of Joseph Warren and Mary Robbins Revere's sons, Edward Hutchinson Robbins Revere (1827–1862) and Paul Joseph Revere (1832–1863) fought and died for the Union cause during the Civil War (the former at Antietam and the latter at Gettysburg). Joseph Warren and Mary Robbins Revere's youngest child, Jane Minot Revere, was the mother of John Phillips Reynolds, Jr., who was instrumental in rescuing his great-grandfather's North End wooden home from destruction in the early 1900s.

68.
See Elizabeth Grundy and Jane Triber's "Paul Revere's Children: Coming of Age in the New Nation," (unpublished research report available at PRMA), for information about the lives of Harriet Revere and Maria Revere Balestier. In 1843, Maria Revere Balestier wrote to her brother Joseph Warren Revere describing the arrival of a bell cast in the Revere foundry in Canton. This bell, which was presented to St. Andrew's Church by Mrs. Balestier, is now in the National Museum in Singapore. See Edward Stickney and Evelyn Stickney, *The Bells of Paul Revere, his sons and grandsons* (Bedford, MA, 1976), 29. For information about John Revere, see Grundy and Triber; previously cited; Goss, 645–46; and Alexandra Lee Levin, "John Revere, M.D.," *Maryland Magazine*, 71 (Autumn 1976): 10–13. For the descendants of John and Lydia LeBaron Goodwin Revere, see Revere and Rodgers, 189–90.

69.
Paul Revere's famous ride the night preceding the battles of Lexington and Concord has been described numerous times, often inaccurately. A good narrative account can be found in Arthur B. Tourtellot, *Lexington and Concord* (New York, 1959). Revere himself composed three accounts of his own activities that night: two drafts of a deposition written just after the events, and a letter written to Dr. Jeremy Belknap of the newly founded Massachusetts Historical Society (1798). All three accounts are in the Revere Family Papers. The Massachusetts State Archives has several bills submitted by Revere for courier (and other) work in 1774 and 1775.

70.
The most complete discussion of Revere's work printing currency can be found in Brigham, 141–63.

71.
The Orderly Book for the Massachusetts State's Train covering the period from June 1777 to December 1778 has been printed in James Kimball, "Orderly Book for the Regiment of Artillery Raised for the Defense of the Town of Boston in 1776," *Essex Institute Historical Collections*, 13 (1876): 237–52; 14 (1877): 60–76, 110–28, 188–211. Paul Revere's Orderly Book for the Second Rhode Island Expedition (1778) is in the Revere Family Papers, Volume 55. Further material on Revere's career in the Massachusetts Militia prior to the Penobscot Expedition can be found in Forbes, 317–45; and Goss, 277–314 (which includes facsimiles of Revere's commissions and extracts from both Orderly Books and other materials).

72.
The Penobscot Expedition has been the subject of a number of articles and scholarly studies, including: William M. Fowler, Jr. "Disaster at Penobscot Bay," *Harvard Magazine* (July-August 1979): 26–31; Russell Bourne, "The Penobscot Fiasco," *American Heritage* (October, 1974): 28–33, 100–101; and Chester B. Kevitt, *Solomon Lovell and the Penobscot Expedition 1779* (Weymouth, Mass., 1976). See also Forbes, 351–65; Goss, 317–93.

73.
PR to MR, 6 October 1781, RFP.

74.
Forbes, 371-72; Goss, 527-30.

75.
See PR to Frederick Geyer, 30 June and 3 November 1783, RFP.

76.
In a letter to Brown and Benson, founders, in Rhode Island, in November 1788, Revere announced that "We have got our Furnass agoing, and find that it answers our expectations." Entries in the back of the Rising States Lodge Record Book suggest that the foundry may have been in operation as early as 1787.

77.
Goss, 530–38, 544–49; Forbes, 391–94. Buhler, *American Silver*, 464–66 (see especially items 414-16).

78.
See Stickney and Stickney. Of more than 300 bells known to have been manufactured by "Paul Revere and Son," 134 are in existence. Of these, 23 are known to have been manufactured during Revere's active involvement in the firm (prior to his retirement in 1811). Revere bells are often to be found in churches in quite small and out of the way New England towns.

79.
Forbes, 424–28; Goss, 553–61.

80.
See Revere Family Papers, vol. 51 (Memoranda book 1796–98) for numerous coroner's oaths. A copy of the 1799 document issued by Revere as president of the board of health which includes instructions for the proper emptying of privies, is in the possession of the Revere family. See also Goss, 589.

81.
In addition to the Massachusetts Charitable Mechanic Association and several Masonic Lodges, Revere was a member of the Boston Library Society, the Boston Humane Society, and the Massachusetts Charitable Fire Society. Receipts for payments of dues to these various societies can be found in the Revere Family Papers. See also Goss, 589–90; Forbes, 482.

82.
Gary Kornblith, "From Artisans to Businessman: Master Mechanics in New England, 1789–1850," (Ph.D. diss., Princeton University, 1983), 54–71.

83.
Kornblith, 72–78; Goss, 451–52; Forbes, 383.

84.
Kornblith, 79–119, *passim*; Goss, 583–88.

85.
The only source for Revere's ambition to be appointed director of the United States Mint or to the Customs Service are two letters written to Revere by Fisher Ames, 26 April 1789, and 24 January 1791. Ames seemed to imply that Revere would not be able to obtain either post due to his known Federalist sympathies. Both Ames letters are in the Revere Family Papers and are also quoted in full in Goss, 460–62.

86.
PR to Thomas Ramsden, 4 August 1804, RFP. Revere includes the following sentiments:

My friend, you know I was always a warm Republican; *I always deprecated* Democracy *as much as I did* Aristocracy. *Our Government is now completely democratic; they turn every person out of office who are not, nor will be of their way of thinking and acting.*

The Revere Family Papers also include this poem or fragment (loose manuscripts undated, listed as 1811):

What great and good men fetters our National Ship/Ore shoals, and thro' Rocks; how they make her to skip/Sage Jefferson's Captain; Brave Madison's mate/Both sailors; both Soldiers; how happy our fate/Secretary Monroe's, a friend to Old-France/He offer'd them money; was willing to dance.

Some of Revere's antagonism to the Jefferson and Madison administrations may have been the result of his difficulties with the government over the copper tariff issue.

87.
See Mark Bortman, "Paul Revere and Sons and Their Jewish Correspondents," *Publications of the American Jewish Historical Society*, 43 (1953–54): 199–229. Harmon Hendricks, Soloman Isaacs, and Haym Salomon, with whom the article is primarily concerned, were wholesalers and manufacturers of copper in the New York area. Isaacs in particular acted as Revere's business agent from time to time.

88.
Draft of a petition to Albert Gallatin, Secretary of the Treasury, enclosed in a letter from Paul Revere and Son to Josiah Quincy, 3 April 1806.

89.
Draft of a petition to the House of Representatives and the Senate of the United States, 12 February 1807, Revere Family Papers, Loose Manuscripts. Revere followed up his petition with a long letter to Josiah Quincy in support of his point of view. In this letter Revere goes into great detail about the technicalities of the copper business, explaining the differences between plates, bars, pigs, and sheets, and surveying the current sources of ore and used copper.

90.
Report of the Committee of Commerce and Manufactures, To Whom Were Referred, On the Second and Thirteenth of November, and the Eighteenth of December Last, the Petitions and Memorial of Paul and Joseph W. Revere, of Boston in the State of Massachusetts, of Sundry Coppersmiths in the City and Liberties of Philadelphia, and of Sundry Manufacturers of Copper in the City of New York (Washington, 1808). (Copy from the collection of the PRMA.)

91.
Gabriel Duvall to Paul Revere and Son, 4 September 1810, Paul Revere and Joseph Warren Revere, Draft of a Petition to Congress to Impose a Tariff on Imported Copper, addressed to James Prince, 10 December 1810, RFP; Bortman, 223.

92.
Agreement dissolving the firm of Paul Revere and Son with Transfer of property to Joseph Warren Revere; Lease of Canton Foundry; Mortgage of Paul Revere and Son Property in Canton and Sharon to Joseph Warren Revere; Agreement between Joseph Warren Revere, Paul Revere Jr., and Thomas Stevens Eayres, Jr. for the continuation of the firm of Paul Revere and Son. RFP, Loose Manuscripts. All of the documents are dated 1 March 1811.

93.
Goss, 610–611.

Figure 10

Front and back of a punch bowl made by Paul Revere in 1768. It commemorates the action of the ninety-two members of the Massachusetts House of Representatives who voted not to rescind their letter protesting the Townshend Acts. H. 5½ in., Diam. (lip) 11 in. Courtesy, Museum of Fine Arts, Boston. Gift by subscription and Francis Bartlett Fund (49.45).

The Revolutionary Revere

A Critical Assessment of
the Silver of Paul Revere

Janine E. Skerry

In popular mythology, Paul Revere, patriot-silversmith, stands as the quintessential American craftsman, the noble embodiment of what every colonial man aspired to be. Rather than an anonymous figure, we have embraced as our ideal of the colonial workman an individual with a history of patriotic political involvement and a legacy of beautiful objects which attest to his skill as an artisan. Certainly, as a patriot and as a businessman, the historical Revere meets our very high expectations. He was indeed public-spirited and contributed both ideologically and physically to the struggle for American independence. And the continued operation into the twentieth century of at least one of his varied business concerns provides ample testimony to his acumen as a capitalist and entrepreneur.

Paul Revere's most renowned work as a silversmith, the "Sons of Liberty Bowl," has been described as a national treasure surpassed in significance only by the Declaration of Independence and the Constitution.[1] The simple, almost hemispherical, shape of this bowl has become synonymous with commemoration, recognition, and tribute in modern America (Fig. 10). Almost every twentieth-century silversmithing firm has produced some variation on the so-called "Paul Revere bowl." Ranging in size from small nut dishes to punch bowls whose proportions exceed even that of their prototype, these replicas of tangible American colonial history are presented to graduates, newlyweds, and visiting heads of state. Certainly, the commercial success of this form is indicative of the popular perception of Revere's standing as a silversmith.

However, just as we are obligated to look beyond the obvious in our assessment of Revere's patriotic and business contributions, so too must we consider the scope of his work in silver beyond the production of the Liberty Bowl. Was Paul Revere an extraordinarily talented artisan? Or was he simply a competent craftsman whose political and social connections fostered a thriving business in the past and kindly remembrance in the present? Other than a punch bowl esteemed for its historical associations, did Revere contribute anything of lasting significance to the history of American design and production in silver? Was he a creative, innovative craftsman, or did he merely produce stock-in-trade to support his ever-growing family? In short, has Revere's artistic output been undeservedly sanctified by an adoring national progeny because of his patriotic exploits?

It is not merely bear-baiting to pose these questions. In the one-hundred-and-twenty-odd years since Henry Wadsworth Longfellow immortalized our subject with his poetry, Paul Revere has moved from relative obscurity to fame as America's most outstanding silversmith. And yet, accounts of Revere's exploits published in the late decades of the nineteenth century do not praise him so much as a craftsman, but as a patriot and a businessman.

In the first book to provide extensive information on the topic of American-made silver, or plate as it was then called, J. H. Buck devotes almost two pages of text to an outline of Revere's family history, education, military involvements, and business enterprises in establishing his brass foundry and copper mill. Although Buck reproduced an invoice from Paul Revere for a silver teapot, it is presented only as evidence of the curious practice of selling silver objects by their weight. Revere's efforts as a silversmith are mentioned but briefly, and then primarily in reference to the large number of pieces of church silver which survive by him.[2]

Buck's treatise was published at a time when the Liberty Bowl was still privately owned and unknown, long before it became a national symbol. Clearly, in this early author's eyes, Revere was just one silversmith among many. Only subsequently did Revere's prominence as a patriotic figure and as a folk hero result in the implicit idealization of his work in silver as well. With the first publication in 1895 of the Sons of Liberty bowl, Paul Revere's silver became sacrosanct through the Colonial Revival/antiquarian interest in objects for their historical associations rather than their artistic merits.[3]

Although biographies of Revere focus primarily on aspects of his life not directly related to his work in precious metal, they clearly convey the message that he was touched with an artistic genius evidenced through his silversmithing. Other than a brief description of the Liberty Bowl, Esther Forbes, for example, does not offer much in the way of a discussion of Revere's silverwork. Nonetheless, she seems enamored of his talent in that area, stating "As a silversmith he was unsurpassed in America."[4]

Throughout the twentieth century Revere has been presented as the consummate American silversmith, and yet little of any substance has been written assessing the aesthetic merits of his work in silver. In his 1917 book *Historic Silver of the Colonies and Its Makers*, Francis Hill Bigelow wrote "the silver wrought by Paul Revere is always sought for, largely for the name it bears."[5] Thirteen years later, Louise Avery accurately assessed the situation when she wrote:

> *Assuredly one does not wish to disparage Revere, but in justice to other Colonial silversmiths, a readjustment of values is called for. Everyone is familiar from childhood with Revere's name and exploits. This familiarity, contrary to the old adage, has not bred contempt, but has occasioned a tremendous demand for his silverwork. Examples, when up for sale, bring three and four times the prices brought by comparable pieces made by other Colonial silversmiths. This is paying a very high price for sentiment. Looked at dispassionately and without bias, Revere's silver is of varying quality, some of it quite distinguished, some of it only average. Incidentally, because of the inflated state of the market, there has come forward more than one piece supposedly bearing his mark that is not his handiwork.*[6]

From the number of objects discussed in her book, Louise Avery certainly seems to have had a firm basis for her analysis of Revere's abilities as a silversmith. And unlike his biographers, Avery's evaluations were not made in a vacuum, but in comparison to the production of other American silversmiths. Perhaps for this reason, there is an unmistakable tone of veracity to her assessment of Revere's workmanship.

Credit must also be given to the late Kathryn C. Buhler for devoting substantial study to the actual objects which bear Revere's name. Aided by the Revere daybooks in the collections of the Massachusetts Historical Society, Buhler researched the extensive holdings of the Museum of Fine Arts, Boston, and established a conclusive chronology of the silversmith's many touchmarks.[7] In terms of published information, her study represents the first definitive analysis of Revere's work in silver.

Still, much remains to be said regarding Paul Revere as a silversmith. His wares have yet to be examined in the context of fabrication techniques, regionalism, patronage, and style. Although Revere's shop employed a number of craftsmen at any given time, the presence or absence of a "shop style" in construction, quality of craftsmanship, and aesthetics has not previously been established. Do all pieces marked with Revere's touch share a kinship in terms of neatness of workmanship and quality of metal? While Revere was active in the shop up to the time of the Revolution, his daily participation after the war declined considerably as his sons assumed a larger role. It is therefore misleading to credit Paul Revere personally with the fabrication of every piece which bears his mark, especially with those objects produced after 1780. Thus, it should be understood that the silverwork was not necessarily executed, or even directly supervised, by Revere.

The Silver of Paul Revere Sr.

In order to assess accurately Paul Revere's contributions to American silversmithing, it is helpful to consider the influence of Revere's father, who was himself a Boston-trained silversmith. During the eighteenth century, the three major hubs of silversmithing in colonial America were Boston, New York, and Philadelphia. The dominance of these urban centers waxed and waned with the economic and political climate, but each remained a vital force in silver production well into the first quarter of the nineteenth century. Throughout the colonies English-style silver held sway as being the most fashionable and desirable, except in New York, which was subject to a strong Dutch influence. The silver which survives by Paul Revere's father, Paul Sr., clearly indicates its New England origins in both style and construction.

The seemingly plain creamer (Fig. 11) made during the last decades of the elder Revere's life is a revealing object. Small pear-shaped, three-legged creampots were common tea accessories produced throughout the major silversmithing centers of the colonies from the 1740s to the 1770s. The example by Paul Sr. is entirely representative of New England creampots in this style, with its bulbous body, cabriole legs, and trifid feet. Typical, too, of its northern colonial origin, is the use of an applied, rather than integral, pouring lip. Although not discernible in the photograph, a solder arc extends approximately one-half inch below the rim into the body of the creamer beneath the lip. At this point the separate, shaped lip was attached to the raised body of the creamer. Rather than a simple butt joint, the adjoining areas of the silver were designed to overlap in a broad angle known as a scarf joint. The overlapping construction guaranteed a stronger solder juncture. Only New England creampots were so fashioned; examples of this form from New York and Philadelphia invariably feature the integral everted lip also found on English prototypes.

Few regional construction variations are evident in eighteenth-century American silver. Generally, the fabrication techniques used for a given type of object were employed throughout the colonies without significant deviation; the seemingly invariable use of applied lips on creampots fashioned by New England silversmiths is a notable exception.[8] It is interesting that this technique was pervasively adopted only in New England, for New England silversmiths generally remained subject to the influence of London in the production of their wares. With its strict regulations, the

Figure 11

Creampot made by Paul
Revere Sr., ca. 1740–1754
(Cat. No. 41). Courtesy,
Worcester Art Museum
(1933.43).

London Goldsmiths' Company would not have sanctioned the use of applied lips on creampots.[9]

This unassuming creampot provides testimony to the fact that, despite his French origins, Paul Revere Sr. thoroughly embraced the working techniques of his New England peers. Further information about Paul Sr. can be derived indirectly from this creampot's history of ownership. It is engraved with the initials "MH," for Mary Hitchborn, youngest sister of Revere's wife Deborah. Revere had married into a prosperous artisan family; the ownership of a piece of plate such as a creampot is indicative of the Hitchborns' comfortable lifestyle.

Among the other objects fashioned by the elder Revere are a pair of gold sleeve buttons of considerable beauty (Fig. 12). The daily work of an eighteenth-century silversmith frequently centered around the production and repair of small personal articles such as shoe, knee, and neck buckles, rings, and sleeve buttons. Although most silversmiths referred to themselves as "goldsmiths," the fabrication of articles in gold was, for the most part, limited to small items. And even then, the majority of these accessories were fabricated of silver, with gold used less frequently.

The engraved border on these sleeve buttons of overlapping leaves surrounding a stylized flower is a common decorative motif on New England silver of this period. Assuming the engraving to be by the elder Revere, rather than the work of a journeyman specialist, they reveal a respectable level of accomplishment in the art of embellishment. The basic shape of these buttons, however, is unusual. Although round sleeve buttons were common in England during the 1600s, octagonal buttons did not become fashionable until the next century. No American-made sleeve buttons are known to survive from the first decades of settlement; those from the first half of the eighteenth century are almost always octagonal like their English counterparts.[10]

The shape of Revere's round sleeve buttons is not only distinctive, but challenging to fabricate as well. Like contemporary octagonal buttons, their edges are folded over to form narrow strengthening borders on their backs. This construction feature is easily fashioned on an octagonal shape, where the angled corners can be snipped to produce eight separate flaps which are folded back. A perfect circle is much harder to manipulate since, in the process of crimping over the edge of the circular form, the basic shape is easily distorted out of round. The successful execution of

Figure 12

Gold sleeve buttons made
by Paul Revere Sr., ca.
1725–1735 (Cat. Nos. 6–7).
Courtesy, Yale University
Art Gallery (1959.17.2).

this deceptively difficult form is indicative of the level of skill in the Revere shop.

Among the larger hollowware forms which survive by Paul Sr. are tankards, canns, and porringers. The drinking vessel illustrated in Figure 13 is typical of mid-century New England tankards. An illusion of verticality is enhanced by the narrow midband encircling the body and by the bell-shaped finial perched on the domed lid. Even the thumbpiece helps to move the eye upward with its elongated, sweeping curve. Vestiges of a rattail can be seen in the rounded drop beneath the hollow handle.

This tankard is particularly revealing of eighteenth-century craft structure in the silversmithing trade. Although it bears the mark used by the elder Revere, the tankard was not made entirely by him or his workshop. The initials "ws" on the upper back of the cast handle terminal suggest that Revere utilized a component part fabricated by another silversmith. Obscured by the curve of the handle, these initials have only recently been observed and are not yet firmly identified. The most likely candidate, however, is William Simpkins (1704-1780), the only known contemporaneous silversmith with the correct initials working in Boston. Little is known of Simpkins's early life and training, but surviving objects by this maker testify to his competence as a silversmith.

Thus, to a certain degree, mass production was in force in American silversmithing by the mid-eighteenth century. Because the initials were cast into the back of the mask pattern, it seems very likely that this component was indeed produced primarily for sale to other silversmiths. Specialist-producers of component parts such as this cast mask terminal provided their fellow craftsmen with the opportunity to offer a wider range of embellishment at reduced expense. It was not necessary for Revere to have the patterns for a variety of cast ornaments, provided he had access to craftsmen such as "ws" who could supply parts.

In his 1976 essay on regionalism in American decorative arts, Charles F. Montgomery speculated that specialization in component production must have been a factor in some urban craft centers by the late eighteenth century.[11] Prior to the discovery of the initials on this handle terminal, the earliest definitive evidence of the use of component parts in American silversmithing was found on a tea service from circa 1815. Although struck with the marks of John or Allen Armstrong and William Thompson, the service is ornamented with milled banding embossed with the name of the diesinker Moritz Fürst.[12] Thus, the evidence offered by the Revere tankard effectively pushes back the verifiable date of such craft specialization in American silversmithing by seventy-five years.

One of the latest pieces of silver fabricated by Paul Revere Sr. is a
sugar dish bearing the "P•REVERE" touchmark used by both the elder Revere and his son (Fig. 14).[13] The sugar dish descended in the Oliver family
of Boston, and was reputedly first owned by Andrew Oliver, Jr. (1731-
1799), son of the loyalist Stamp Act agent.

Eighteenth-century American silver sugar dishes are comparatively
rare; the earliest such dishes have long been described as being copies of
Chinese ceramic prototypes. The body of this example was raised from a
disk of silver, and its edge was reinforced with an applied molding. The
simple stepped foot was cast, cleaned, and soldered in place; evidence of
Paul Sr.'s working techniques can be seen in his use of a thick solder, still
visible after skimming, on the inside of the footring. The lid was fashioned
in much the same manner as the body, although the reel handle was
swaged and seamed rather than cast.

Compact yet graceful, the sugar dish testifies to Paul Sr.'s confidence
and ability with the Queen Anne style. The success of his design is due in
part to the masterfully engraved stylized acanthus leaves which adorn the
lid of the dish. This motif is a throwback to the earlier Baroque period,
but it is executed here in a manner which is entirely sympathetic to the
new aesthetic of controlled simplicity. Although not unique, this sugar
dish is certainly one of the most compelling examples of Boston Queen
Anne silver.[14]

The four illustrated pieces of silver by Paul Revere Sr. document his
training in English-influenced aesthetics and New England construction
techniques. He was a capable, even talented, silversmith who produced a
variety of objects in an economical fashion. Undoubtedly Paul Revere
Sr.'s reputation today is based primarily upon his association with his
namesake, but it is important to recognize his own considerable talent,
especially when assessing the work of the son he trained.

Revere's Shop: The Early Years

Shortly after his father's death in 1754, Paul Revere took over the
family business. Little is known of Revere's silversmithing career in these
early years. However, the waste and memoranda books which survive
from 1761 to 1797 vividly depict the operation of a silversmith's shop.[15]
After only seven years on his own, the shop records indicate that the
young Revere was conducting a brisk business. His first recorded transac-

tion was the making of a jewel, or medal, for a fellow Freemason. Also listed are the numerous repairs that were the mainstay of a silversmith's activities. Entries abound from the first pages to the last for "mending sundrys," such as putting a new lid on a tankard, "taking out bruises" from a well-worn piece of plate, or cleaning and burnishing salts.

Less common activities are recorded as well. In February 1762, for instance, Revere charged Thomas Brackett for "putting two Silver Handles to two Shells for Spoons," and two years later, in September 1764, he charged Andrew Oliver for making a sugar dish out of an ostrich egg. Among the unusual forms listed are a silver "pudding bason," a "silver panikan," several silver spatulas fashioned for a doctor, a silver extinguisher for candles, and a pair of silver spredders.[16] Some activities not directly associated with silversmithing are also noted. Revere cut a branding iron for his cousin William Hitchborn on 6 October 1762, and mended a glass dessert pyramid for Perez Morton in 1786.

Numerous entries in the daybooks testify to the seemingly endless production in both silver and gold of small personal items such as buckles, buttons, and rings. As noted earlier, this work constituted a major source of business for silversmiths. Lamentably, few of these accessories survive. Among the known examples of such smallwork by the Revere shop are two gold rings and a gold thimble, all unmarked but with histories of ownership in the Revere family.[17]

Revere was apparently well connected within the silversmithing community in eastern Massachusetts. As early as 1762 he debited the silversmiths Nathaniel Hurd and Benjamin Green for purchases in his daybooks. It seems likely that these craftsmen were not acquiring objects for personal use, but instead were filling out orders for their own clients. Among the many silversmiths listed over the years in the Revere books are Samuel and John Avery, William Taylor, John Coburn, Jonathan Trott, and Samuel Minott. The latter turned to Revere on several occasions for ornamentally chased items, including a waiter and a sugar bowl.

It has long been recognized that Revere's shop produced some objects which were re-marked and sold by other silversmiths. Perhaps the best-known example of this is a teapot and stand which were overstruck with the mark of Josiah Austin. Because Revere's touchmark is still legible there is little doubt that the pair were made in the Revere shop but retailed by Austin.[18] This type of symbiotic relationship between early American silversmiths has not been explored in great depth. The elder Revere's use, in at least one instance, of component parts produced by another silversmith and Paul Revere's willingness to sell his wares wholesale to other artisans highlight a cooperative aspect of this craft. Considerable research remains to be done on this aspect of craft structure in colonial American silversmithing.

When Revere began training in his father's shop, the rococo style was in vogue. Although Boston remained a major center of silver production during this period, it never embraced the lighthearted whimsy of the rococo as fully as either New York or Philadelphia. This was true of Boston's furniture as well as its silver.

A large number of the objects from the Paul Revere shop which predate the Revolution are ubiquitous forms which do not vary significantly from one stylistic period to another. Canns and porringers, for instance, remained much the same throughout the eighteenth century with only minor variations in detail. Nonetheless, several pieces survive by Revere which speak of a sensitivity for the rococo aesthetic not generally associ-

ated with Boston silversmithing.

The salver illustrated in Figure 15 is one of three very similar circular footed trays made in 1760 and 1761, prior to the time covered by Revere's silver shop waste and memoranda books. All three of the salvers share the same cast rim of shells and scrolls, but each differs in its engraved embellishment.[19] On this example, a narrow border of tightly spaced wriggle-work echoes the undulating line of the salver's rim, and a circle of chevrons encloses the asymmetrical coat of arms. The reverse of the salver is engraved with the presentation inscription *The Gift of James Tyng to his / Sister Sarah Tyng*. Like the other two salvers, this example was given as a marriage gift.[20]

Although salvers or small trays seem like easily constructed items, they presented more of a challenge to the silversmith than is immediately apparent. Hammering a billet of silver into the flat sheet from which objects were raised was both time-consuming and labor-intensive. In most instances minor variations in the uniformity of the gauge, or thickness of the metal, were to be expected. In the process of raising a hollowware form a silversmith could generally compensate for such irregularities. But in fabricating a salver, the metal had to be of an extremely uniform thickness, without deviations, ripples, or overworked areas. The art of making a salver is dependent upon the production of a perfectly flat, even surface. Further care must then be taken to insure that the body of the salver does not warp when the cast feet and rim are soldered in place. The greater the expanse of the surface, the more likely warping becomes.

A creampot and sugar dish Revere made in 1761–1762 for Lucretia Chandler (Fig. 16) proves his success in the rococo style was no mere fluke.[21] The somewhat broad, heavy shape of these double-bellied objects is typical of the New England interpretation of the rococo taste, but the

Figure 16

Creampot and sugar dish made by Paul Revere, 1761–1762 (Cat. Nos. 64 and 65). Courtesy, Museum of Fine Arts, Boston. Pauline Revere Thayer Collection (35.1781 and 1782).

lavish use of floral repoussé ornament is quite exceptional. Repoussé, or high relief, chasing was not frequently employed on mid-century Boston silver. Although silversmiths in New York and, particularly, Philadelphia seemed to delight in the extravagances offered by chased rococo ornament, Boston silversmiths remained immune to its charms. Relief chasing, when found on Boston-made objects, is relatively flat and rigid. Revere's efforts on the Chandler sugar dish and creampot are acceptable in comparison to similar decoration produced in Philadelphia. In terms of Boston rococo silver, however, these pieces are exceptional in their exuberant interpretation and technical execution.[22]

Throughout its history the Revere shop fabricated numerous presentation pieces to commemorate significant events and acknowledge individual effort. The so-called Sons of Liberty Bowl, thought to have been made in 1768, is certainly the best-known piece of presentation silver by this maker. Less readily recognized but equally distinguished objects were commissioned from the Revere shop in that same year. The tutorial tankard illustrated in Figure 17 is a fine example of Revere's less publicized commission work.

As the name implies, tutorial silver was presented to academic teachers, or tutors, by their grateful students. The practice of commissioning such silver had a long history in the colonies; several pieces made for the faculty members at Harvard and Yale still survive today. This tankard by the Revere shop is typical in its use of Latin for the presentation inscription. The lines may be translated: "Presented to Stephan Scales by his students at Harvard in the year 1768. Having passed two years under his tutelage, they give this drinking vessel as a symbol of their gratitude." The dedication is engraved within a large rectangular cartouche capped, appropriately, by two small books entitled *Locke's Efsay* and *Price's Mor.*[23]

In design and execution, the Scales tankard is a splendid example of both Boston silversmithing and Revere's work. Like all American tankards of the seventeenth and eighteenth centuries, this vessel was raised, or hammered up, from a disk of flattened silver. The stepped baseband, midband, and two-part hollow handle were then soldered onto the finished

Figure 17

Tankard made in 1768 by
Paul Revere (Cat. No. 94).
Courtesy, Museum of Fine
Arts, Boston. Gift of Ed-
ward N. Lamson and Bar-
bara T. Lamson, Edward
F. Lamson, Howard J.
Lamson, and Susan L.
Strickler (1986.678).

body; seam lines where the base and midbands begin and end are faintly
discernible on this tankard to the left of the handle. Although tankard
designs change little in Massachusetts after the mid-eighteenth century,
features such as the high-domed lid and swirled finial corroborate the date
of the inscription.

The condition of the Scales tankard is excellent and offers an opportunity to examine the work of Revere's shop without the deviations wrought
by repair or alteration. The metal is clean and smooth (that is, free from
the marks left by poorly maintained tools), and seems to be of a very
uniform gauge. The final planishing of the silversmith's hammer marks
was carefully executed, so that clear evidence of raising is visible only
inside of the lid. Typical of most pieces bearing Revere's mark, the juncture of the bezel, or narrow vertical rim, and the inside of the lid was left
with excess solder.[24]

Four years later, in 1772, Revere's shop made the coffeepot (Fig. 18)
which was presented to Jonathan Derby by his father, Richard. Still privately owned, it is the only known marked American three-legged coffeepot. Although similar coffeepots were uncommon in England, another

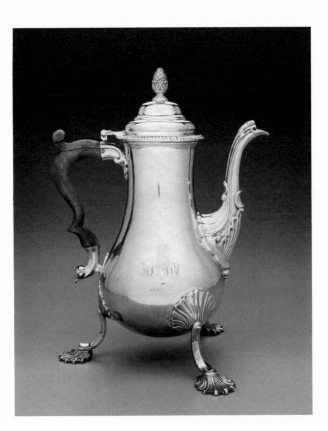

Coffeepot made by Paul Revere in 1772 (Cat. No. 68). Privately owned. Photograph courtesy, Museum of Fine Arts, Boston.

Salem family owned a double-bellied example which had been made in London in 1759. Thus, it has been conjectured that the English example may have served as a design influence for Revere.[25] Ironically, three-legged coffeepots were commonly produced in France, from whence Revere's father hailed. Numerous Gallic examples of this form testify to its popularity on the Continent. While an early church cup and a later set of tumblers, copied by Paul Revere from French prototypes, survive, there is no evidence that he had access to a French coffeepot of this design.[26]

The three-legged form presents a challenge to the silversmith because of its inherent tendency to appear awkward and ungainly. While French silversmiths mitigated this problem by fashioning smaller, more slender coffeepots, Revere followed the English formula of simply updating a basic coffeepot body by adding three large shell and scroll legs. The handle sockets, lid, and finial on the Derby coffeepot are identical to those used on a vessel of circa 1760, and the same cast spout is found on his later coffeepot of 1781, made for Paul Dudley Sargent.[27] Details such as the alternating gadroons around the rim of the lid, the graduated pendant drop beneath the spout, and the carved reed of the wooden handle forming an extension of the silver scroll on the upper socket all contribute to a unified design. The ample curves and generous proportions of the handle and spout balance the wide stance of the coffeepot's feet. Although decidedly unfamiliar to the American eye, Revere's interpretation of this continental form is quite successful.

The Revere Shop After the War

After the disruption of the Revolutionary War years, the Revere shop resumed its production of silver at an accelerated pace. With the increasing prosperity of the new nation came the desire for the trappings of a genteel society. The demand for older communal drinking forms such as tankards declined, but newly fashionable table items were eagerly sought.

Tea- and coffeepots were especially popular, and the practice of ordering all the necessary equipage en suite arose.[28]

As the war wound down, Revere began to produce silver in the fashionable neoclassical style which had been popular throughout Europe for over a decade. Much lighter and more restrained than its predecessor, neoclassicism was equated with an intellectual celebration of the republican virtues of democracy and enlightenment. As such, the new nation and Revere embraced it with patriotic fervor. Among the earliest examples of neoclassical hollowware by the shop is the drum-shaped teapot (Fig. 19) made in 1782 for Stephen and Isannah Bruce. Four other such pots by the Revere shop survive, all of similar date and with only minor variations in detail.[29] Although a broader, more horizontal interpretation of this form was produced in the mid-Atlantic region from Philadelphia to Baltimore, no other drum-shaped teapots by Boston-area silversmiths are known to survive.[30]

Close examination of Revere's drum-shape teapot elucidates the working techniques of the period. Although the basic cylindrical form suggests that the body was fashioned from a sheet of silver rolled into a tube and soldered closed, this is not the case. All five of the surviving drum teapots from the Revere shop were raised, or hammered up, from disks of flat silver.[31] Thus, the vertical sides of the pots are extensions of their flat bottoms; the gadroon or bead borders encircling the base of each pot serve to strengthen, as well as embellish, the most exposed point of the metal.[32]

Although the body of Revere's drum-shaped teapot is raised, its spout and handle ferrules are fashioned of seamed cylinders ornamented with chased reeding. The shaped and soldered spout and ferrules were filled with a pitch-resin compound for support, and then were hand chased, or hammered, with a narrow, blunt-edged tool to produce parallel convex reeds. When the chasing was completed, the spout and ferrules were heated so that the pitch would once again liquify and thus be poured out. The finished components were then soldered in place onto the body.

The reeded elements, together with the high neck and tapered sides of the teapot, foster an illusion of verticality which is similar to the stance of contemporary New England tankards. The large, open script initials within a delicate garland of leaves embellishing the Bruce teapot signal a change in engraving styles. Revere's daybooks record the charges for the fabrication of this teapot, and make specific use of the term cypher to describe its cursive lettering. In both style and execution, the Bruce teapot is indicative of the Revere shop's early prowess in the neoclassical taste.

Other than the Liberty Bowl, few forms are more closely associated with the Revere shop than the fluted oval teapot. This quintessential neoclassical form was produced almost exclusively in the Boston area, and yet is now synonymous with American Federal silver as a whole.[33] Although numerous teapots survive, only one service by Revere in this style is known to survive en suite (Fig. 20).[34] Made for John Templeman, the service includes a teapot on stand, covered sugar urn, creampot, punch strainer, caddy spoon, tea caddy, stand, and tongs. Revere's ledger entry of 17 April 1792 also lists six silver tablespoons and twelve teaspoons; the tongs which are illustrated are a later addition to the service. The most unusual forms are the "silver tea shell," or caddy spoon, and the tea caddy.[35]

The fluted teapot form takes full advantage of the silversmithing technologies available in America at the end of the Revolutionary War. Although there is little evidence to indicate that Revere had access to a reliable source of rolled sheet silver prior to the mid-1780s, it seems likely that he was well supplied by the end of that decade. All of the known fluted teapots from his shop were fashioned in an identical manner, using metal of a highly uniform gauge. It is likely that the silver used for these teapots was flattened by a rolling mill rather than by battery force.[36]

The construction of the Revere shop's fluted teapots follows a standardized format. A rectangular sheet of silver was hammered into an oval and then both soldered and riveted together at the overlapping juncture. The resulting seam can be seen slightly to the left or right under the handle on the finished teapot. The area of overlap is quite narrow, approximately one-quarter inch in depth. Several small rivets approximately one-sixteenth inch in diameter further strengthen the solder joint.[37]

Although the fluted teapot form exploited the advantages of sheet silver and allowed the Revere shop to fabricate hollowware with comparatively little effort, fluted sugar urns and creampots, such as those in the Templeman service, were highly labor-intensive constructions. A tapered body shape cannot be fabricated by seaming a rectangle of sheet silver into a cylinder. Prior to the introduction of lathe spinning into silver production in the nineteenth century, rounded and tapered hollowware bodies could only be fabricated by hand raising. The Revere shop's skill is evident in the even hand-hammered fluting which embellishes the sugar urn and creampot without distorting their basic body shape.

Among American silversmiths, only the shops of Paul Revere, Benjamin Burt, and Joseph Loring, all located in Boston, are known to have produced this type of fluted oval teapot. The example which survives by Burt in the collections of the Museum of Fine Arts, Boston, is larger by approximately one-eighth inch in all dimensions than its counterparts by Revere.[38] The fabrication of the teapot from the Burt shop, however, is identical to that employed by the Revere shop, including the otherwise unique use of rivets in the soldered seam of the body. Rather interestingly, a detailed comparison of the swag and tassel motif indicates that the same engraver ornamented the Burt teapot and a Revere teapot made for Jonathan Hunnewell in 1796.[39]

Joseph Loring has been credited with the fabrication of the fluted teapot form on the basis of a teapot and stand in the collections of the Museum of Fine Arts, Boston.[40] The teapot is unmarked, but the stand bears the semiscript full name touch used by Loring. In its construction, this

teapot is identical to those produced in the Revere shop. The body dimensions of the teapot ascribed to Loring correspond precisely to those of
marked Revere examples, even to the depth and curvature of each of the
sixteen hand-hammered concave flutes.

In comparison to its matching teapot, the silver stand marked by Loring exhibits crude and inept workmanship. The shaping of its rim in particular lacks depth and definition. It is hard to accept the supposition that
the stand and teapot were produced by the same shop. Given Revere's
cooperative relationship with other silversmiths noted earlier, it is entirely
plausible that the unmarked fluted teapot attributed to Joseph Loring was,
in fact, fabricated by the Revere shop and sold to Loring for his retail.
The marked stand, however, was probably made by Loring. If this speculation is correct, Benjamin Burt was Paul Revere's only Boston rival in the
production of high style neoclassical fluted tearwares.

Members of the Derby family of Salem, Massachusetts, were among
the many wealthy merchants who patronized Revere. In 1797 the shop
fashioned a newly stylish form, the two-handled tea tray or waiter, for
shipowner Elias Hasket Derby (Fig. 21). Although the broad scallops and
ever-so-slightly asymmetrical shells of its border are motifs commonly associated with the rococo style, the waiter is thoroughly neoclassical.[41]
Revere elongated the tight, curving lines of the earlier style to produce a
harmonious, graceful expression of the new taste. Even the shells have
been reduced and simplified to suggest more of a delicate embellishment
than a bold flourish.

The sweep of the waiter's twelve broad arcs provides the perfect coun-
terpoint to a fluted teapot, covered sugar urn, and creampot. Thus juxta-
posed, it is clear that this tray was intended to complement such forms.
The outermost rim was cast in pieces; three slightly different patterns
were used to obtain the desired curvature. The cast rim elements are
soldered onto a hammered booge, or inner rim, which is integral with the
flat center surface of the tray.

Revere's use of handles on this large waiter also indicates its late date. Cast as single pieces and soldered in place, the handles have been knocked slightly askew by almost two hundred years of use. With their gently swollen center bars, they are similar to the bail handles of furniture brasses; the seashell-like scrolls at the terminals of the bars do not have a readily apparent corollary, however.

The engraved monogram in a pendant oval suspended from a bowknot is a neoclassical convention. The lettering used here is a simplification of that found on the 1782 drum-shaped teapot made for the Bruce family (Fig. 19). In this instance, however, Revere's daybooks record this feature simply as "engraving" rather than as a "cypher." Perhaps the latter term was used exclusively for script letters, while the former suggested a wider variety of embellishment.

As noted earlier, the fabrication of a large tray presented a challenge to the silversmith's skills. The back of the Derby waiter bears witness to the technical difficulties of this form, for the metal shows numerous stress marks and surface cracks, as well as extensive firescale. However, the size and weight of the waiter, together with its graceful design, provide an admirable testimony to the silversmithing prowess of the Revere shop.

Following George Washington's death, the Grand Lodge of Masons in Massachusetts commissioned a gold urn to hold a lock of the first president's hair. The urn (Fig. 22), fashioned between 1800 and 1801, survives today in the possession of that same institution as a relic of not only the first American president, but also of the most famous masonic silversmith.[42]

As Edith Steblecki notes, Revere's association with Freemasonry was lengthy and significant. He served in various capacities in the Lodge of St. Andrew and in the Grand Lodge, and fashioned or procured numerous items for masonic use, including ceremonial equipage such as silver jewels and ladles.[43] Thus, it is wholly appropriate that his brother Freemasons would have turned to him for this important commission.

Unfortunately, the gold memorial urn is unmarked, or at least bears no visible marks today. Long credited to Revere, it is worth reviewing the evidence that supports this attribution. Upon receiving word of Washington's death a committee consisting of the three past Grand Masters—John Warren, Paul Revere, and Josiah Bartlett—was selected to write a letter of condolence to Washington's widow. In that missive of 11 January 1800, they expressed their sorrow and requested a lock of the president's hair, which would be preserved in a golden urn at the Grand Lodge of Massachusetts. Martha Washington granted their petition on 27 January 1800; the curl of hair is still enclosed under glass within the memorial urn, and is visible when the lid is removed.[44]

A day-long ceremony organized by the Freemasons of Massachusetts was held in Boston on 12 February 1800 to mourn the death of Washington. Paul Revere was among the pallbearers who carried a draped pedestal and a white marble urn in the accompanying memorial procession. From descriptions of the service, it appears that this marble urn served as a temporary repository for the lock of Washington's hair.[45]

An entry in the transcribed transactions of the Grand Lodge of Massachusetts further links Revere with both the marble and gold urns. The minutes for 8 June 1800 note that Revere had temporary custody of the urn used in the funeral procession. A committee charged with finding a suitable depository for the urn suggested that the urn and regalia remain with Revere while permanent housing was sought. The committee further noted at the same time "that the procuring [of] the Gold Urn is in great forwardness."[46]

Later reports in the transactions of the Grand Lodge indicated that Revere retained possession of the white marble urn until at least as late as 1809. Although the records do not provide complete information on the commission to fabricate the gold urn, it was noted on 9 March 1801 that "The committee appointed to procure the Golden Urn reported; the Urn was then recommitted as before, to devise a suitable inscription and report [at] the next meeting." This rather cryptic transcription suggests that the urn had indeed been fabricated by this date, and was presented for approval; the urn was then returned to its maker (presumably Revere) while an inscription for engraving was being considered.

The urn has had several mishaps since its original fabrication. As a result of being dropped, its domed lid is slightly compressed beneath its double-ball finial. While the object as a whole is in a very good state of preservation, evidence of past restoration can be seen on the underside of its foot. Generally, such a circular stepped, splayed foot was either raised or cast and then soldered in place. The silversmith's touchmark is frequently found inside of the hollow foot on the bottom of the body. In this instance, however, it is impossible to determine if a mark is present because at some point in the past the hollow foot was fitted with a brass plug to provide additional support to its base. Furthermore, because the glass disk which encloses the lock of hair is fixed in place at the upper rim of the body beneath the lid, it cannot be determined if an echo of a touchmark is visible from within the piece. Thus, although it is possible that the urn is indeed marked, this cannot be verified without reversing past restorations.

The urn form became exceedingly popular during the neoclassical period and was adopted for a variety of hollowware forms, from tea urns to sugar bowls and, as seen here, memorials. This particular example, however, is closest in both scale and ornament to the spice casters produced by the Revere shop. A pair of marked Revere casters dated circa 1790-1800 feature square plinths beneath a similar foot, and sport a more elaborate twisted finial.[47] Despite these differences and a more elongated body shape, the similarities between these marked examples and the gold urn are obvious.

The evidence for attributing the gold memorial urn to the Revere shop consists of a combination of the silversmith's association with Freemasonry in general, and his role in the acquisition of the lock of George Washington's hair in particular. Further support is offered by the fact that Revere was entrusted with the safekeeping of the white marble urn which initially housed the lock of hair. Finally, silver casters marked with Revere's touch exhibit similarities in design. Although the combined evidence is certainly not irrefutable, in the absence of dissenting information, it argues persuasively for an attribution to the Revere shop.

Evaluating Revere's Silver: Sentiment or Skill?

After examining silver made by the Revere shop, it is necessary to return to the initial inquiry. Was Revere the extraordinarily skilled craftsman whom we have so enshrined in our national consciousness? In deifying Revere as the quintessential patriot/silversmith, a man of straw has been created. This has clearly had a prejudicial effect on our perception of his artistic output. By virtue of its touchmark alone, Revere's silver is oftentimes overvalued both aesthetically and monetarily. This is particu-

Figure 22

Gold memorial urn made
ca. 1800–1801 and attrib-
uted to Paul Revere (Cat.
No. 217). Courtesy, Grand
Lodge of Masons in Massa-
chusetts, A.F. & A.M.

larly lamentable because by prejudging it, Revere's work has not generally been considered critically.

Although there are inevitably some exceptions, on the whole works from the Revere shop are well crafted. The silver made before the war may be stylistically and technically ranked in the forefront of its Boston peers. The shop's proficiency with the rococo style is evident in such items as the tea service made for Lucretia Chandler and the salver presented to Sarah Tyng. And the facility with the essentially foreign form of the three-legged coffeepot suggests a command of craft exceeding the bounds of familiarity and provincialism.

Revere's more exceptional talents for the adaptation to and exploitation of technological changes in silversmithing are most evident in the post-Revolutionary silver. The enduring appeal of the fluted oval teapot provides ample testimony to Revere's success at mass-producing aesthetically satisfying objects. During this period the hint of expeditious production methods provided by his father's use of component parts blossoms and Revere the entrepreneur-craftsman emerges. The Revere shop fashioned a more limited range of forms in its later years, but among its production were such exceptional items as the waiter made for Elias Hasket Derby.[48]

To return to C. Louise Avery's earlier assessment of the patriot's artistic production, Revere's silver is of varying quality. On the whole, it compares favorably with that of his peers. Although many objects are virtually indistinguishable from the works of any number of contemporaneous silversmiths, some of Revere's production is exceptional. In terms of craftsmanship, his wares are generally among the best of the period and often set the standard. It is, however, in such areas as stylistic interpretation, technological innovation, and entrepreneurial marketing that Paul Revere excelled. Our ingrained affection for the patriot/silversmith is not unfounded, but it is overly simplistic. Revere was a talented artisan, but an even more talented technical innovator and businessman. He played an active role in not one, but two, revolutions: the War for Independence, and the nascent industrialization of American silversmithing.

Notes

1.
Walter Muir Whitehill et al., *Paul Revere's Boston: 1735–1818* (Boston, 1975), 118.

2.
J. H. Buck, *Old Plate, Ecclesiastical, Decorative, and Domestic: Its Makers and Marks* (New York, 1888), 54–56.

3.
The Sons of Liberty punch bowl was the subject of an article which appeared in the *Boston Sunday Herald* of 20 January 1895, subsequently reprinted as Benjamin F. Stevens, *The Silver Punch Bowl Made by Paul Revere* (Boston, 1895).

4.
Forbes, 105. See also Goss.

5.
Frances Hill Bigelow, *Historic Silver of the Colonies and Its Makers* (1917; reprint New York, 1941), 212.

6.
C. Louise Avery, *Early American Silver* (New York, 1930), 87–88.

7.
See Kathryn C. Buhler, *American Silver, 1655–1825, in the Museum of Fine Arts, Boston*, 2 vols. (Boston, 1972), 2:384–472.

8.
Rather curiously, New England silversmiths abandoned applied lips on creampots when the body shifted from a pear-shape to a double-bellied or urn form. At this point, New England smiths conformed to the techniques employed by their New York and Philadelphia brethren, and fashioned creampots with integral lips everted from the raised body of the pot.

9.
Although it is not clear if the London Goldsmith's Company controlled construction techniques, hallmarking regulations would have required that an applied lip be marked, thus defacing yet another area of the object.

It is possible that some provincial English silversmiths, far from the reach of the London guildhall, used unmarked applied lips on creampots. The technique is more economical in terms of both silver and labor, and thus provided a means of economy for the silversmith. In *Starting to Collect Silver* by John Luddington (Suffolk, England, 1984) a George II creampot with an applied lip is illustrated on page 117. Although it is presented as a later repair easily overlooked by an unwary novice collector, it may indeed be an example of a period deviation in construction technique. In the absence of any hallmark information which would clarify the date and origin of the creampot, it is difficult to assess.

10.
In the exhibition catalogue *American Gold, 1700-1860* (New Haven, 1963), Peter J. Bohan notes (p. 17) that the majority of gold sleeve buttons which survive from the first half of the eighteenth century seem to have been made in Boston.

11.
Charles F. Montgomery, "Regional Preferences and Characteristics in American Decorative Arts: 1750–1800," in Charles F. Montgomery and Patricia E. Kane, eds. *American Art: 1750–1800, Towards Independence* (Boston, 1976), 50–65.

12.
The tea service is in the collections of the Yale University Art Gallery, New Haven, Connecticut. Since its acquisition, several other pieces of American silver embellished with the same milled border marked by Moritz Fürst have also surfaced in the marketplace. Fürst was a diesinker and medal engraver from Hungary who worked in Philadelphia between 1807 and circa 1840 making dies for medals, seals and, apparently, milled borders. All of his signed banding which has surfaced thus far appears to have been produced from a single set of engraved rollers in a grapevine pattern. For more information on this diesinker, see Georgina S. Chamberlain, "Moritz Fürst, Diesinker and Artist," *The Numismatist* (June 1954):588–92.

13.
Although pieces with this mark are often difficult to attribute firmly to either father or son, it is most likely that Paul Sr. made this example during the last two years of his life. Stylistically the sugar dish is in the Queen Anne taste which was fashionable during the height of his career. As a young single man, Andrew Oliver, Jr. would not have owned silver teawares prior to his marriage at age twenty-one in 1752. Since the eighteen-year-old Revere was still serving his apprenticeship, he would not have been eligible to independently fabricate silver at that time. Ironically, as an apprentice in his father's shop, Paul Revere probably did assist in some way with the fabrication of this sugar dish.

14.
A virtually identical sugar dish marked by John Coburn is in the collections of the Museum of Fine Arts, Boston. Although there is no documentary evidence to support a business relationship between Paul Revere Sr. and John Coburn, numerous transactions recorded in the younger Revere's waste and memoranda books testify to the fact that Coburn purchased silver and services such as engraving from the 1760s onward. On that basis it may be speculated that, like his son, the elder Revere occasionally provided goods and/or services for Coburn, perhaps including even the sugar dish which bears Coburn's mark. See Buhler, *American Silver, 1655-1825*, 1:303.

15.
The books, which cover the years from 1761 to 1775 and 1779 to 1797, are among the Revere Family Papers in the collections of the Massachusetts Historical Society in Boston.

16.
The Revere daybooks also offer a treasure trove of period terminology for the decorative arts historian. For example, in 1763 Revere recorded the fashioning of a pair of butter cups, a rare form which was soon superceded by sauceboats. A December 1771 entry lists a silver scalloped tureen ladle of five ounces and ten pennnyweight; an October entry two years later refers to a "large soop spoon" of seven ounces and ten pennyweight. The heavy weights for these items suggests that they were both the large ladles which we generally associate with punch today. A February 1768 notation records "large gravie spoons" and "butter ladles" in the same entry. The former were probably basting or stuffing spoons, while the latter may have been either sauce or gravy ladles.

17.
These items are in the collections of the Museum of Fine Arts, Boston. The same institution also owns an enameled gold mourning ring set with an amethyst; although this ring bears no mark, it was made for one of Revere's patrons, and is therefore attributed to the patriot-silversmith.

18.
The teapot and stand, engraved with the monogram of Hannah Carter of Newbury, Massachusetts, are owned by the Museum of Fine Arts, Boston. A set of six fluted teaspoons with the same engraved initials, but marked only by Austin, are in the collections of the Yale University Art Gallery. Because the Revere daybooks record a charge against Nathaniel Austin (Josiah's nephew) for the making and engraving of twelve "scoloped teaspoons" it has been assumed that the spoons were also fashioned by Revere, although not stuck with his mark.

19.
The other salvers are in the collections of the Paul Revere Life Insurance Company and the Museum of Fine Arts, Boston. The former was given to William Phillips in 1760, and the latter was given one year later to Lucretia Chandler. See Wendy A. Cooper, *In Praise of America* (New York, 1980) 82, 84, 85 and Buhler, *American Silver, 1625-1825*, 2:393.

20.
Sarah Tyng (1720/21-1791) of Dunstable married John Winslow (1708-1788) of Chelmsford in September, 1760. The salver was presented to Sarah in 1761 by her younger brother, James Tyng (1730/31-ca. 1775). *Sibley's Harvard Graduates*, 5:651-53 and see also Brother Anthony of Padua, *The Tyng Family in America* (Poughkeepsie, NY, 1956), 29-30.

21.
The sugar dish is engraved on the bottom of its foot "B. Greene to L. Chandler." Although Kathryn Buhler dated this pair to the year of Lucretia Chandler's marriage in 1761, the 11 March 1762 record of a charge for the sugar dish against Benjamin Green in Revere's daybooks suggests that the gift may have been actually fabricated in the year following her wedding. See Buhler, *American Silver, 1655-1825*, 2:394-95.

22.
The creampot is also of interest as one of the first examples of an integral lip on such a New England vessel. As was stated previously, the applied lips found on New England pear-shaped creamers gave way to integral lips with the introduction of double-bellied and urn- shaped bodies. The cast handle on the Chandler creampot, although contorted from its original shape, appears to be identical to the handle found on the earlier style creampots by both Revere Sr. and Paul Revere.

23.
The latter title refers to the British theologian Richard Price's 1758 publication *Review of the Principle Questions in Morals*. Stephen Scales was a graduate of Harvard College, receiving his baccalaureate in 1763 and a master of arts degree in 1766. He served as a tutor at his Alma Mater from 1767 to 1770 while studying law. Apparently, this tankard was not the only gift bestowed upon Scales by his grateful charges in 1768; a pair of canns, fashioned by Revere and bearing the same presentation inscription, also survive. The canns were at one point owned by R. T. Halsey and were on extended loan to the Metropolitan Museum of Art in New York City. They are now in the collections of the R.W. Norton Art Gallery. See *American Silver and Pressed Glass: A Collection in the R.W. Norton Art Gallery* (Shreveport, LA, 1967), 21.

24.
Large gobs of silver wire solder, or snippets of silver sheet solder, were often left intact under the base or inside of vessels where components such as footrings and bezels were attached. This sort of rough soldering, which would not have been permitted by the London goldsmiths' hall, is frequently found on hollowware by Revere (as well as on work by other American silversmiths). Occasionally, pieces marked by Revere show evidence of filing and cleaning which suggest that not all of the craftsmen in his shop finished their work in the same manner.

25.
Henry N. Flynt and Martha Gandy Fales, *The Heritage Foundation Collection Of Silver* (Old Deerfield, MA, 1968), 125. See also, Martha Gandy Fales, *Early American Silver*, rev. ed. (New York, 1970), 119–20.

Note: The latter publication states on page 119 that Revere updated the English design by fashioning a double-bellied, rather than pear-shaped, body. This is incorrect; as is indicated by the photographs in Flynt and Fales, the English coffeepot is double-bellied, and Revere's is indeed pear-shaped.

26.
The church cup, which was commissioned for the Old South Church of Boston circa 1759, is currently on deposit, along with its French prototype, at the Museum of Fine Arts, Boston. Both pieces are discussed in E. Alfred Jones, *The Old Silver of American Churches*, 50. In 1795 or 1797 Revere fashioned engraved silver cups for Elias Hasket Derby of Salem. They were copied after a set of French tumblers owned by Derby. Four of the Revere cups and two of the French prototypes are now in the collections of the Metropolitan Museum of Art, New York. Another portion of the set is also owned by the Society of Colonial Dames in Washington, D.C.

27.
Buhler, *American Silver, 1625–1825*, 2:391–92, 418–19.

28.
Before 1780, silver tea- and coffeepots were only rarely purchased in sets with other items such as creamers and sugar bowls. It was far more common to acquire the component parts of a tea service individually, over the course of several years. Thus, prior to the Revolution, a family's silver teapot, sugar bowl, and creamer might all be of different design.

29.
Another drum-shaped teapot from 1782, made for Thomas Hitchborn, is owned by the Museum of Fine Arts, Boston; its finial has been replaced. See Buhler, *American Silver, 1625–1825*, 2:420. A second teapot, made in April 1782 for Captain Joseph Henshaw, is owned by the Henry Ford Museum & Greenfield Village, Deerborn, Michigan. A third teapot, commissioned by Moses Michael Hayes in 1783, is privately owned. The fourth drum-shaped pot, which has been dated to 1782–1785, is in the Mabel Brady Garvan Collection at the Yale University Art Gallery. The latter teapot, which does not have an established provenance, exhibits a particularly heavy, mottled firescale similar to that frequently found on Revere's later seamed beakers. See Kathryn C. Buhler and Graham Hood, *American Silver, Garvan and Other Collections in the Yale University Art Gallery*, 2 vols. (New Haven, CT, 1970), 1:189–90.

30.
Janine E. Skerry, *Regionalism in American Neoclassical Silver*, The 1987 Washington Antiques Show Catalog (Washington, D.C., 1987), 72–75.

31.
This construction technique was also used by mid-Atlantic silversmiths of the same period. Every eighteenth-century drum-shaped teapot of American origin examined by the author was fashioned by raising rather than seaming. Oval teapots, however, which were popular throughout the new nation by 1790, were invariably fabricated by the latter, more expeditious, method.

32.
The slightly later fluted oval teapots (discussed at length further in this essay) produced by the Revere shop do not generally feature a protective border at the right angle junctures where the sides of the teapots meet their flat bases. Today these oval teapots almost invariably offer testimony to their hard use and abuse through the numerous patches to their bases and lower sides. If a flat-bottomed, straight-sided vessel is not placed squarely against a horizontal surface such as a tabletop, the right angle formed by the juncture of the sides and base will be dented. Because of the oval shape of Revere's fluted teapots, damage was most frequently concentrated at the bases of the spouts and handles. A fluted oval teapot recently given to the Museum of Fine Arts, Boston provides evidence that Revere may have been aware of this inherent weakness. Unlike the other examples, the teapot made for William Dall circa 1797 sports a flat, narrow reinforcement band at the edge of the base. The band, which appears to be original to the teapot, is both inconspicuous and effective. Unlike the majority of its contemporaries, the Dall teapot has not suffered gross dents and damage to the base of its spout and handle.

33.
Revere's inspiration for this form was drawn from English silver examples and pattern books.

34.
Although Revere made other fluted tea services, the Templeman assemblage is the largest which remains intact in one institution today. A partial service consisting of a coffee urn, teapot and stand, and sugar urn, together with a tureen ladle, is in the collections of the Museum of Fine Arts, Boston. See Kathryn C, Buhler, *American Silver, 1655–1825*, 1:442–47.

35.
The stand supporting the tea caddy in the illustration is not listed among the items in Revere's 17 April 1792 entry in the waste and memoranda books. John Templeman was charged on 22 March 1793 for a silver stand, however, there is no indication that it was intended for use with the tea caddy.

In *American Silver* (Cleveland, 1950), Kathryn C. Buhler states on page 59 that Revere recorded only one tea caddy in his waste and memoranda books. I would like to thank Deborah Federhen for bringing to my attention the 14 July 1792 entry for a tea caddy charged to Mr. Joseph Blake, Esq.

36.
As is noted in Edgard Moreno's essay on the copper mills at Canton, Paul Revere paid Solomon Munroe for his work in "putting up a plating mill." While it is possible that the mill in question was intended for copper sheet production, the principles involved in rolling sheet are the same for either metal. See Solomon Munroe to Paul Revere bill, 17 November 1785, RFP.

37.
This same fabrication technique is also found on all of Revere's plain and serpentine oval teapots. Since Revere's ovoid teapots date from the post-1785 period, it may be assumed that the Revere shop used rolled sheet silver, which was more readily available after the war, for the fabrication of these vessels. Although the majority of objects were still fabricated by means of raising, the production of seamed oval forms, such as teapots, was greatly facilitated by the use of sheet metal.

38.
Buhler, *American Silver, 1655–1825*, 1:350–52.

39.
Ibid., 2:456. Deborah Federhen's research into the Revere daybooks suggests that at least three different engravers were employed by the shop at various times.

40.
Buhler, *American Silver, 1655–1825*, 2:486–89.

41.
A number of publications that illustrate this waiter erroneously imply that it is rococo in style, or is a "transitional" piece. See, for example, Whitehill et al., 190–91; and Michael Clayton, *The Collector's Dictionary of the Silver and Gold of Great Britain and North America*, 2nd. ed. (Suffolk, England, 1985), 442.

42.
This gold urn has long been ascribed to Revere. Among recent publications which so attribute it are Fales, *Early American Silver*, 164–65; and Whitehill et al., 214–15. See also Edith J. Steblecki, *Paul Revere and Freemasonry* (Boston, 1985), 60–63. I am indebted to Steblecki for information and assistance on the topic of Revere's associations with Freemasonry.

43.
The Lodge of St. Andrew owns three brass candlesticks which are attributed to Paul Revere; they were given to the Lodge by Brother Thomas Dakin in 1785. Although unmarked, they are fabricated in a manner consistent with late eighteenth-century manufacture. Given the evidence currently available, it is impossible either to confirm or refute their attribution to Revere. Certainly the bell foundry that Revere operated would have been capable of fabricating such items. However, the ledger books for the foundry do not list candlesticks among the wares produced. Records from the Revere hardware business do contain occasional references to imported brass candlesticks, indicating that the three candlesticks owned by the Lodge of Saint Andrew may have been procured by Revere. Entries in a Revere memorandum book of 1784 to 1793 (owned by the Grand Lodge of Masons in Massachusetts) list objects made or obtained for the Lodge of St. Andrew and for the Rising States Lodge; candlesticks are among the items noted in both lists.

44.
Goss, 2:488–91.

45.
For an account of the memorial procession, see *Proceedings of the Most Worshipful Grand Lodge of Ancient Free and Accepted Masons of the Commonwealth of Massachusetts in Union with the Most Ancient and Honorable Grand Lodge in Europe and America, According to the Old Constitutions. 1792–1815* (Cambridge, 1905), 157–60. Although the current whereabouts of the white marble urn is unknown, it is described in detail in Goss, 2:493–95.

46.
Proceedings, 1792–1815, 168.
47.
These casters are in the collections of the
Fogg Art Museum at Harvard University.
See Kenyon C. Bolton et al., *American Art
at Harvard*, catalogue for an exhibition
held at Harvard University from April 1972
to June 1972 (Boston, 1972), cat. no. 175.
48.
For a discussion of this object in relation to
Revere's overall post-Revolutionary output, see Deborah Federhen, "Revere Re-
examined," *Winterthur Newsletter* (Summer 1985).

Figure 23

Portrait of Paul Revere painted ca. 1768–1770 by John Singleton Copley (1738–1815). Oil on canvas, 35 x 28½ in. Courtesy, Museum of Fine Arts, Boston. Gift of Joseph W., William B., and Edward H. R. Revere (30.781).

From Artisan to Entrepreneur

Paul Revere's Silver Shop Operation

Deborah A. Federhen

For over forty years, Paul Revere's silver shop formed the cornerstone of his personal and professional life, providing an outlet for his creative talents and for dramatic expression of political convictions. In addition, the shop's success enabled Revere to expand and diversify his business interests in the areas of importing and retailing English goods, metal founding, bell casting, the copper industry, and other speculative ventures. Revere's career as a silversmith is broken into two distinctly different periods of shop operation separated by a four-year term of military service during the Revolution: the early period running from 1757 until 1775, and the second beginning in 1779 and ending around 1800. Both periods are extraordinarily well documented by the survival of many of Revere's business records as well as hundreds of his silver objects. With this information it is possible to investigate the shop's organization, the changes in Revere's business as he diversified, and the ways in which the silver he produced reflected these changes.

Paul Revere inherited from his father both his knowledge of silversmithing and a fully equipped silver shop. With the death of Paul Sr. in 1754, the young silversmith was inhibited neither by lack of capital nor lack of equipment from practicing his trade. There is substantial evidence that Revere was casting elements from his father's molds throughout his career, but especially during the first decade. For example, a caster made by Revere circa 1755–1760 used the same molds to cast the foot and bowl that his father had used for a caster ten years earlier (Figs. 24 and 25). Revere continued to use his father's molds for porringer handles until the end of the century.[1]

Similarly, the network of business relationships established by his father proved vital to Revere's early success. Revere Sr. purchased household goods and shop supplies from the Boston merchant Benjamin Greene between 1739 and 1753, offering a variety of silver objects in exchange for the merchandise. Greene became one of the younger Revere's earliest customers, ordering a sugar dish on 27 February 1762. Payment was made with a combination of cash, silver, and household goods.[2] Greene and his son, Benjamin Greene, Jr., continued to patronize Revere until 1796.

Revere's early period of shop operation is distinguished by the great variety in the types of silver made and the services offered by the shop. He produced ninety different kinds of objects—including cups, canns, and casters, buckles, buttons, and butter boats; tea sets, trays, thimbles, and tankards; and a variety of flatware forms, as well as children's whistles, pistol grips, an Indian pipe, a set of surgeon's instruments, and a squirrel chain. Many of Revere's most unusual forms including candlesticks, cranes, a chafing dish, an extinguisher, a funnel, and cases for miniatures, were commissioned during the earliest period of his shop operation—before a lull in production in 1769 and 1770. These items reveal Revere's impressive skill and versatility as both a designer and a craftsman. The preparation of intricate patterns and molds for casting special-

ized forms was an expensive and time-consuming process, particularly for one-of-a-kind objects.[3] The concentration of these unique forms occurs in the early years of Revere's shop when he was eager to expand his business, demonstrate his skill, and please his patrons. In later years, when his business and reputation were well established, it was not necessary to accept commissions that would require substantial investments of time and materials for the design and construction of unusual objects.

Revere's daybooks include a detailed record of payment rendered in addition to objects ordered. Patrons were assessed according to the weight and value of the silver and the labor required to make the object with additional fees charged for extras, like wooden handles or engraving. Epes Sargent's order for a coffeepot on 4 March 1769 illustrates this system:

Epes Sargent Esqr	D^r	
	Oz	
To a Silver Coffee Pot at w^t 27 : 5		
To the Making		4.0
To Engraving the Arms		0.16.0
To the Wooden Handel		0.3.4

Sargent supplied Revere with 23 ounces 4 pennyweight of silver to partially offset the fee in his order.[4]

Setting the Tables of Well-to-Do Bostonians

Prominent among the objects produced in Revere's shop were an assortment of hollowware and flatware articles for the dining tables and tea tables of well-to-do Bostonians. Over half of his total production was comprised of objects for dining and drinking (Table A). Spoons of varying sizes, sometimes specified as tea, table, or salt spoons were produced in increasing quantities during the 1760s and 1770s. While some of these tablewares have modern equivalents, others have become obsolete. Salvers, chafing dishes, and ladles remained in common use throughout the nineteenth and twentieth centuries, experiencing occasional changes in form but retaining their eighteenth-century functions as implements for serving food. Revere's graceful butter boats are similar in form and function to modern sauce boats; however the "butter cup," an oversized double-bellied cup with a raised open-ended handle, is now a rare archaic form. Revere provided silver shakers for the various other condiments favored by his patrons: mustard, pepper, and sugar.[5] These casters appeared regularly during this first period of shop operations, but were not so common during the 1780s and 1790s. Porringers, likewise, enjoyed their greatest period of popularity before the Revolution. The daybooks record the production of fifteen porringers between 1768–1775, half that many after the war, and none at all after 1787.

Most of the hollowware forms made by Revere were connected with the preparation and consumption of beverages. The fifty-eight tankards and canns commissioned during this period indicate a robust, communal quaffing of beer, ales, spirits, and wine punch. These impressive, capacious objects reflected the conviviality of the "choice spirits" who gathered around the tables in taverns, lodges, and parlors for card playing or political debates.

The tea ritual offered a less boisterous but equally important occasion for social interaction.[6] Tea was introduced into Europe from the Orient during the early seventeenth century as part of the trade in spices, silks, and ceramics fostered by the Dutch, Portuguese, and English East Indies Companies. Though at first a rare and costly luxury, tea gained adherents rapidly as trade increased during the seventeenth and eighteenth centuries. Bostonians eagerly adopted the practice of drinking tea, consuming over sixteen thousand pounds of tea in 1759 alone.[7] The ritualized consumption of this exotic beverage demanded specialized accoutrements. Revere supplied a variety of silver items specifically for the tea ceremony: teapots, creampots, sugar dishes, sugar tongs, tea tongs, and teaspoons, and it is no surprise that in his portrait by John Singleton Copley, Revere holds a pear-shaped teapot typical of the type made in his shop prior to the Revolution (Fig. 23).

Tea drinking became a politically charged issue in the years immediately preceding the war with Great Britain. On 29 June 1767 the Townshend Revenue Act was passed, imposing duties on glass, colored pigments, lead, paper, and tea exported to the American colonies. The outraged merchants, traders, and citizens of Boston urged a boycott of the taxed goods to protest the taxation of the American colonies without colonial representation in Parliament. The success of the boycott resulted in the repeal of all the Townshend duties in 1770, except the tax on tea. The continuing controversy was escalated by the Tea Act of 1773 which granted the financially troubled East India Company a virtual monopoly in the exportation of tea to the colonies by allowing it to offer tea at prices considerably lower than the London markets. However, merchants resented the restriction of their trade by monopolies, and many colonists regarded the low prices as a subtle means of collecting the disputed duty on tea. At a mass meeting held in the Old South Meeting House, five thousand Bostonians voted unanimously to refuse payment of the tax.

Revere's silver production reflects this burgeoning political crisis. Until 1767 Revere made one or two teapots per year. From 1769 until 1775, when Revere closed his shop to serve the cause of American liberty, his production of teapots was reduced to two commissions in 1773. An entry in the daybook for 2 September 1773 records the order of a forty-five-piece service by Dr. William Paine of Worcester. Intended as a commemoration of Paine's marriage to Lois Orne, the silver was marked with the coat of arms of the Orne family and the bride's initials, "L. O." This service included a teapot, tea tongs and eighteen teaspoons, in addition to two canns, one tankard, two porringers, two butter boats, one creampot, one coffeepot, four salt spoons, and twelve large spoons. Paine's purchase of such a monumental tea service at the height of the furor over tea clearly and extravagantly proclaimed his Loyalist sympathies. In fact, in June 1774, Paine coauthored a protest of the Boston Tea Party, published in the *Massachusetts Gazette* and the *Boston News-Letter*, in which he denounced the "baneful influence" of the committees of correspondence and deplored the waste of "teas of immense value, lately belonging to the East-India Company [which] were not long since, scandalously destroyed in Boston."[8] The Paine service is a compelling example of the practical separation of business and politics. Revere did not allow his political differences with his patrons to jeopardize a profitable commission. He may even have enjoyed the irony of a Tea Party "Indian" making a teapot for a Loyalist.

Many Bostonians who boycotted tea during this period turned to other beverages, such as coffee. Revere had made only two coffeepots by 1767 when the tea crisis began to simmer. However, in 1769 when British warships challenged entry into Boston harbor, British soldiers were quartered on the common and in Faneuil Hall, and an angry populace boycotted English goods, Revere's patrons purchased six coffeepots in that year alone. Another four were ordered in 1772 and 1773 (Table A).

Trying Times

The volume of transactions handled by Revere's silver shop fluctuated widely during the 1760s and 1770s. Both the turbulent political climate of Boston and, to a lesser degree, domestic crises adversely affected Revere's work. On 18 February 1756, Revere left his work as a silversmith and accepted the commission as a second lieutenant for a local artillery regiment raised to defend British interests during the French and Indian War. Revere's enlistment lasted from the spring of 1756 until the end of that year. [9] A more personal trauma was responsible for a reduction in output during February and March 1764, as explained by a notice in the records of the Boston selectmen. On 16 February, Revere reported that one of his children had contracted smallpox, the Revere family was quarantined in their house for the duration of the illness, probably a couple of weeks.[10]

Revere's business suffered during the postwar depression which followed the cessation of the French and Indian War. With the decline in the mercantile trade in 1765, many of the merchants who had patronized the silversmith were no longer able to afford luxury items which they had purchased in such quantity only a year earlier.[11] To bring in extra cash, Revere rented part of his shop. An entry in his daybook for 15 April 1765 states, "This Day Lett Part of My Shop to Mr. Thomas Beney. The Rent to be Paid Quarterly at four Pounds a Year." However, in the fall of 1765, Revere's estate was confiscated for a debt of £10 to Thomas Fletcher.[12] Although he was able to settle his debt without legal action, the economic situation for Revere, and indeed for Boston, remained grim for another five or six years.

Table A

	1761–1775		1779–1797	
	Number	Percent	Number	Percent
Silver Objects				
Flatware	410	35.8%	2,069	49.15%
Tea and Coffee Wares	61	5.3%	198	4.7%
Table Wares	129	11.3%	177	4.2%
Personal Items	449	39.2%	623	14.8%
Harness Fittings	0	0.0%	1,044	24.8%
Miscellaneous	96	8.4%	99	2.35%
Total Objects	1145	100.0%	4,210	100.0%
Services (orders)				
Engraving	65		306	
Printing	73		45	
Number of Prints	8163		17,699	
Repairs	82		332	
Tools and Supplies	8		18	
Dentistry	1		0	
Brass/Pewter	0		84	

Revere's political activities account in part for the dramatic reduction in his silver shop transactions between 1767 and 1770. As a member of the North End Caucus, the Long Room Club, and the Sons of Liberty, he was actively involved in directing the resistance to the Townshend Act. In the years just prior to the outbreak of hostilities at Lexington and Concord, Revere frequently rode express to Philadelphia and New York for the committees of correspondence, often being absent from Boston for eleven or twelve days at a time. Business in the silver shop slowed considerably due to his extended absences in September, October, and December 1774. Overall, however, the shop experienced an increase in productivity during 1773 and 1774, probably due to the influx of English officers into Boston, prewar speculation, and the assistance of at least two new apprentices including his son, Paul Jr.

In spite of the fluctuations in production due to illness or insurrection, it is still possible to determine a recurrent pattern of seasonal peaks. The first annual surge seems to have occurred during February, March, and April, with a second developing between August and November. These periods coincided with the arrival of the most up-to-date goods from England in the spring and fall. Periods of active mercantile trade were beneficial to craftsmen like Revere in several ways; generous supplies of specie in circulation encouraged the commission of luxury goods such as silver and provided silversmiths with a source of raw material. In addition, many of Revere's clients were merchants who placed their orders for silver objects in the wake of a prosperous seasonal trade. These imported goods and the constant influx of new merchandise kept colonial craftsmen abreast of the latest London fashions and were an important style source for American silversmiths.

Many customers requested the addition of engraved ornament to their objects, frequently arms, monograms, or inscriptions, an optional feature for which they were charged extra. The earliest entry in the daybook

Figure 26

Bookplate for Gardiner
Chandler, engraved ca.
1760–1770 by Paul Revere
(Cat. No. 100). Courtesy,
Paul Revere Memorial
Association.

which itemizes engraving is an order for a teapot on 17 February 1762:

```
Mr Saml Treat Dr
To a silver Tea Pot Wt Oz at 7/p Oz      6.7.9
                            18.5
To the Making Tea Pot                              3.6.8
To Engraving Tea Pot                               1.6.7
To a Wooding Handle                                0.3.4
                                                £11.4.5
```

Revere occasionally added engraving to items brought in by his patrons. In 1765 he added arms on two salvers for Zachariah Johonnot, put
arms on a teapot for Edward Procter, and engraved two crests for Doctor
Philip Godfred Kast.[13] Most of the elaborate coats of arms were engraved
during the 1760s and 1770s. Heraldic engraving on silver contributed not
only to an object's beauty, it enhanced the status of the owners by associ-
ating them with English nobility and served as a reliable means of identification in the event of theft. Revere's heraldic engraving was not confined
to silver. He engraved bookplates for at least fifteen customers, of which
eleven examples have survived.[14] The coat of arms that appeared on the
bookplate for Gardiner Chandler (Fig. 26) is the same as the arms engraved on Lucretia Chandler's silver (Fig. 27).

The use of heraldry in America was not governed by the strict regulations which prevailed in England. The jurisdiction of the College of Her-
alds did not extend to the colonies, and as a result, Americans displayed
arms with considerable freedom. John Guillim's *A Display of Heraldry*,
well known in the colonies during the eighteenth century, presented
hundreds of illustrations to those wishing to adopt a family coat of arms.
Originally published in 1611, Guillim's voluminous survey of English heraldry had been revised and reissued four times before 1724, when the
sixth edition was published.[15] There is no documentation for Revere's
ownership of this volume; however, there is substantial evidence that he
possessed a detailed knowledge of heraldry. For example, the Sargent
arms on a bookplate that Revere engraved for Epes Sargent in 1764 conform to Guillim's specifications for the name of Sargeant, "Argent, a chevron between Dolphins naiant embowed Sable," despite the absence of a
line drawing to accompany the description.[16]

Figure 27
Salver made in 1761 for Lucretia Chandler by Paul Revere. Diam. 13⅛ in. Courtesy, Museum of Fine Arts, Boston. Gift of Henry Davis Sleeper in memory of his mother, Maria West-cote Sleeper (25.592).

Figure 28
Clifford coat of arms from John Guillim, *Display of Heraldry*, London, 1724. Courtesy, Henry Francis du Pont Winterthur Museum Library: Collection of Printed Books.

Patrons whose family name did not appear in *A Display of Heraldry* may have adopted the arms associated with a similar name or a related family branch. The latter possibility might explain the use of the Clifford arms (Fig. 28) by members of the Chandler family.[17]

The arms displayed on the tea service ordered by William Paine in 1773 to commemorate his marriage to Lois Orne, demonstrate a creative disregard for the rules of heraldry. Since the Orne family apparently had not been granted a coat of arms, Revere adapted the arms of the Forster family, a design of "a Chevron Vert, between 3 Bugle-horns stringed Sable" which was probably suggested by the phonetic similarity of Orne and horn.[18] The Forster arms were already known to Revere before the Paine commission, since his father had engraved a variant of this design on a teapot for the Foster family circa 1740.[19] Revere's stylistic debt to the elder Revere is clearly evident in much of his engraving. The cartouche, foliate mantling and banner that appear on a bookplate which Paul Sr. engraved for himself in the 1720s was reused by the younger Revere in the 1760s for the Chandler and Sargent bookplates among others.

Building a Name: Common Objects for Daily Life
Only one-half of Revere's production from 1761 to 1775 was made up of elegant, richly engraved tea- and tablewares. Miscellaneous odd forms and small personal items comprised the other half. Unusual items like candlesticks, snuffers, masonic jewels, children's whistles, funnels, cranes, and thimbles formed only 8 percent of his total production. The 449 personal items (39 percent) produced by Revere between 1761 and 1775, however, constituted a significant category. Revere supplied his patrons with hundreds of buckles for their shoes, coats, stocks, and breeches, as well as gold, silver, and stone buttons for their garments. Revere's work in gold was confined to small objects: buttons, broaches, beads, bracelets, and rings. These small unpretentious articles contributed substantially to the financial success of Revere's shop. Their value as advertising far outweighed their unassuming character since they carried the Revere name into the daily life of Bostonians of many economic levels.

Diversification was essential in order for a silversmith to overcome a fluctuating economy, an intermittent market, a decline in maritime trade, and a deteriorating political situation. The scarcity of silver and the subsequent decline of commissions during the postwar depression of the mid-

1760s motivated Revere to offer several auxilliary services. Orders for repair on silver, including cleaning and burnishing, peaked during 1763 and remained numerous until 1766, increasing again in the four years just before the Revolution. Copperplate engraving and printing developed into an important facet of Revere's business. Revere's interest in printing was evident early in his career. In December 1761, he paid Isaac Greenwood £5.15.0 for "half of a Roiling Prefs."[20] A notice placed in the *Boston News-Letter* 11 May 1769 announcing the sale of "a large rolling-press, for printing off a copper plate," identifies the equipment owned by Revere, and confirms his commercial interest in copperplate engraving even before his daybook records any printing commissions.[21] Orders for prints rose into the thousands after 1770. An account with Edes and Gill, a firm of printers for whom Revere occasionally engraved mastheads, shows that they supplied the silversmith with large quantities of paper stock between August 1770 and April 1772.[22] Revere received his largest engraving commission from Isaiah Thomas, a close friend and a fellow member of the Masons and the Sons of Liberty. Thomas, publisher of the radical *Massachusetts Spy*, founded a new conservative Whig publication, the *Royal American Magazine*, in 1774. Revere supplied the engravings for each issue. His ability as an engraver lay in his meticulous craftsmanship rather than in his creative powers. Many of his political prints were copied from English broadsides. The earliest of his political cartoons, "A View of the Year 1765" was copied from an English caricature; a portrait of the Reverend Jonathan Mayhew in 1766 was taken from a mezzotint by Richard Jennys, and "A Warm Place—Hell" engraved a year later was modeled after an English cartoon entitled "A Warm Place—Hell" satirizing the Scots.[23] The derivative nature of Revere's engraving was not unusual for the eighteenth century; artists borrowed freely from every available design source until the establishment of copyright restricted this option. Revere's reliance on predominantly English sources for his engravings is a compelling indication of the overwhelming influence of English culture on the colonists, in spite of growing political differences.

Dentistry was another service that Revere performed. Having learned this trade from Dr. John Baker, a surgeon-dentist who practiced in Boston 1767-1768, Revere immediately advertised his ability to replace missing teeth with artificial ones in the *Boston News-Letter*, 25 August 1768, and the *Boston Gazette*, 19 September 1768.[24] Revere billed Samuel Hewes in 1771 for engraving a copperplate, running off seven hundred prints, and fastening his teeth.[25] Three years later a daybook entry records that John Jay had his teeth cleaned and purchased a pot of dentifrice from the silversmith.[26]

A Silversmith's Shop: Opportune Alliances

The quantity and variety of products and services offered by the Revere shop indicates a business of substantial size and scope. The shop of Boston silversmith Zachariah Brigden, a contemporary of Revere's, provides an interesting comparison. Zachariah Brigden produced much less hollowware than Revere during the period 1765–1775 and relied heavily on repair work in his business. Even so, Brigden's accounts record his transactions with fifteen shop assistants—journeymen and apprentices.[27] Revere also staffed his shop with unskilled apprentices and experienced journeymen. Apprentices would have begun their training by assuming responsibility for routine menial tasks such as cleaning the shop, collecting silver filings for refining, and tending fires, gradually performing more difficult jobs as they became more adept. Journeymen, skilled craftsmen who lacked the means to establish their own shops, were able to assist the master silversmith with the design and fabrication of intricate objects. Some supplied specialized skills, such as casting, engraving, or jewelry making. However, since only the master's mark would appear on the finished object, the work of many of these men, and in most instances their very identities, remains anonymous.

Revere's daybook provides clues to the identities of four of his assistants. The earliest mentioned is his younger brother, Thomas. Born in 1739/40, Thomas would have been of the age to start his apprenticeship when Paul Sr. died in 1754. Both convenience and necessity suggest that Thomas was trained by his older brother Paul. When his seven year apprenticeship ended, Thomas continued to work for his brother as a journeyman. An entry for 9 April 1761 charged Thomas £9.19.0 for "Sundays out of the Shop," cash lent, fourteen weeks board as well as some articles of clothing, and a wig. As an apprentice, Thomas would have received room and board with his master's family as part of his contract; this bill probably marks his shift in status from an indentured youth to a day laborer.[28] Two more possible journeymen were charged for board in 1762, Samuel Butts was assessed for five weeks on 19 May and Mathew Metcalf for two weeks on 8 September. The Metcalf entry includes a line for "Ballance of Old Acct" indicating that this was not a new relationship. Butts continued to appear in the daybook until 24 August 1764 when he settled his account with Revere for three weeks and five days board and shop supplies. He had received a share of his father's estate a week earlier and possibly ventured out on his own, since he does not reappear in the Revere accounts.[29] In 1774 Revere received an anxious letter from Josiah Collins of Newport expressing concern over the status of his son's apprenticeship. "It greaves me to be obliged to inform you that I Cannot pay you for the Board of my d[r] Child till my Returne or the Returne of the Vefsel, which will be about 3 Months . . . This, I hope will not be the means of my poor Childs Suffering."[30] Although Revere undoubtedly had more assistants working in his shop prior to the Revolution, their identities are still unknown.

Revere frequently relied on fellow craftsmen to furnish him with specialized objects, services, or shop supplies, and in turn, his particular talents were utilized by his colleagues. The turner, Isaac Greenwood, provided Revere with a variety of services from 1757 until 1774. Revere's accounts with Greenwood include payments for "turning" coffeepots, teapots, casters, and canns; for making a pattern for a wine cup; and for making wooden handles for coffeepots, teapots, and ladles.[31] In the 1760s, Revere collaborated with jeweller Josiah Flagg on several songbooks. Flagg used his musical abilities to set the tunes in scores; Revere engraved the plates. Revere charged his partner £150 for one-half the engraving costs, but covered the other half as his share of the expenses of the book.[32]

Prior to the Revolution, Revere's accounts record transactions with thirteen silversmiths. Subcontracting difficult orders to silversmiths with special talents or to large shops was a mutually beneficial practice. Successful, skilled craftsmen like Revere profited through the expansion of their business and the enhancement of their reputation. Silversmiths with less diversified shops were able to offer their clientele a variety of articles which they had neither the patterns, equipment, skill, nor time to make or produce. One of the earliest mentioned, Samuel Minott, commissioned

Revere to make three salvers and a "chased" sugar dish, probably indicating repoussé ornamentation.[33] Special skills are necessary to create successfully the flawlessly flat surface of a salver or the complex texture of repoussé work. Revere's proficiency at making these difficult objects was well recognized by his colleagues; John Coburn, Nathaniel Hurd, and John Symmes also ordered "chased" objects or salvers from Revere in 1762 and 1767.[34] Many of the objects which Revere made for other silversmiths were unusual or unique forms, evidence of the professional respect accorded his craftsmanship and his skills in design.

Revere's transactions with John Welsh are indicative of a different sort of professional relationship involving the exchange of services for goods. From 1760 until 1765 Revere obtained shop supplies from Welsh including salt petre, borax, pumicestone, gold foil, picture glass, crucibles, gravers, files, shoe chapes and flukes, black pots, and binding wire. In payment he engraved jewelry and made spoons, spectacles, and odd buckles for his colleague. One of Revere's most curious objects, a squirrel chain, was commissioned by Welsh on 21 November 1772.[35]

Revere's clientele included many others besides his professional colleagues. His early success was due as much to social and familial connections as to his obvious talent. James A. Henretta's study of the mercantile and social systems of colonial Boston concluded that "there was a direct relation between permanence of residence and economic condition." Henretta observed, "Even in an expanding and diversifying economic environment the best opportunities for advancement rested with those who could draw upon long-standing connections, upon the credit facilities of friends and neighbors and upon political influence."[36] During the early years of his career, Revere received many orders from his maternal relatives, the Hitchborns. Six members of this family appear as customers in the first daybook, including his uncle, Thomas Hitchborn, and his cousins, Nathaniel, Robert, and Thomas Jr., all boat builders, Benjamin, a lawyer, and William, a hatter. Another client, Nathaniel Fosdick, was related to Revere through his marriage to Frances Hitchborn. Revere also found a number of patrons among his neighbors on Clark's Wharf. Besides his cousin Thomas Hitchborn Jr., Revere made objects for Ezra Collins, the Webb family, and the Cochrans. Isaac Greenwood, who performed services as a turner for Revere, and John Webb, who furnished Revere with shop supplies, likewise lived very close to Clark's Wharf.

Social, political, and religious organizations provided Revere with further opportunities to develop business contacts. Josiah Flagg and Joseph Snelling, who as boys had served as bell ringers with Revere at Christ's Church, became his patrons as adults. Revere became a Freemason by joining the Lodge of St. Andrew in 1760. His fellow masons proved to be loyal customers with over a dozen lodge members appearing in the first daybook.[37] The very first entry in his daybook, 3 January 1761, records the order of a Freemason's medal for James Graham.[38] Revere produced masonic medals and jewels for his lodge brothers and engraved notifications of meetings. He received some commissions from neighboring lodges as well. On 15 June 1773 the Tyrian lodge requested an engraved copperplate and four hundred prints for meeting notifications and two Steward's jewels.[39] Many of Revere's patrons were actively involved in the same political organizations of which he was a member; the Sons of Liberty, the Long Room Club and the North End Caucus.

Revere's clientele encompassed many other facets of Boston society including prominent merchants (Thomas Greene, Thomas Brattle, Zachariah Johonnet, the Quincys, and the Amorys) as well as artisans and tradesmen. Despite his own fervent stand as a patriot, Revere's business relationships transcended political affiliations, and he numbered among his customers such notable Tories as John Coffin, Epes Sargent of Gloucester, and the Chandlers and Paines of Worcester. Before the outbreak of the Revolution disrupted Revere's career, he had established himself as a successful silversmith with the respect of his colleagues, a diverse and influential clientele, and an active role in the political and social life of Boston.

The Second Shop Period, 1779–1797

During the second period of his shop operation, Revere's output changed dramatically, both in number and type of objects produced. Over four thousand objects are recorded in the daybooks between 1779 and 1797, almost four times the amount fabricated during the earlier period (Table A). While an equal number of different forms were made during this later phase, slightly fewer hollowware forms were produced— thirty as compared to thirty-four. Flatware forms, on the other hand, proliferated. Revere made fourteen types of spoons including spoons for mustard, marrow, capers, ragout, dessert and pap, as well as the more usual tea-, tablespoons, and salt spoons. In quantity, production of both hollowware and flatware increased during the second period; however, hollowwares decreased significantly as a percentage of the total output whereas flatware comprised over 49 percent of the total (Table A). There were fewer of the unusual forms which characterized Revere's pre-Revolutionary production. The objects made after 1779 are predominantly standard forms, a change in production which allowed Revere to establish patterns and procedures which his journeymen and apprentices could execute, releasing him from direct involvement in the design of each object and enabling him to diversify his business interests, while still drastically increasing the silver shop's output.

The types of objects ordered from Revere's shop during this period suggest that some changes may have occurred in the culinary habits of his affluent Boston patrons. The increase in the number of spoons designed for specific foods suggests that dining was becoming more ritualized requiring elaborate table settings to consume a progression of separate courses. Revere imported significant quantities of English knives and forks for resale in his retail shop. Over six thousand knives and forks are recorded in his shipping invoices for 1783.[40] An intriguing variety of handle types were available: split bone, "green Japanned," sham stag, white bone, and Chinese. These enormous quantities of imported flatware were undoubtedly ordered by Revere in response to the needs of his customers, and are another indication of the development of an increasingly complex and formal dining ritual. Revere made very few silver forks or knives in his career. The English imports, relatively inexpensive and plentiful, were a more practical solution to the escalating demand for specialized flatware. William Foster paid Revere £7.11.6 on 18 November 1784 for a set of six silver forks engraved with crests. In contrast, Revere paid only £4.16.- in October 1783 for 576 "white Bone table Knives & forks."[41]

Porringers began to decline in popularity as a utensil for general use and were more frequently associated with children. Between 1762 and 1774 Revere made sixteen porringers, of which only one was identified as a child's porringer; during the later period, he made eight standard porringers between 1781 and 1787 and six child's porringers, all ordered after

1792. Revere produced his only set of silver dishes in 1796, a set of four ordered by Edward Gray, each weighing about twenty-four ounces, slightly heavier than a teapot.[42] Very costly and easily scratched, Gray's silver dishes may have been admired, but it seems were never copied by Revere. The waning popularity of silver porringers and dishes at the end of the eighteenth century coincides with the increased importation of English ceramic tablewares into America, particularly the cream-colored earthenwares produced in Staffordshire. Revere bought "1 Crate Cream Col^d ware" and "one crate blue ware" for his retail shop in 1791 at a fraction of the cost of producing similar wares in silver.[43] As English ceramics became more readily available, Bostonians eagerly furnished their dining tables with decorative, reasonably-priced earthenware table services.

Revere continued to produce a wide variety of drinking vessels during the 1780s and 1790s, including canns, tankards, and cups. These objects essentially retained their mid-century form and construction methods and varied from these earlier counterparts only in the style of the engraving. Tankards diminished slightly in number during this period and cups more than doubled, another instance of the replacement of traditional communal vessels with an individual one. Goblets, which first appeared as a daybook entry in 1782, were an elegant new addition to the drinking paraphernalia made during this period. A set of six goblets made for Nathaniel Tracy in 1782 are among the most graceful objects ever made by Revere.[44]

By far the largest group of Revere's silver objects were designed for the preparation and consumption of tea, a beverage which wealthy Bostonians once again consumed with dedicated regularity and conspicuous elaboration. Following his visit to Boston in 1781 the Baron Cromot du Bourg reported that Bostonians "take a great deal of tea in the morning . . . [and] about five o'clock they take more tea, some wine, madeira [and] punch."[45] According to his daybook Revere made fifty teapots during the last two decades of the eighteenth century, a dramatic increase over the nine he produced prior to the Revolution. The earliest teapots of this period are cylindrical in form rather than pear-shaped, conforming to the neoclassical style popular in England at this time. Teapots made for Thomas Hitchborn in 1782 and Moses Michael Hayes in 1783 are of this type, with straight sides, applied convex shoulders, low domed lids and straight fluted spouts.[46] The spouts and shoulders are made of seamed metal, but the body is raised in the traditional fashion. The Hitchborn pot features gadrooning on the edges of the body and the cover, while the others have newer style beaded edges. By the mid-1780s, Revere was making teapots of seamed sheet silver in several styles—oval, paneled, and fluted. Delicately engraved with oval medallions, wreaths, drapery sags, floral garlands, and foliate bands, these lovely teapots display the restrained ornamentation, symmetrical design, and balanced proportion espoused by the English neoclassical style.

New Technology and the Liberal Craftsman

The development of machinery for the production of sheet silver revolutionized the craft of silversmithing. Rolled sheet silver could be cut to shape and seamed rapidly and easily, thereby eliminating the costly and time-consuming process of raising holloware. Chambers's *Dictionary*, published in 1853, commented on the changes that the rolling mills had affected on the silversmith's art:

The business of the goldsmith formerly required much more labour than it does at present, for they were obliged to hammer the metal from the ingot to the thinness they wanted but there are now invented flatting-mills, which reduce metal to the thinness that is required at a very small expense.[47]

In *The Colonial Silversmith: His Techniques & His Products*, Henry J. Kauffman has suggested that while many silversmiths trained in traditional techniques may have resisted the use of prefabricated metal sheets, "it is probable that the change was very welcome to those with more liberal views and a keener eye for favorable bank balances."[48] Revere, undeniably possessed of liberal views, an inventive spirit, and financial ambitions, began to investigate the potentials of sheet silver almost immediately following the reopening of his shop. The cylindrical teapots Revere made during the early 1780s have spouts and handle sockets of sheet silver attached to raised bodies. Although he had not acquired sufficient confidence with the new material to construct an entire object with it, his eagerness to explore fully the possibilities of sheet silver is evident from the fluting of seamed parts. Revere's success with these early experiments encouraged him to expand his use of rolled silver, a venture that culminated in the intricate shapes of Revere's paneled and fluted sheet silver teapots.

Flatting mills were present in the colonies as early as 1733, when one was listed in the inventory of Philadelphia goldsmith Cesar Ghiselin.[49] Philadelphia craftsmen seem to have adopted this new technology before the other colonies. Another Philadelphia silversmith, Joseph Richardson, wrote to England in 1760 for a pair of replacement rollers for his own flatting mill and for that of a colleague.[50] During the 1770s, Philadelphia's newspapers carried advertisements for flatting mills and rolled metals and on 23 October 1789 the *Pennsylvania Packet* announced the opening of The American Bullion and Refining Office which supplied artisans with both refined and plated metals.[51] Revere had acquired a plating mill by late 1785 when he was billed 8 shillings by Solomon Munro for "one day work a putting up plating mill."[52] Munro charged Revere a further 1 shilling and 8 pence for the "16 foot joist" he used to build a platform for the plating mill, suggesting a mill of considerable size. Diderot's *Encyclopedie* includes several illustrations of flatting mills, some small enough to fit on a work bench, others requiring their own framework. Revere's plating mill would probably have looked very similar to these wooden frames with metal rollers which could be regulated with screws to control the thickness of the metal (Fig. 29). After 1785, Revere would have been able to supply his own sheet silver, freeing him from a reliance on irregular shipments of costly imported metals.[53]

Revere experimented with several seaming techniques for sheet silver. Some of his late teapots are seamed with the traditional butt joint. However, the majority are constructed by overlapping the edges to be soldered.[54] Not only is this a stronger method for attaching two sheets of very thin metal, but less training and experience are required in order to form a clean lapped joint. By altering his construction method, Revere was able to delegate much of the work in his silver shop to journeymen and apprentices, a savings in both time and money. Variations in the placement of the seams, the amount of overlap, and the direction of overlap indicate the presence of more that one craftsman at work. Revere's willingness to adopt new technology and abandon traditional construction techniques allowed him to increase the output of his silver shop dramatically and maintain a high standard of quality while simultaneously devoting more of his time to other business ventures.

The tea ceremony became increasingly complex at the end of the eighteenth century, requiring correspondingly augmented tea services. After 1790 teapots were frequently accompanied by teapot stands and containers for sugar and cream. Seven teapots were ordered en suite with a creampot and a sugar dish during the 1790s compared to only one such set before this time.[55] Revere made many tea accessories as separate items for his patrons, presumably to enhance their existing tea services. Between 1781 and 1797 Revere sold fifty pairs of sugar tongs, fifty-eight creampots, eighteen sugar bowls and twenty-one teapot stands. Teapot stands, intended to disperse the heat of the teapot so as to avoid burns on the table top or table linens, had become almost a standard feature during the last decade of the century. Variations in terminology for these objects reveal a great variety in the shape and style of the containers in which Bostonians served their sugar and cream. Revere made jugs, buckets, pots, and pitchers for cream, the last two with both plain and fluted surfaces. Tea drinkers dipped sugar tongs into silver sugar baskets, dishes, bowls, and urns designed for the sweetener.

Revere made one of his most extensive tea services for John and Mehitable Templeman on 17 April 1792. The Templemans ordered a teapot and stand, tea caddy, sugar urn, creampot, punch strainer, tea shell, six tablespoons, and twelve teaspoons. Additional pieces were added over the next year; a cann, four salt spoons and a coffee urn in 1792, a stand in 1793, and six large spoons, twelve teaspoons, and a stand in 1793.[56] The Templeman service includes several unusual forms. The tea caddy is one of only two such sets made by Revere; the tea shell is unique.[57] Punch strainers, although less rare, occur only sporadically throughout Revere's career; four of the seven recorded were made after the Revolution. The Templeman punch strainer supports Baron Cromot du Bourg's observation that wine punch often accompanied tea at a festive evening gathering. The ostentatious display of an elaborate and formal tea etiquette was not restricted to Boston. Revere supplied tea wares to patrons in surrounding towns like Worcester, Salem, Newburyport, New Bedford, and Roxbury, and farther afield in New Hampshire, Maine, Connecticut, and New York.

The consumption of tea reached staggering proportions in the late eighteenth century, particularly following the opening of the China trade to American ships in 1784; coffee, however, retained a consistently modest popularity. Twelve coffeepots and coffee urns appear in the daybooks for the second period, the same number as in the earlier period. Coffeepots made during the 1780s and 1790s differ little from their earlier counterparts in form or construction. By 1791, Revere had updated the appearance of the traditional coffeepot with engraving in the neoclassical style, ribbons, swags, and floral garlands surrounding an oval medallion.[58] Coffee urns are a radical departure from the traditional form for coffee. Only three are recorded in the daybooks in 1783, 1792, and 1793. A pair of punch urns made for John Codman in May 1795 are probably similar in shape. These elongated urns raised on footed pedestals with sweeping loop handles and soaring conical lids are the ultimate ceremonial vessels dispensing beverages with graceful dignity and costly splendor.

The bulk of Revere's shop output, however, was comprised of small objects and stock goods, rather than monumental coffee urns or elegant fluted teapots. He produced simple hollowware forms out of sheet metal

Figure 29

Diagram of a plating mill (figs. 25 and 26) from Denis Diderot, *Encyclopedie, ou dictionnaire des sciences, des arts et des metiers, 1751–1772.* Vol. II, plate II. Courtesy, Henry Francis du Pont Winterthur Museum Library: Collection of Printed Books.

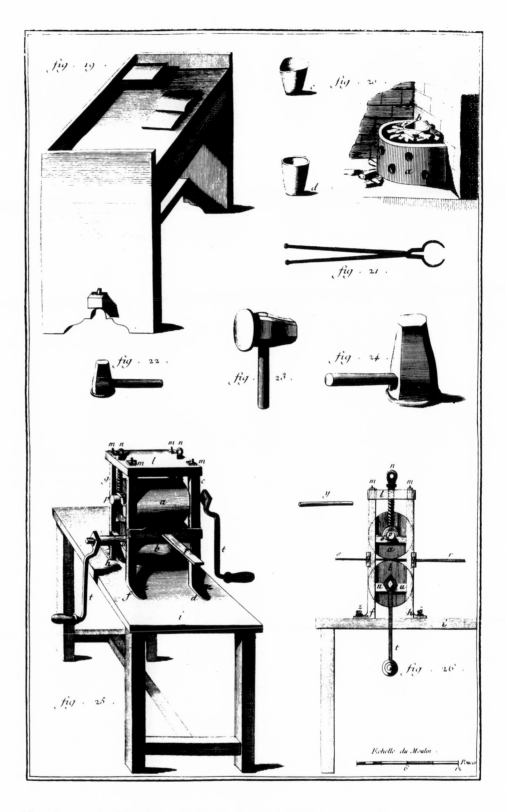

like the seamed beakers made for Ozias Goodwin around 1800. Personal items, especially buckles and buttons, made up almost 15 percent of his production. Between 1780 and 1797 his patrons ordered 318 silver and gold buckles to fasten their boots, shoes, sleeves, and breeches. The daybooks record another 115 plated buckles during these years.

Harness Fittings and Hat Bills: Collaboration with Other Artisans
Revere initiated extremely profitable associations with four saddlers

and harnessmakers in 1787. For seven years he supplied Zachariah Hicks, John Dyer, Edward Cole, and John Winneck with a staggering number of silver and plated harness fittings—1,044 saddle nails, stirrups, slides, and bridle buckles and tips in several sizes. Although none of them have survived, contemporary paintings of horses portray vividly the quantity and variety of metal fastenings needed to outfit a horse for riding or driving. An accurate idea of the size and shape of Revere's harness buckles can be found in his Memoranda Book, 1788–1795, which contains patterns for four sizes of plated harness buckles, with a notation of how much silver was required to plate each kind. Revere made other equestrian accoutrements, such as breast plates, "winker" plates, spurs, and chaise ornaments.[59]

Although Revere imported a variety of plated Sheffield wares from England after the Revolution, his orders do not appear to include any buckles. There is ample evidence that Revere was manufacturing his own silver-plated objects.[60] His Memoranda Book for 1788–1795 includes a recipe for plating silver onto copper:

Receipt to Silver Copper pl
Take half an ounce of Fine Silver fillings put it into an oyl flask, put one ounce of double Aqua Fortis to it and dilute it with some warm water till the silver disolved frequently shaking it. then turn it into a glass tumbler, and put in some pulverized sal-amoniack to precipitate the silver, it will settle like a curd at the bottom, after it is all settled, wash it with warm water till there is no taste in the water, put it into some glazed vessel, then add ¾ an oz of pul^{zd} Sal-Amonia put them in a small quantity at a time in the above proportion, stirring them with a clean stick till it becomes a paste, rub the paste on your copper with your finger after you have prepared your copper by pumicing it & rubing it smooth with a fine stone, taking care to keep your finger clean, first whet it, & dip it into the tarter & sal-amoniac rub the copper before you put on the paste.[61]

In addition to the paste method, there is evidence to suggest that Revere could produce fused plate with his plating mill. A plating mill could easily function as a flatting mill to create sheet silver, but included in the design was a method for heating the rollers to provide the combination of heat and pressure necessary to fuse sheets of silver and copper together into silverplate. Revere consistently refers to his mill as a plating mill; although terminology alone is not conclusive evidence, Revere's identification of his mill as a plating mill rather than a flatting mill presupposes his familiarity with the technology of fuse plating. Furthermore, the sudden escalation of Revere's production of small plated wares after 1786 to over eleven hundred objects suggests that he had acquired a fast and efficient method for producing plated silver.

Revere's plating mill would have been invaluable in producing large quantities of silver and plated buckles quickly and efficiently. The hundreds of bridle buckles which Revere made between 1787 and 1793 were probably cut out of small sheets of silver plate which he produced with his mill. The patterns for plated harness buckles in his Memoranda Book are simple three-sided rectilinear forms, which could easily be cut from sheet metal; the small size is shown nested inside the large buckle, no doubt to utilize the maximum amount of the plated sheet metal. Among the silver residue which Revere sent to London for refining in 1791 were "clippings of plated buckles." This probably refers to the scraps of sheet metal left over after the buckles had been cut out, as well as debris created by trimming the rough edges of these buckles. Buckles plated with the paste method would receive their finishing touches before the application of the silver mixture, and, therefore, would not require additional trimming after being silvered. Buckles for personal adornment which featured raised decorative surface ornamentation could not be cut from sheets of silver plate, and were undoubtedly plated by the paste method. Apparently he only fabricated small plated objects in the silver shop since rings, chains, buckles, trunk hardware, electrical points, and jackets for glass sconce arms are the only plated objects sold in the daybooks.[62] It was probably cheaper for Revere to import plated hollowware from Sheffield than to produce it himself.

Revere's relationship with a family of hatters, the Boardmans, began in 1773 when he sold William Boardman three hundred hat bills—small printed makers labels affixed to the inside of hats.[63] Before the Revolution, Revere made five hundred hat bills for this customer. After the war, business escalated for Boardman, now in partnership with his son on Ann Street. On 20 August 1783 they ordered a copperplate and two hundred hat bills from the silversmith.[64] During the second period of his shop operation, Revere printed 8,522 hat bills for the Boardmans.[65] Hat bills appear with some consistency throughout both daybooks, but not in any overwhelming quantity until 1792. In that year, Revere established a business relationship with hatter William Williams, also located on Ann Street. By the close of the second daybook in 1797, Williams had ordered 8,700 hat bills.[66] Orders from a few other hatters brought the total number produced during this period to over 17,000. In spite of the astounding number of hats with Revere labels worn by Bostonians at the end of the century, not a single example of these small advertising labels has survived.

Not all of Revere's output was custom work. A sampling of hollowware and an assortment of small objects would be made in advance and arrayed in the shop window or display cases to entice potential customers and to demonstrate the silversmith's skill and versatility. One of the first things that Revere did upon reopening his shop in August 1783 (now both a hardware store and silver shop) was to prepare such objects for display. An extensive entry for August lists the "Stock Ready made in the Cases" and includes buckles, buttons, broaches, gold rings, pins, a gold necklace, spurs, teaspoons, tablespoons, salt spoons, sugar tongs, creampots, casters, a soup ladle, and a punch ladle.[67] Large hollowware forms involved a greater financial investment in labor, materials, and design, and were therefore not appropriate as a stock item. Even though most of the articles were small, the display stock still represented a considerable investment, valued at over £117.

While there are no eighteenth-century depictions of the interior of an American silver shop, Diderot's *Encyclopedie* provides a glimpse into the interior of a silversmith's shop of approximately 1771 (Fig. 30). One corner of the room is devoted to retailing the objects made within the shop, and is furnished with a sales counter and glass-fronted wall cases filled with a miscellany of small items. Revere's cases may have looked similar to these, although probably somewhat less grandiose.

Revere's second period of shop operation shows a fairly regular influx of transactions, without the large gaps which occurred during the turbu-

Figure 30

Silver shop interior, ca. 1771 from Denis Diderot, *Encyclopedie, ou diction-naire des sciences, des arts et des metiers, 1751–1772.* Vol. VIII, plate I. Courtesy, Henry Francis du Pont Winterthur Museum Library: Collection of Printed Books.

lent pre-Revolutionary years. Partnerships for the production of specialty goods, like harness fittings and hat bills, and a steady business in stock goods compensated for irregularities in orders for custom work. The greatest concentrations of transactions occur between 1787 and 1792, coinciding with the period of Revere's contracts with the saddlers and harness-makers. Fluctuations in the number of orders received by the shop still occurred seasonally, in the fall and spring, corresponding to the arrival of the newest imported mechandise in the Boston retail shops. Foreign trade was extremely important to Boston's domestic economy. Revere complained about the adverse effects of the disruption of trade in a letter to his agent in England on 15 April 1784:

> *We have had the most tedious Winter I ever knew; our harbour has been froze up, the greatest part the time; and the forming of a Bank here which is not opened yet, has made a great stagnation of money, that we have been able to do but little business.*[68]

From the records it seems that Revere's shop received only two orders in March 1784 and none at all during April, a compelling illustration of the interdependence of the domestic economy and the mercantile trade.

A Continuing Dependence

Commercial ties with England were essential to Revere's work as a silversmith in several ways. He relied on trade to obtain shop supplies, secure refining services not available locally, acquire household goods for resale in his hardware store, and apprise him of the latest London styles. Revere did not completely sever these ties even during the Revolution. Several exiled Boston Tories served as his contacts in England and Revere still occasionally made silver for some of his expatriated patrons. One agent, John Joy, offered to accept a dozen dessert spoons as compensation of the silversmith's £18 debt.[69] In his eagerness to receive supplies from England, Revere anticipated the Treaty of Paris by several months. The treaty ending the war with England was signed on 3 September 1783. However, in July 1783, two months before the resumption of legal trade with England, Revere received six casks of imported hardware, flatware, and miscellaneous small metal objects valued at £444.17.2, for which he had paid a 20 percent advance.[70] This shipment included some metalworking supplies—twenty-four dozen files, twenty dozen scissors, and twenty-seven dozen iron chapes for shoe and knee buckles. His agent, Frederick William Geyer, shipped twenty-five casks of nails on 22 August 1783.[71] Revere purchased a large quantity of shop equipment from Geyer during September 1783 and February 1784.[72] In 1784 Revere began to order tools from John Sampson, a London jeweler. Evidently tools were considered contraband even after the Treaty of Paris, and Sampson wrote to advise Revere of the difficulty in shipping these commodities in early 1785:

> I am Duly favᵈ with your very obliging letter of 9 Decʳ the Commissions wherein you have been so kind as to favour me with shall claim my particular attention and I flatter myself they will give you entire satisfaction and will be shiped by the very next Ship that sails. if the Invoices are unavoidably excised by the quantity it may remain until you have occasion for any thing further in my way. it is with Difficulty we are able to get any tools shipt as they fall under the Denomination of prohibhitted wares you will oblige me by keeping it unknown to the Captain who conveys them as my future conveniency in shipping may be hurt.[73]

In addition to metalworking tools, Revere stocked a comprehensive selection of household wares. Although he bought some of his goods locally from merchants or at auction, the bulk of this inventory too was imported from England. He advertised his hardware services in the *Massachusetts Centinel* on 10 December 1785:

> Imported and to be Sold, by Paul Revere, Directly opposite Liberty-Pole, A General assortment of Hardware, consisting of Pewter, Brass, Copper, Ironmongery, Cutlery, Jappaned and Plated Wares, Among which are a few neat Brass Sconces, of one, two and three branches, 3-pint plated Coffe-Urns, and Goblets, Very neat jappaned Tea-Trays, in sets Brass Candlesticks, Looking-Glasses, Patent-Jacks, Carving Knives, &c. &c. All which will be sold at the lowest advance for cash. The Gold and Silver-Smith's business carried on in all its Branches.

Coins remained one of the most prevalent sources of metal for the silversmith.[74] Samuel Dillaway is credited with "silver & 4 dollars" toward his order for a new silver teapot, sugar dish, pair of casters, and spoon in 1787.[75] There were other sources of silver available as well. Patrons brought in old silver objects which were damaged or out-of-style to be melted down and reshaped into newer forms. In September 1796 Mary Jarvis supplied Revere with fifty-three ounces of silver including an old tankard and cann, from which he fashioned a teapot, four silver salts, eighteen teaspoons and six creampots.[76] Revere and his shop assistants carefully collected the scrap silver generated in the shop; leather "aprons" attached to the edges of the workbench caught the filings and clippings as the silversmith worked (Fig. 31). The floor was swept each night to collect any casting scraps or clippings. Occasionally, Revere used these stray bits and pieces of silver residue to pay for imported goods. He sent his agent Geyer a combination of "Gold lace burned & melted," "silver Ditto" and "a composition of mettals the Sweep of a Goldsmith's

Figure 31

Silver shop workbench, ca. 1771 from Denis Diderot, *Encyclopedie, ou diction-naire des sciences, des arts et des metiers, 1751–1772.* Vol. VIII, plate VIII. Courtesy of the Trustees of the Boston Public Library.

shop" with instructions for him to assay the metal and "write a particular account of the value of what each piece Fetched per Ounce for I expect it will be in my power to make considerable remittances in such things."[77] A memorandum dated 8 December 1791 states, "Sent by Cap[t] Tristram Barnard bound to London a quantity of metal the filings & clippings of plated buckles & a quantity of pumice dust containing silver, to git refined & to purchase a plating mill. I expect near 30 oz silver."[78]

From Goldsmith to Gentleman: Revere's Business Network

Before the Revolution Revere's silver shop had been the sole focus of his activities; now it had become a cog in a larger business network. After 1787, Revere stopped calling himself a goldsmith on official documents like deeds and began styling himself "Esquire." He used the goldsmith shop as a reliable source of capital to finance the expansion of his business through various speculative ventures.[79] From 1783 until 1789 there are numerous entries in the daybook for cash taken out of the shop amounting to hundreds of pounds. A few are identified as payments for rent or supplies. The vast majority, however, are unspecified. The supply of ready cash generated by his silversmithing activities enabled Revere to experiment professionally. One of the earliest digressions was a partnership with Simon Willard to manufacture clock jacks. Willard sent Revere a brief message in 1782, "I am happy to inform you that Jack-Business goes on beyond my Expectations."[80] Though business flourished over the next few years the partnership was terminated in 1785 at a loss to Revere.

His next enterprise, a more ambitious undertaking, expanded his expertise into other realms of metalworking. In 1788, he opened a foundry on Lynn Street in Boston for the smelting of iron and brass. In November 1788 he wrote optimistically to Mess[rs] Brown & Benson, furnace owners from Providence, Rhode Island, "We have got our furnass agoing, and find that it answers our expectations, & have no doubt the business will do exceedingly well in the Town of Boston . . . I should be glad that you would ship as soon as possible ten tons of Pigs by the way of Nantucket without there should be a vessell coming here from Providence." Revere was very anxious to obtain a steady supply of raw materials for his foundry, and offered to sell a share of his furnace to Brown & Benson in exchange for pig iron.[81] The trade card for the foundry illustrates the primary product lines manufactured there, shipbuilding materials, canons, and bells. Funding was probably provided by profits from the silver shop. There are frequent entries in the second daybook for withdrawals of cash. Entries "To Cash" began in 1783 and end abruptly in 1789. Although Revere did not establish any additional businesses in the 1790s, he did explore new markets for his products, particularly in the South. Samuel Paine, a shopkeeper in Richmond, Virginia, sold some of Revere's hardware goods in his store in 1790.[82] Newspapers in Savannah, Charleston, Alexandria, Richmond, Norfolk, and Baltimore informed their readers of Revere's work in iron and brass at the foundry and at the copper rolling mill he opened in Canton in 1800.

The expansion of Revere's business empire after the Revolution provided increased opportunities to purchase English goods. Revere relied heavily on plated wares and pattern books imported from Sheffield as models for the design and ornamentation of his silver objects. He received a large shipment of forty different types of plated goods in January 1784 including an illustrated pattern book. Revere wrote enthusiastically to Geyer extolling the potentials of the trade catalogue and asking that another be sent to him,

> *They enclosed me in the case of plated ware a book with drawings which is a very good direction for one to write by. I should be very glad if you would send me eight pair of plated branches, four of No. 103 and four of No. 178 as marked in said book. If they have drawings different from the book I received should be glad they would send me one more book.*[83]

The impact of these Sheffield designs upon Revere's silver was phenomenal. In many instances Revere seems to have copied his designs directly from Sheffield prototypes. Models for many of the unusual forms listed in the second daybook can be found in Sheffield pattern books including the punch urn, hooped cann, and tea shell. Vessels for making tea and coffee dominate the catalogues in an astounding variety, providing Revere with inspiration for the design and construction of his own wares (Fig. 32).

Revere drew upon other style sources, in addition to imported English silver, silverplate, and Sheffield pattern books. Creamware pitchers with transfer-printed decorations of landscapes, ships, or political emblems were imported from Liverpool in increasing numbers toward the end of the eighteenth century. Interest in French arts intensified following the alliance with France during the American Revolution. Derby, a prominent Salem merchant, acquired a set of four silver beakers made by Parisian silversmith Denis Colombier in 1789 (Fig. 33). Six years later, Derby commissioned Revere to augment his set of cups with eight copies (Fig. 34).[84] Revere easily duplicated the straight sided cup and the applied rim mold-

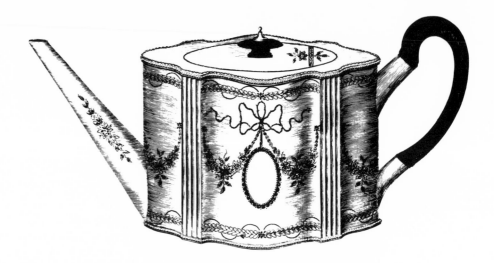

Figure 32

Illustration of a teapot (plate 110) from Love, Silverside, Darby & Co., *Trade Catalogue*. Sheffield, England, ca. 1785. Courtesy, Henry Francis du Pont Winterthur Museum Library: Collection of Printed Books.

ing. His treatment of the engraved decoration, however, is a simplified version of the original, alternating shells and roses separated by a wavy band. The Derby cups are a good example not only of French influence on American silver, but of the importance of customer preference in determining the style of an object.

Journeymen, Apprentices and Relatives:
The Craftsmen in Revere's Shop

Variations in the construction of the objects marked with Revere's stamp during the 1780s and 1790s indicate that a number of craftsmen—journeymen, apprentices, and relatives—were employed in Revere's shop. Workmanship can vary significantly during this period; the silver is not hammered to a consistent gauge; covers do not always fit perfectly; and a number of variations in seaming techniques are in evidence in addition to the differences in the engraved decoration.

As Revere diversified his business interests, he relied increasingly on his son, Paul Jr., to manage the silver shop. The Revolutionary War interrupted Paul Jr.'s formal apprenticeship with his father; however, he was left in charge of the house and shop during Revere's exile in Watertown, a compelling indication of Revere's confidence in his young son's abilities. By 1782, the younger man had completed both his military service and his unconventional apprenticeship. Revere wrote proudly to his cousin John Rivoire on 1 July 1782, "My eldest son has left the army, and is in business for himself." Father and son had reunited in a partnership by August 1783 when he appears regularly in the new daybook for the silver shop. A receipt from Isaac Greenwood on 27 November 1793 acknowledges the partnership as "Paul Revere & Son."[85] A sporadic notation of hatch marks, naughts, and crosses in the margins of the daybook is partially explained on a page for June 1789 as denoting responsibility for the order.[86] Revere's mark, slanting hatch marks, occurs most frequently during the 1780s, but declines after 1791 when presumably he spent more time at the newly opened foundry. The younger Revere's marks, horizon-

Figure 33

Beaker made by French goldsmith Denis Colombier in 1789 (Cat. No. 61). Courtesy, Metropolitan Museum of Art. Mr. and Mrs. Marshall P. Blankard Gift, 1967 (67.94).

Figure 34

Pair of beakers made in 1795 or 1797 by Paul Revere (Cat. Nos. 62–63). Courtesy, Metropolitan Museum of Art. Mrs. Russel Sage Gift, 1958 (58.3.1–2).

tal hatchmarks or a cross, occur quite regularly throughout the book. Notations for father and son rarely appear beside large orders or orders for hollowware, which probably required the attention of several shop members. Paul Jr. continued his silversmithing activities until 1806, maintaining the Revere tradition while his father devoted himself to new pursuits at the Canton rolling mill.

Another son, Joseph Warren Revere, was also trained as a silversmith. Joseph, twelve when the foundry opened, made his career in the family's copper and brass industries. However, Revere considered training in a traditional metalsmithing craft to be a means of ensuring a livelihood. Revere provided his son with both the opportunity to experiment in a new field and the skills to succeed in a secure profession.

David Moseley, memorable as a troublesome apprentice and an irresponsible craftsman, ran away from Revere to sign on as a shipmaster's apprentice. Revere eventually recovered Moseley, an action he may have regretted bitterly later when Moseley's marriage to Revere's sister, Betsey, extended his responsibility for the errant artisan beyond the term of his apprenticeship. Moseley's account in the ledger for the retail shop documents a very one-sided relationship. Moseley obtained shop supplies from his brother-in-law, without payment, and was unable to overcome alcoholism. By 1796, Revere's memoranda book indicates that money for the couple was delivered to Betsey.[87] Revere was eventually appointed administrator of the Moseley estate in an effort to improve their bleak financial situation.

Another apprentice, Thomas Stevens Eayres, married Revere's daughter, Frances, in 1788. Eayres, however, earned praise for his commitment and ability and Revere readily supported his son-in-law when the younger man tried to establish a business in Worcester. He wrote warmly to his friend Isaiah Thomas on 8 May 1791 that Eayres "has a need to carry on his business, which is a Goldsmith, in the Town of Worcester . . . I recommend him as an Industrious and Ingenious Tradesman and of good morals, and I dare say, he will be an acquisition to the citizens of any town he may settle in, your Kind notice and advice to him will be received as done to myself."[88] Eayres's attempt to relocate to Worcester in 1791 was unsuccessful. The Worcester town meeting voted to rescind the taxes for "Thomas S. Eayres, a Madman gone to Boston."[89] In spite of his illness, Eayres established a silver shop on Essex Street upon his return to Boston. By 1802, however, his deteriorating condition necessitated the appointment of a guardian, a position which Revere filled willingly until Eayres's death in 1813.

Several names emerge from the records as possible journeymen in the Revere shop. David Ripley boarded with Revere in October 1789 and received payment of sixteen shillings and six pence.[90] Ripley was born in Hingham, Massachusetts, 27 August 1767, and had established himself as a silversmith, clockmaker, and bookbinder in Greenfield by 1801. The daybook entry for Ripley's board includes charges for 14½ ounces of silver and chapes, suggesting that Ripley may have been making buckles for Revere. William Homes received cash payments from Revere in 1791 and 1803 totaling over £21.[91] Homes's shop on Ann Street was very close to Revere's shop and some collaboration between the two silversmiths would have been convenient. Thomas Kettell was paid the considerable sum of £77 in 1803. Kettell and Homes, both established silversmiths by this time, were probably involved with Revere in a specific project rather than working as journeymen.

As with the earlier period, Revere exchanged services with other Boston craftsmen. His long-term relationship with Isaac Greenwood continued into the 1780s, as a receipt dated 27 November 1783 for "five shillings in full of all accounts to this date" from Greenwood to Paul Revere & Son attests.[92] He supplied shop equipment, raw materials, and finished products to many of his colleagues, including his cousin Samuel Hitchborn, Benjamin Burt, Nathaniel Austen, Caleb Beal, Stephen Emery, Samuel Minott, Joseph Loring, and George Trott. His reputation as an engraver continued to attract patronage from his peers. Burt, a skilled designer, commissioned Revere to engrave a dish, a cup, a pair of gold buttons, teaspoons, and a pair of tea tongs in May and October 1792.[93] A fluted teapot, covered sugar urn, and creampot in the Museum of Fine Arts, Boston, were made by Burt, but have the distinctive tassel and swag engraving found on Revere silver and were probably sent to the Revere shop to be decorated. Revere also produced some silver objects which were restamped and retailed by several of his colleagues.

The staggering escalation in Revere's silver output following the Revolution was not the result of a corresponding growth in the number of his patrons. In quantity, Revere's clientele increased only slightly, from 300 before the war to 312 in the later period; in character, however, his patronage changed significantly. Many of his early business relationships were terminated by the war, and only forty-six customers patronized Revere during both periods of his shop operation. He continued to make silver for his Hitchborn relatives, including his uncle Thomas, and cousins Samuel, a silversmith, and Benjamin, a Harvard-educated lawyer. Another cousin, Phillip Marrett, and a son-in-law, Amos Lincoln, both placed orders with Revere. Some of his most loyal supporters were fellow masons; of the fourteen who appear in the second daybook, half were carryovers from the earlier period, including Samuel Barrett, Stephen Bruce, Michael Moses Hayes, John Lowell, Perez Morton, Edward Proctor, and Dr. John Warren. Friends established during Revere's political activities as a patriot, like Moses Gill and Thomas Dawes, became patrons during the peaceful and prosperous aftermath of the Revolution. Merchants continued to dominate Revere's list of patrons. Forty-eight of his customers called themselves merchants, and no doubt many of those listed in the city directories without a profession or as "Esquire" were involved in trade as shipowners or importers. Perez Morton, Harrison Gray Otis, and Elias Hasket Derby were prominent members of the new emerging elite, the "gentleman-trader." The most significant change in Revere's clientele during this period was the increasing number of craftsmen.[94] Some of these men were purchasing silver for their own use; others, like the saddlers and hatters discussed earlier, were business associates. Revere sought long-term contracts for specialty items with craftsmen in other professions as a means of stabilizing the flow of transactions into the shop and increasing production.

As his own business identity shifted from an artisan to an entrepreneur, the character of Revere's silver shop, silver products, and patrons altered to accommodate his new goals. Emphasis shifted from the erratic production of custom goods, to a more standardized line of objects and specialty items, regulating the operation of the shop so that it would function smoothly and efficiently within a larger business network.

Notes

1.
Compare the handle of a porringer made by Revere Sr. in the Museum of Fine Arts, Boston, with porringers by the younger Revere at Yale and the MFA, Boston.

2.
Benjamin Greene Ledger, 1734–1758; Revere Waste and Memoranda Book, 1761–1783, 6–7, RFP.

3.
Barbara McLean Ward's research on early Boston goldsmiths suggests that cast objects like candlesticks which required complex molds were made primarily by a few silversmiths who specialized in casting. Surviving examples appear to have been made by a small number of craftsmen using similar molds. See Barbara McLean Ward, "Boston Goldsmiths, 1690–1730," in Ian M. G. Quimby, ed., *The Craftsman in Early America*, (Winterthur, DE, 1984), 147.

4.
Revere Waste and Memoranda Book, 1761–1783, 35, RFP.

5.
Younge, Greaves and Hoyland, *Trade Catalogue* (Sheffield, England, ca. 1790). The price list for this trade catalogue identifies the contents of the bottles in a cruet frame as "Soy, Ketchup, Cayan, Tarragon, Lemon and Elder." It lists other sets which combine casters and glass bottles, providing silver containers for the dry spices, cayan, pepper, and tarragon and glass cruets for the liquid condiments.

6.
Rodris Roth, "Tea Drinking in Eighteenth-Century America: Its Etiquette and Equipage," *U. S. National Museum Bulletin*, 225 (1961): 63.

7.
John Marshall Phillips, *American Silver* (New York, 1949), 98.

8.
Revere Waste and Memoranda Book, 1761–1783, 46. For quote see Louisa Dresser, "American Silver Given in Memory of Frederick William Paine, 1866–1935," *Worcester Art Museum Annual* 2 (1936–1937): 90.

9.
Forbes, 42, 44.

10.
Ibid., 76–77.

11.
James A. Mulholland, *A History of Metals in Colonial America* (Alabama, 1981), 90.

12.
Forbes, 107.

13.
Revere Waste and Memoranda Book, 1761–1783, 5, 25, 26, RFP.

14.
Collections of Revere's bookplates are held in the Yale University Library. The eleven surviving examples are illustrated in Clarence S. Brigham, *Paul Revere's Engravings* (New York, 1969).

15.
Barbara McLean Ward and Gerald W. R. Ward, *Silver in American Life* (New Haven, 1979), 76.

16.
Revere Waste and Memoranda Book, 1761–1783, 23, RFP; John Guillim, *A Display of Heraldry*, 6th ed. (London, 1724), 240.

17.
Guillim, 407.

18.
Guillim, 315.

19.
John Gardner's bookplate illustrated in Brigham, plate 52, uses a similar design of three stringed horns and a chevron with a tincture.

20.
Isaac Greenwood Account, 1757–1761, RFP.

21.
George Francis Dow, *The Arts and Crafts in New England 1764–1775* (Topsfield, MA, 1927), 21.

22.
Edes and Gill Account, January 1696–November 1772, RFP.

23.
Jane Ross, "Paul Revere—Patriot Engraver," *Early American Life* 6 (April 1975): 36–37. The most extensive analysis of Revere's design sources for his engravings can be found in Brigham's *Paul Revere's Engravings.*

24.
Dow, 55; Forbes, 130.

25.
Samuel Hewes Account, January - April 1771, RFP.

26.
Revere Waste and Memoranda Book, 1761–1783, 49, RFP.

27.
Brigden Daybook, 1780–1785, Brigden Papers.

28.
Family ties do not seem to have affected Revere's accounting of business relationships. Revere charged his mother, Deborah Revere, for 12 months board on 10 December 1762 and for 52 weeks board on 12 December 1763 and 25 December 1764 and kept records of both the goods she supplied and money spent on her behalf. See Revere Waste and Memoranda Book, 1761–1783, 14, 21, 25, RFP.

29.
Ibid., 1761–1783, 9, 12, and 23, RFP.

30.
Josiah Collins to PR, Letter 22 November 1774, RFP.

31.
Revere Waste and Memoranda Book, 1761–1783, 11, 25, 49; Greenwood Account 1757–1761, RFP. In her book *Joseph Richardson and Family, Philadelphia Silversmiths*, Martha Gandy Fales provides further documentation of the interrelationship of turners and silversmiths. She cites (p. 283) the *Boston Chronicle* 1–8 August 1768 in which turner Isaac Fowls advertises "Turns work for Gold-Smith, viz. Tankards, Canns, Casters, Salts."

32.
Elbridge Henry Goss, 1: 54. Goss included a bill from Revere to Flagg for silver show buckles, a silver creampot, a pair of "turtle shell" buttons, "one half of Engraving Copper Plates for Singing Book," and various amounts of silver, gold, and cash.

33.
Revere Waste and Memoranda Book, 1761–1783, 11, 12, 13, RFP.

34.
Ibid., 1761–1783, 8, 13, 33, RFP.

35.
John Welsh to PR, Account 1761–August 1765; Revere Waste and Memoranda Book, 1761–1783, 42, RFP.

36.
James A. Henretta, "Economic Development and Social Structure in Colonial Boston," *William and Mary Quarterly* 22 (January 1965): 77.

37.
Masons who ordered silver from Revere include Samuel Barrett, Stephen Bruce, Capt. Cochran, James Graham, M.M. Hayes, John Lowell, Perez Morton, Edward Proctor, John Symmes, Isaiah Thomas, John Warren, Joseph Warren, and Joseph Webb. These names were identified in Forbes, Goss, and records of the Lodge of St. Andrew.

38.
Revere Waste and Memoranda Book, 1761–1783, 5, RFP.

39.
Ibid., 1761–1783, 45, RFP.

40.
Capt. Nathaniel Fellows to PR, Shipping invoice July 1783; Frederick Wm. Geyer to PR, Shipping invoice, 1 October 1783, RFP.

41.
Revere Waste and Memoranda Book, 1761–1783; Revere, Shipping Invoice, 1783, RFP.

42.
Revere Waste and Memoranda Book, 1761–1783, 150, RFP.

43.
Lewis Hays to PR, Invoice, 20 September 1791; Josiah Vose to PR, Invoice, 6 October 1791, RFP.

44.
Revere Waste and Memoranda Book, 1761–1783, 69, RFP.

45.
Roth, 66.

46.
Revere Waste and Memoranda Book, 1761–1783, 72, 73, RFP.

47.
Quoted in Fales, *Richardson and Family*, 282–83.

48.
Henry J. Kauffman, *The Colonial Silversmith: His Techniques & His Products*, (New York, 1969), 128.

49.
Harrold E. Gillingham, "Cesar Ghiselin, Philadelphia's First Gold and Silversmith, 1693–1733," *The Pennsylvania Magazine of History and Biography* 57 (1933): 248.

50.
Fales, *Richardson and Family*, 232, 234.

51.
Ibid., 283; Kauffman, 127–28.

52.
Solomon Munro to PR, Bill, 17 November 1785, RFP.

53.
Many of the objects made during the later period exhibit a considerable amount of firescale. Revere may have increased the amount of copper in his silver alloy; the addition of copper lowers the melting point of the alloy which would make the silver more responsive to the plating mill. The finished object would be pickled to remove the impurities on the surface and leave a thin layer of pure silver. Over time, successive polishings have revealed the irregular coloration of the alloy beneath the surface layer.

54.
Research by Janine Skerry and Edgard Moreno has suggested that possibly all of the Revere shop's seamed silver teapots have lapped joints which have been secured with silver rivets rather than butt joints.

55.
Kathryn Buhler, "Three Teapots with Some Accessories," *Museum of Fine Arts Bulletin* 61 (1963): 58.

56.
Revere Waste and Memoranda Book, 1783–1797, 119, 120, 129, RFP.

57.
Revere's daybook records a large service ordered by James Blake which includes a tea caddy. Revere Waste and Memoranda Book, 1783–1797, 93, 94, 100, 111, 122, 127, 129, 130, 150, RFP.

58.
Revere was not singular in his retention of the rococo coffeepot form. Ephraim Brasher made a double-bellied coffeepot in 1780–1790 which he updated with neoclassical engraving and an urn-shaped finial. This coffeepot, now in the Metropolitan Museum of Art, is illustrated in Safford, "Colonial Silver": 54–55.

59.
Harness fittings provided a constant and reliable source of business for another eighteenth-century metalworker. Connecticut clockmaker Daniel Burnap owned a small plating mill, with rolls of 1¾ inches and 2¼ inches, which he undoubtedly used to make buckles. His record books contain instructions for several methods of silver plating, two specifically designated for plating buckles. Penrose R. Hoopes, *Shop Records of Daniel Burnap, Clockmaker* (Hartford, CT, 1979), 73, 100, 121, 125.

60.
Revere, Shipping Invoices, 1783–1791, RFP.

61.
Paul Revere, Memoranda Book, 1788–1795, RFP.

62.
The daybook records other plated objects brought to Revere for repair, including candlesticks and tea wares, but there is no evidence that Revere ever made any of these items. For quote, Revere Memoranda and Journal, 1788–1795, RFP.

63.
Revere Waste and Memoranda Book, 1761–1783, 43, RFP.

64.
Ibid., 1783–1797, 78, RFP.

65.
Ibid., 1783–1797, 57, 71, 73, 83, 98, 106, 112, 114, 117, 122, 126, 130, 134, 141, 147, 148, 155, 157, 162, 165, RFP.

66.
Ibid., 118, 121–23, 128, 130, 132, 134, 140–41, 148, 151, 154, 161, RFP.

67.
Ibid., 4, RFP.

68.
Goss, 530.

69.
Forbes, 371.

70.
Revere, Shipping Invoice, July 1783, RFP.

71.
Frederick William Geyer to PR, Shipping Invoice, 22 August 1783, RFP.

72.
Ibid., Shipping Invoice, 20 September 1783; 12 February 1784, RFP.

73.
John Sampson to PR, Shipping Invoice, 10 March 1785, RFP.

74.
Revere was not the only silversmith to obtain silver from foreign coins. Zachariah Brigden's daybook contains an entry for "10 crowns to make a Tankard" in 1780. Zachariah Brigden, Daybook 1780–1785, Brigden Papers.

75.
Revere Waste and Memoranda Book, 1783–1797, 51, RFP.

76.
Ibid., 87, RFP.

77.
Ibid., 94, 95, 96, RFP.

78.
Goss, 528.

79.
Revere Memoranda & Journal, 1781–1785, RFP. Donald L. Fennimore's work on Fletcher and Gardiner of Philadelphia determined that they also used their silver shop as a revenue producing element in a large business enterprise. Donald L. Fennimore, "Elegant Patterns of Uncommon Good Taste: Domestic Silver by Thomas Fletcher and Sidney Gardiner," Unpublished master's thesis (University of Delaware, 1972).

80.
Simon Willard to PR, 1782, RFP.

81.
Goss, 531–32.

82.
Samuel Paine to PR, Shipping Invoice,
January 1784, RFP.
83.
PR to Frederick Wm. Geyer, 19 January
1784, RFP.
84.
Revere Waste and Memoranda Book,
1783–1797, RFP.
85.
Isaac Greenwood to Paul Revere & Son,
Receipt, 27 November 1793, RFP.
86.
Revere Waste and Memoranda Book,
1783–1797, 77, RFP; Buhler, *American
Silver*, 2: 433.
87.
Paul Revere, Memoranda Book, 1796–
1798, RFP.
88.
PR to Isaiah Thomas, 8 May 1791, RFP.
89.
Harry N. Flynt and Martha Gandy Fales,
*The Heritage Foundation, Collection of
Silver* (Old Deerfield, MA, 1968), 211.
90.
Revere Waste and Memoranda Book,
1783–1797, 82, RFP.
91.
Revere Memoranda Book, 1788–1795;
Revere Memoranda Book, 1795, RFP.
92.
Greenwood to Revere & Son, Receipt,
27 November 1793, RFP.
93.
Revere, Memoranda Book, 1788–1795,
RFP.
94.
It is somewhat difficult to draw very concrete conclusions about changes in the
professions of Revere's clientele during his
two periods of shop operation because documentation for the earlier period is limited. The "Taking Books" compiled by the
Assessors of the Town of Boston in 1780 is
the earliest city-wide census, with city directories appearing regularly after 1789.
There are no comparable documents for
the pre-revolutionary years.

Figure 35

Undated pen and ink
sketch of the Revere property in Canton, Massachu-
setts attributed to Paul
Revere (Cat. No. 38).
Courtesy, Massachusetts
Historical Society.

Patriotism and Profit

The Copper Mills at Canton

Edgard Moreno

In December of 1800, rounding out his sixty-fifth year, Paul Revere began an enterprise unique to our emerging nation. Through his own initiative, Revere established a successful factory for the production of a material of vital national importance: sheet copper. The copper mill at Canton, Massachusetts, founded and directed by Revere until his retirement in 1811, foreshadowed the metal industries of the nineteenth century which would transform the demographic, economic, and political directions of the United States.

Revere's prototypical factory faced many of the same issues as those encountered by the larger enterprises that were to follow later in the century. The need for supportive government interaction, the perfection of technology, the procurement of skilled labor and raw materials, the development of reliable sources of energy and transportation, and the legislation of commercial protection were vital to Revere's success. In his transition from the simple artisan captured in John Singleton Copley's portrait of the late 1760s (Fig. 23), to Saint-Memin's depiction of a well-to-do industrialist of 1800 (Fig. 36), Revere embodied the upward mobility that would become the hallmark of the nineteenth century. At a venerable age, Revere embarked on a venture of colossal magnitude.

The refining of copper was a largely unknown technology, with little information available to those outside the coppersmith's trade. Revere's knowledge of silversmithing would have been only marginally useful in his mastery of the processes employed in the mass production of sheet copper.[1] The mechanics for rolling copper on a large scale only recently had been perfected in England, and were a closely guarded secret. The procurement of either raw ore or refined copper was difficult even during the best of times and competition for it was fierce. Additionally, the amount of capital needed for this kind of venture was significant. Revere undoubtedly knew that should he fail, his assets would not cover the notes of credit. Revere was not the first to attempt the domestic manufacture of sheet copper, but he was the first to master it.

The surviving documents among the Revere Family Papers pertaining to the copper mill at Canton provide a window into the workings of early nineteenth-century American business and politics. Examining correspondence to and from Revere allows firsthand information to be assembled. As a businessman Revere displayed a dynamic and engaging personality struggling for the realization of a risky, and as yet unproven, venture. The factory's ledger books amplify the day-to-day operations, providing multiple insights into the nature of the clientele, quantity of business, profit margins, types of products, labor needs and payment, and technological problems and solutions. The paucity of substantive published information makes these papers, so rich in data, extremely important to understanding early domestic copper production.

Figure 36
Profile of Paul Revere drawn ca. 1800 by Philadelphia artist, Charles Balthazar Julien Fevret de Saint-Memin (Cat. No. 28). Courtesy, Museum of Fine Arts, Boston. Gift of Mrs. Walter Knight (47.1055).

Prelude: A Brief History of Copper Production

The refining of copper was man's first attempt at metal production.[2] Archeological evidence indicates usage as far back as circa 7500 B.C., making copper the oldest worked metal. Knowledge of copper technologies was consolidated over time; by the eighteenth century a limited amount of published information was available regarding the refining of copper ore. The specific metalworking techniques involved changed but little over the centuries. Copper ore, which is usually extracted by mining, is a material containing mineral complexes in which copper is an ingredient. In the refining process, the ore is crushed into small chunks by a water driven trip hammer. The small pieces can be densely packed into the furnace, thus providing a larger heating surface that results in a more controlled burning process. The ore, now ready for its first heating, is placed in a roasting furnace and heated to just below melting point. The heat, in combination with atmospheric oxygen, eliminates sulphur and other impurities from the copper ore. This process is known as oxidation. The ore, or charge, is then removed from the roasting furnace and packed in layers with fluxes, or oxidation retardants, in a high temperature reverberatory furnace.

The actual melting process, called smelting, commences at this stage. When the charge reaches approximately 1990 degrees Fahrenheit, it becomes a viscous liquid with a combination of flux, carbon, and minerals floating on the top. This surface scum is periodically drained off via a tap-hole in the upper side of the furnace. On the bottom, impure metallic copper settles, and through a different tap-hole is allowed to flow into hand-held ladles. The content of the ladles is called the "matte," which is an iron-copper sulfide with a smattering of gold, silver, lead, and traces of a half dozen other metals. A second smelting eliminates the majority of

these impurities. After the final smelting, the matte is transferred to a
crucible which is placed in an air furnace. As air is forced over the crucible by means of bellows, iron, sulphur, and other impurities such as silica
and alumina, float to the top as slag. The purified liquid at the bottom of
the crucible is then poured into rectangular molds. In this manner, a bar
weighing from thirty to one hundred pounds results. The outer surfaces of
these bars, or pigs, exhibit the excritas of the many gases which escape as
the metal cools, hence the name "blister copper." Most metallic copper
transported during the colonial and post-Revolutionary period was in the
form of pigs.

It is beyond the scope of this essay to enumerate all of the attempts at
domestic copper mining and refining. As early as 1707 mines in Connecticut produced limited quantities of copper. Subsequent mines and refineries in Belleview and Pluckamin, New Jersey, and Frederick County,
Maryland, also proved to be of short duration with only limited production
of refined copper. Some of these refineries did have the ability to produce
sheet copper, but their output appears negligible.[3] The fact that these
ventures were short-lived and ended rather badly for their proprietors is
indicative of the tremendous difficulties that faced copper producers.

In fact, prior to the establishment of the Revere mill at Canton, sheet
copper was either imported from England or scavenged and reworked
from discarded imported products. Newspaper advertisements attest to
the eagerness of coppersmiths to purchase old copper articles.[4] And as
will be shown, Revere used imported English copper sheet for his first
client.

As early as 1721 copper production had been restricted in the colonies. The amendment of that year to the 1660 "Act for the Encouragement
and Increase of Shipping and Navigation" decreed the sole destination of
copper ore to be England. This was of little economic significance to the
colonies due to the limited production of copper, though it does demonstrate that England held copper in equal esteem to the other strategic
naval materials such as lumber and tar. During the first half of the eighteenth century, constricting legislation tightened English control over colonial metals production. The "Iron Act" of 1750 specifically prohibited
the construction in the colonies of a furnace for iron smelting, or of rolling
and slitting mills. At least on paper, this law echoed the mercantilist philosophy aptly stated by a member of the English Board of Trade in 1726:

> Hence it follows that all advantageous projects which are truly prejudi-
> cial to and inconsistent with the interest of the Mother State must be
> understood to be illegal and the practices unwarranted, because they
> contradict the end for which the Colony had being.[5]

Thus, England's flourishing iron trade would be protected from competition. The colonies, by the same act, could ship domestically mined ore
to London duty free, but they could not manufacture it. They were com-
pelled to import manufactured iron from England. But similar to other
laws, the "Iron Act" proved to be unenforceable and by 1770 the colonies
had a greater number of forges and furnaces than England and Wales
combined.[6]

Why then did the colonists fail to attack the production of copper with
the same alacrity? The mechanics of refining and working iron are equivalent to those used in copper production. The demand for sheet copper is
demonstrated by the vast array of skillets, pans, pots, and kettles adver-

tised in eighteenth-century newspapers. Production of copper metal in the colonies, however, remained limited and sporadic. Ultimately, neither England's laws nor a lack of colonial ingenuity was responsible for the limited domestic production of copper. Market demand simply could not provide a lucrative return on this type of capital-intensive production. Pots and pans alone could not make copper production viable.

Colonial production remained limited until the introduction of sheet copper into the shipbuilding industry coincided with the need for an American navy. Copper sheathing of ship bottoms was a late eighteenth-century development which allowed for the greater speed and navigability essential to our developing navy. Revere was in an auspicious position at the proper time to take full advantage of this coincidence.

Copper Sheathing for Ship Hulls

The first documentation of English naval use of copper was in 1758 when the *H.M.S. Alarm*, a ten-gun frigate, was experimentally copper sheathed.[7] Previous attempts to mitigate the effects of the marine worm *teredo navalis*, which bores into the bottom planking of ships and destroys their water seal, had been unsuccessful. Applications of tar, hair, and paper in different combinations had been tried. Lead sheathing was found to be too heavy, and deal wood planking, though rarely successful, was exorbitantly expensive.[8] Worms were not the only bothersome creatures for ships' hulls on long voyages. The accretion of barnacles substantially reduced the speed and so the economic gain of a mercantile voyage. More importantly, barnacles and worms hampered the duration and efficiency of military vessels in the water.

In 1761 the Lords of the Admiralty ordered an examination of the *H.M.S. Alarm* to "observe the effect of worm" and to evaluate if the "bottom was clean or fouled of barnacles and weeds which usually collect on ship bottoms on long voyages."[9] In August of 1763 the Naval Board reported that the planking was free of both worms and barnacles. By the Revolution most ships were provided with the protective qualities of copper.

During the years between the Revolution and the beginning of the nineteenth century, our new nation continued to import copper from its reluctant trade partner and former oppressor. This dependence seems abnormal given the patriotic fervor of the new nation. However, the effects of the war were felt long after America's victory. Each sector of the American market felt the aftershocks caused by the transition from a war to a peacetime economy. Inflation was rampant; by late 1777 the rate of exchange for 1775 paper currency was three dollars to one. Within the next year the exchange rate had escalated to five 1775 dollars to one 1778 dollar. By the spring of 1779 it was sixteen to one, and by the late 1780s seventy-seven to one, after reaching a high of $169.50 in mid-1781.[10]

In this inflationary environment, the risks associated with capital investment, whether personal or borrowed, escalated dramatically. Concurrent with this financial chaos, New England's, and specifically Massachusetts', maritime trade suffered a double blow. The great mercantile wealth based upon codfish trade was abruptly cut off. Native fishing schooners that had not been burnt, sunk, or captured during the war were few in number; those which had been dry-docked needed extensive repair. The whaling industry had fared no better: of over two hundred whalers from Nantucket and Dartmouth, less than half a dozen remained.[11]

Additionally, the lucrative trade routes and their markets established while under English rule had been undercut during the war and were not successfully reopened in the following years. In order to stimulate her home market, England barred the West Indies ports to American cod importation. American whalers were likewise prohibited from English home ports. By 1786 Massachusetts was exporting one-fourth of the quantity of goods which it had in 1774. The reduced markets open to our trade, combined with American economic instability, caused the demand for new ships to become negligible.[12] European nations were quick to take advantage of the resulting depression of American shipbuilding activity in the late 1770s and 1780s. Dutch, Austrian, Swedish, and German ships thronged American harbors.

The 1790s demonstrated the resilience of America's maritime trade. Goods imported to and exported from China brought increasing amounts of much needed hard currency. A stable economy provided the incentive for expanded capital investment. The legislation of tonnage duties for foreign vessels docking at each port in America guaranteed a competitive edge for domestic shippers. Construction accelerated in Massachusetts shipyards; in the North River yard an average of twenty-three ships were built per year from 1799 to 1801.[13]

During the last decade of the eighteenth century, England's renewed hostility with France decisively set the stage for American production of sheet copper. France's 1793 declaration of war on England reopened the Anglo-French conflict after a ten year hiatus. Lord Howe had previously developed a British naval strategy during his tenure as first lord of the admiralty (1783-1788). It was actively implemented by him after taking over the Channel Fleet in 1790. England's open blockade of French ports provided both defensive protection against invasion and offensive advantage against French importation of necessary supplies. By necessity a great number of English ships were built or refitted to carry out the blockade effectively. The copper sheathing of ships became even more crucial to England's success in light of French Navy Minister Castries's 1780 order to copper all French warships.[14] Demand in England for domestically produced copper rose accordingly.

As the British concentrated on the war, their mercantile trading position weakened. The United States quickly seized the opportunity to expand its market share, thus stimulating maritime trade and ship construction. More shipbuilding created greater demand for sheet copper; increasing amounts were imported until 1798, when Great Britain's "Orders In Council" of that year restricted British copper exportation.[15] The subsequent sudden depletion of the richest copper mine in the empire, Anglesca, located in Wales, coupled with the high wartime demand, resulted in amended restrictions which further limited exportation. Coincidentially, a new and powerful client desirous of obtaining copper sheet entered the American market to compete with private shipbuilders. The United States Navy was created by act of Congress in the spring of 1798.

With private and public interest now competing for a limited supply of sheet copper the stage was set for its profitable mass production. From his vantage near the newly active shipyards of Boston, Revere was poised to begin his daring entrepreneurial venture.

Figure 37

Trade card engraved by Thomas Clarke, ca. 1796–1803, for Paul Revere and Son (Cat. No. 116). Courtesy, Paul Revere Memorial Association.

Creating an American Copper Industry

By 1800 Paul Revere's business activities centered on the manufacture of base metal objects. At his foundry located in the North End, he operated a profitable business producing cast bells and cast and drawn copper hardware for ships (Fig. 37). Imported copper pigs were melted, alloyed, and fabricated into various sized nails, bolts, clips, and other ship accessories. Revere's competition was limited to English products of equal or lesser quality. Despite a handsome return from this business, Revere chose to expand his production. Revere's correspondence shows a premeditated and obvious, though unstated, goal; to be the first successful American producer of sheet copper. The American government needed a stable domestic source for copper sheathing for her new navy. Within two years, the aspirations of each party coalesced into a new domestic industry.

On 11 March 1800, Paul Revere writes to the Honorable Harrison G. Otis in Philadelphia:

> *if the government would send me a quantity [of ore] and pay my expenses I would make furnaces and make myself master of this business [of smelting copper].*

Such unbridled optimism seems cocky coming from a man who admits later in the same letter:

> *I have never tried to smelt the ore because I have could never find any of it.*[16]

Perhaps this brash confidence, coupled with the navy's dire need, persuaded the government to consider his offer. This was not the first time the government had entertained proposals regarding the manufacture of naval hardware from domestic ore. At least two other contracts had been awarded: one to Benjamin Hentrey of Philadelphia for production of sheet copper from the "Gap Mine or other mines in the United States" and another shortly thereafter on 23 August 1799, to Jacob Marks and Nicholas Roosevelt.[17]

The Roosevelt attempt to refine native ore and produce bolts, spikes, nails, and sheet was an abysmal failure. Located near the Schuyler Mines north of Newark, New Jersey, the site produced copper spikes which were judged by the government to be unsatisfactory.[18] Although instructions and acceptable samples were sent to Roosevelt by Secretary of the Navy Benjamin Stoddert, the prototypes could not be reproduced. By January of 1801, the government had loaned the exorbitant sum of 51,800 dollars without receiving a suitable product. The new administration of 1801 terminated Roosevelt's contract, resulting in his bankruptcy, and substituted Revere's plan for copper production.

The government's unsuccessful partnership with Roosevelt clarified two points. The production of copper sheathing required extensive machinery "beyond the reach of individual capital and enterprise."[19] Further, America needed the "establishment of the domestic manufacturing of copper on a scale proportional to the probable demands of the United States for the Navy Department."[20]

As early as 12 April 1794, Joshua Humphreys advised Secretary of War Henry Knox of the radical changes, including copper sheathing, which would be incorporated into the construction of naval ships. Benjamin Stoddert, secretary of the navy, concurred, subsequently voicing his opinion that "the use of flannel soaked in tar on which the copper will be placed" should be employed.[21]

The advantages of an impervious surface on a ship's hull were obvious. Less apparent was the tremendous financial gain to be made by supplying this protection. A 1798 estimate of copper to be used on a seventy-four-gun ship was 1,620 tons. This was broken down by cost as follows:

6,600 feet bolts, 110,000 spikes   *$10,960.00*
3,600 copper sheets
(4' x 14" 36oz. to the sq. foot)   *$17,440.00* [22]

A clearer perspective is given by the following table:

Cost of a warship with:	*16*	*20*	*22 guns*
Total cost of ship	*36,670*	*56,110*	*64,354*
Total cost of copper	*5,150*	*8,980*	*10,200*
% of copper cost to total cost	*14*	*16*	*15.8* [23]

Using the figures given for the cost of bolts versus sheet for the seventy-four-gun ship, it can be calculated that approximately 60 percent of the total copper cost would be due to copper sheathing. The magnitude of these figures suggests the potential for substantial monetary gain. Given the government's desire to build a navy, Revere's plans to establish a copper rolling mill were both patriotic and potentially lucrative.

Revere had problems as early as December 1798 in procuring raw copper. He no doubt realized the government had the power to requisition native ore and imported pigs to meet the military needs. The letter to Harrison Gray Otis which requested the government to supply him with ore, cited previously, was the opening move in Revere's business strategy. No mention was made of sheet production; the initial emphasis was on establishing the contact and guaranteeing a source of raw material.

Apparently Revere received some encouragement since two months later, in May 1800, he traveled to the capital at Philadelphia. At navy secretary Stoddert's office, Joshua Humphreys offered to send Revere a quantity of ore for a trial smelting. From the secretary, Revere secured a contract to supply the bolts and spikes for two ships, one being built in Boston and the other in Portsmouth. More important, he was also engaged to "roll a portion [of the refined copper] into sheets provided [he] could attain it."[24]

By 17 January 1801 Revere sent the secretary a piece of sheet produced from native ore.[25] The ore, which had been sent in a barrel weighing over four hundred pounds, was reduced to about thirty pounds of pure copper after smelting by Revere. The refined copper was rolled into sheets using a silversmithing mill.[26] Revere's account of this experiment mentions repeatedly that the yield would have been greater, perhaps doubled, if the proper machinery were available.[27] In the letter sent with the copper sheet he complained that the ore had to be pounded by hand; that the melting furnace he used was for refining large quantities of copper (eighteen hundred pounds at a time), not for small amounts; and that the size of the sheet, although small, was as great as the largest mill in Boston could produce. Still, Revere had succeeded in refining and flattening copper sheet.

In the Stoddert letter of 1801, the first reference is made to a government loan to cover the expense of erecting a complex for the smelting, refining, and manufacturing of copper. Revere wrote to the secretary, stating that Mr. Higginson, naval agent, has informed him that "[the] government will advance me from 8,000 to 10,000 dollars to assist me in procuring a mill." Having already obtained the mill and having completed the order for bolts and spikes for one ship, Revere asked that a prompt payment be made since he had placed himself in great debt.[28]

The election of a new administration caused delays in the approval of Revere's request for his loan. Throughout the spring, Revere wrote the attorney general and the outgoing and incoming secretaries of the navy a series of letters requesting the promised assistance. These letters are almost identical in content, and give a clear picture of the intended government contract. The advance of ten thousand dollars was interest free, with a payment to be made in sheet copper sold to the government at a cost of fifty cents per pound. The terms stipulated that Revere was to credit twenty-eight cents per pound to the government's account for the raw material that they were to provide.[29]

By the time Revere finally received the long-promised ten thousand dollar advance, he estimated that the mill had cost him "at least $15,000."[30] With the loan in hand, however, Revere's situation dramatically improved. Although the exact date of Revere's receipt of the loan is not known, from his correspondence we know that it must have occurred after 29 June 1801. In May of 1802, Revere completed the contract for ten thousand dollars worth of sheet copper. In less than a year he had rolled approximately twenty thousand pounds of copper. The completion of this contractual obligation yielded sufficient profits to eradicate one-third of the original debt incurred by Revere in establishing the factory. The mill at Canton was up and running two years after Revere's first proposal to the government and only slightly more than a year after he first smelted copper. Few other American enterprises of this magnitude could boast of this accomplishment.

The Canton Mill

The land at Canton was bought by Revere from Messrs. Robbins, Leonard, and Kinsley in January of 1800 for six thousand dollars. Included in this transaction were the deeds to several buildings, among them a slitting mill (Fig. 38). Leonard and Kinsley had for many years operated a large ironworks on a portion of the property they sold to Revere. A stream running through the property provided power for "slitting" iron into work-

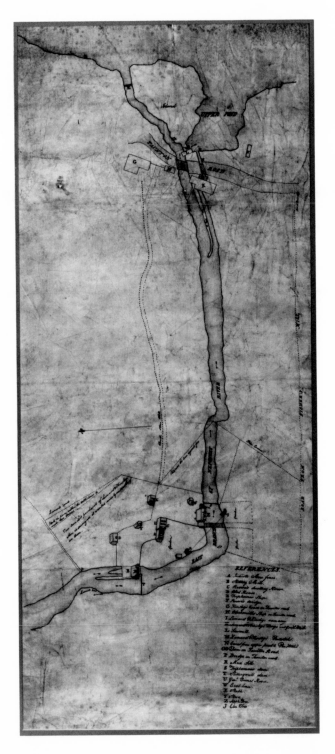

Figure 38

Map of the copper rolling mill in Canton, Massachusetts, ca. 1801–1818, attributed to Paul Revere (Cat. No. 132). Courtesy, Paul Revere Memorial Association.

able bars or rods. Revere wrote to Joshua Humphreys on 22 January 1801 that he had a mill "that I am preparing for rolling copper after the English methode."[31] The work on the mill was expected to be completed by that June. The renovation of the mill significantly reduced the amount of capital investment, thus allowing profits to accrue more rapidly.

No inventory survives for the contents of the mill during the early years at Canton. It is entirely possible that the earliest machinery was similar to the two milling devices Revere listed in 1809:

one for rolling copper sheets, the other a tongue and trip hammer, the first has two master wheels as feet meters [,] the other one wheel 18 feet, a wire machine for drawing square wire rods into spikes. And two air furnaces besides machinery for boring cannon and turning them.

This configuration would be the minimum necessary to manufacture spikes and sheet copper, both of which were produced at Canton from the start. As has been stated, the rolling mill was converted from an iron slitting mill. Trip hammers, used in both iron and copper production, frequently were located near iron slitting mills. At Revere's copper mill, these water-driven hammers crushed the ore before it was roasted and smelted in air furnaces.[32] The refined molten copper was then poured into flat blanks which were fed between the wringer-like iron cylinders of the milling machine. Sheet copper of varying thickness resulted from numerous passes between the cylinders or rolls.

One of Revere's main problems was the lack of high-quality, domestically made rolls. The rolls had to be cast iron with an unblemished surface. The process of casting iron tends to leave surface pits caused by escaping gas bubbles. If not removed, these pit marks are transferred to the sheet metal as it passes between the rolls. With each pass the metal becomes increasingly thinner and increasingly marred. Pitting affects the sheet's uniformity; a small variation in thickness can result in a distorted edge on the sheet.[33] It would have been necessary to replace the rolls as they deteriorated from use, yet few mentions of replacement rolls are found in the daybooks. This may be due to the relatively small quantity of copper rolled.

The first reference to rolls is to be found in a 13 January 1801 letter to Mr. Eber [?] Luis. Revere wrote to his friend, then traveling to England, to ask that he explore the possibility of buying English rolls twenty inches in length and nine inches in diameter. Although admitting that rolls could be bought in America, Revere felt that their quality was not comparable to English ones. It is unclear whether the first set of rolls used at Canton was indeed brought from England. As Revere knew, there were restrictions against precisely this kind of exportation. No further references to English rolls exist in Revere's correspondence; all rolls mentioned subsequently were manufactured domestically.

The next reference to rolls in Revere's correspondence is a 31 May 1802 order for rolls to be cast in Plymouth, Massachusetts. On 19 January 1804, Revere wrote again to Nathaniel Goodwin in Plymouth stating that he has heard nothing from him but that he was still interested in acquiring rolls. In May of the same year, he rejected rolls from Messrs. Thacher and Hayward. In April 1806 he instructed Thacher and Hayward to cast only one roll, since he had "a different opinion of rolls cast in clay." Writing to W.B. Lyman of Plymouth on 20 August 1806, Revere stated that the rolls bought from Old Iron in Danvers, Massachusetts, cost between one and one-half and two dollars per pound of iron, and were not yet paid for. It is not clear whether these rolls were fabricated for the Canton mill or for resale.[34]

The number of rolls used during the first ten years of the mill's operation is not revealed in the Revere papers. However, the width of sheet copper produced increased from twelve to thirty-six inches during this period, each increment necessitating a new pair of rolls. Since concrete information concerning the original rolls is not available, we can only approximate the costs involved in their fabrication.

The dimensions given to Mr. Luis for the rolls were a diameter of twelve inches and a length of twenty inches. These dimensions were determined by the particular mill that Revere was renovating, and so therefore can be assumed to be the size of the first pair of rolls. The dimensions do not take into consideration the side extensions which held each roll within the mill frame. The roll's total weight can be extrapolated since Revere was given an estimated weight for a roll of seven inches in diameter and one foot long.[35] The original pair of rolls would have weighed between nine hundred and one thousand pounds. Using the lower 1806 cost per pound the rolls would have cost between 1,350 dollars and 1,500 dollars; at the higher price the cost would range between 1,800 dollars and 2,000 dollars. This high cost would help to explain the 15,000 dollar start-up cost since the building and mill frame only came to 6,000 dollars. It would be reasonable that the remainder could have been made up of improvements to the buildings and furnace and waterworks construction. Added to this was Revere's contractual obligation to pay for all wastage, which he figured at twenty thousand ounces, or approximately 500 to 600 dollars.

Other costs of operation such as labor, energy, and raw materials can be compared to recorded yearly sales, thus allowing the growth, direction, and profitability of the company to be traced. Each aspect of the business covered in the ledgers contributes specific information regarding the day-to-day operation of the Canton works. This data provides a remarkable window into the structure of an early nineteenth-century factory.

Labor, Energy, and Raw Materials: Operating the Canton Mill

Information on employment at the mill was gathered from the first ledger book, which covers the period from 1802–1806. Additionally, workers' names during the 1805 to 1811 period were cross-referenced to the first wastebooks which list the starting date of employment, wages, and absenteeism.

As can be seen from the employment table (Table 1), the small number of workers during the early years suggests, at best, limited specialization of work. In addition to smelting, the mill's production from 1801 to 1803 included the production of copper sheet and, to a greater extent, copper bolts, nails, and spikes (Fig. 39). After 1803 Revere's casting operations for bells and cannon were added to the Canton works. With such diverse production, and the variable demand for sheet copper, it can be assumed that workers were transferred from one area of the operation to another as production demanded.

From 1802 to 1809 the payroll increased slightly more than 100 percent, with the number of workers increasing from five to twelve.[36] Willaby Dexter was Revere's foreman for the first two years; his brother Jeremiah took over the position the following year. At least until April 1803, most of the workers boarded at the Revere house on the factory grounds. Willaby was charged by Revere for workmen's accommodations; presumably, the workers reimbursed their foreman.[37]

There is little to indicate an apprenticeship system within the mill. The term appears once in 1803 in the context of board for "Mr. Nathaniel Morton and Apprentices." The lack of further references or contractual documents leaves great doubt concerning a traditional apprenticeship system. Although no definitive correlation has been established, the names included in the employment table (Table 1) suggest a strong familial relationship between many workers.

The salaries of both Dexters, better than double those of fellow workers, reflect their managerial positions. Just how long Jeremiah's tenure as

Employment Records
Table 1

1802:	Payroll - $1276.08
	5 workers (W. Dexter, J. Dexter, A. Fales, J. Vose, J. Story)
1803:	Payroll - $1107.60
	5 workers (J. Dexter, Jos. Pettee, A. Smith, S. Allen, J. Story)
1804:	Payroll - $1001.55
	5 workers (J. Story, A. Smith, Otis Withington, Jason Clap, J. Dexter)
1805:	Payroll - $1573.28
	7 workers (J. Dexter, J. Story, A. Smith, J. Clap, E. Withington, Benj. Wilder, T. Tattersole)
1806:	Payroll - $1831.44
	7 workers (J. Dexter, A. Smith, E. Withington, T. Tattersole, I. Bosworth, T. Allen, J. Johnson)
1807:	Payroll - $2291.96
	10 workers (J. Dexter, A. Smith, E. Withington, T. Tattersole, I. Bosworth, J. Withington, Nat. Withington, C. Cromwell, E. Hood, Simone Hews)
1808:	Payroll - $1490.32
	6 workers (J. Dexter, E. Withington, I. Bosworth, C. Cromwell, A. Howard, L. Everton)
1809:	Payroll - $3420.04
	12 workers (J. Dexter, I. Bosworth, C. Cromwell, A. Howard, S. Freeman, J. Snow, T. Sheppard, D. Cushman, D. Horton, D. Perkins, A. Thompson, E. Horton)
1810:	Payroll - $3641.17
	12 workers (J. Dexter, I. Bosworth, T. Sheppard, D. Cushman, A. Thompson, E. Horton, B. Allen, F. Soiner, J. Bosworth, T. Perkins, Nat Pratt, Moses Fuller)

foreman lasted is difficult to determine. Although he worked through 1810, by 1809 his salary was only half that of several newly hired workers. It is possible that Revere's son Joseph Warren took over more of the day-to-day operations during 1809 in anticipation of the 1810 agreement to purchase his father's share of the business.

The wage disbursements in the 1802 to 1805 period were usually based on a monthly salary for a six-day work week. Both Dexters are the only workers paid from the earliest entries at a daily wage. Only after 1805 is the rate on a per diem basis for all workers. The company oftentimes acted as a bank for its employees. Full wages were seldom demanded; the earnings were carried forward for months and occasionally for years. Small debits were recorded for each worker on a weekly basis. Some of these were paid to third parties at the employee's request. There are also limited instances of credits for wood or copper scrap which individual full-time workers accrued.

Debits were recorded in the ledger books for days missed. It appears that American work habits have improved with time; unexplained absenteeism of up to a week per month was not unusual throughout the ranks of workers. One workman was even listed as absent for three months! Several records indicate that workers transporting goods to or from Boston unaccountably did not reappear for several days. The worst of these offenders was perhaps Mr. Tattersal, whose three-month-long absence, and frequent infractions of attendance, no doubt contributed to his status as the lowest paid full-time employee. The fact that these workers were not fired on the spot, but rather were kept on despite their infractions, may indicate that such behavior was not an unacceptable deviation from the norm.

During the period from 1809 to 1810 when Joseph Warren Revere was assuming control of the company, there were major changes in employ-

Figure 39

Copper ship fittings made at the Canton rolling mill, ca. 1819, for *U.S.S. New Hampshire* (Cat. No. 123). Courtesy, Paul Revere Memorial Association.

ment. The number of employees increased and substantially higher salaries were recorded. Between May and July three workers were hired at the high salary of three dollars per day. Of the three men, only one appears to have worked at the mill for a full year. Their high salaries, when compared to the majority of concurrently hired workers, may indicate some previous experience in the manufacturing of copper. It remains an intriguing question why this sudden and short-lived change in employment habits occurred at this point.[38]

Much of the energy required for the mill was provided by water-driven wheels. As stated previously, each pair of rolls was powered by "feet meters." Independent powering greatly reduced the stress placed on the rolls and gears. The trip hammer listed by Revere was also water driven. Additional non-water-generated energy was required to anneal sheet copper. The number of times a sheet needed to be heated to relieve the stress of compression is not determined easily.

Revere used both hot and cold rolling methods in sheet manufacture, the difference between the two being the increased stiffness of the sheet when cold rolled. The thickness of the blank at the start of milling, the metal's purity, and whether the sheet was hot or cold rolled would all influence the number of times the sheet needed to be annealed or softened. As early as 6 July 1803, Revere knew of problems associated with applying cold-rolled copper.[39] For this reason, it is likely that the Canton mills primarily produced hot-rolled copper sheet.

In order to assess the factory's energy demands all reference to wood or coal purchases for the mill during 1806 were tabulated. Small purchases of two to three cords from a few suppliers occurred frequently throughout the year, the preferred woods being oak and chestnut, though large quantities of pine were also bought.[40] The 1806 yearly fuel consumption was $986.64. Of this amount, $160.23 consisted of coal purchases, which have been included in the total fuel costs, even though it is probable that a quantity was used in the smelting process.

The price of copper pigs varied over the ten years under consideration. Although at times as low as eighteen cents per pound, the average price was approximately twenty-five cents, with the 1801 to 1803 government credit of twenty-eight cents per pound being one of the highest recorded raw material cost. The mill paid for the transport of its raw material. It came to Canton primarily from the docks in Boston via independently owned ox carts. The 1806 rate for transportation averaged 14 dollars per ton per trip.[41] This translates to an approximate cost of 900 dollars per year for transportation of raw materials used in the production of sheet copper.

Specific references to insurance or advertising were not found in the company books. Revere did advertise while working at his various careers in Boston, and it would be expected that he did the same for the Canton mill. In real terms, however, this cost along with possible expenditures for items such as chemicals, machine lubricants, and sand for casting, are not significant compared to the overall gross figures. This is especially true for the rolling operation where, other than labor, copper, rolls, and heat for annealing the copper, little else was needed.

Becoming Competitive

Sales generated by the mill were meticulously recorded in the waste-books. The books actually start in May of 1799, before Revere owned the property in Canton. Copper bolts and nails and bells, common products of the Revere shop in Boston, made up most of the early transactions. The 21 May 1799 issue of the *Massachusetts Mercury* states that the thirty-two-gun frigate *Boston* was "the first copper-bottomed ship built in America whose bolts and spikes (drawn from malleable copper) have been manu-factured in the United States." Indeed, in the foundry wastebook ending in April 1799, large quantities of these two fasteners were charged to this ship.

Among the first sales recorded in the books is a charge on 28 May 1799 to the ship *Boston* of $12.49 for twenty-five pounds of sheet copper. Such a small amount of metal was probably ordered for repairs to her hull. This copper sheet could not have been fabricated by Revere since he did not yet possess the means of rolling it. Presumably, Revere acted in this in-stance as a retailer of imported English rolled copper. This is not surpris-ing, since Revere's previous career as a hardware store owner would have exposed him to a multitude of copper articles imported from England.

Revere ordered some of these articles from Harmon Hendricks of New York. At the end of the eighteenth century Hendricks was the largest importer of copper and brass objects, copper sheet, and copper pigs. The archives of the New York Genealogical Society preserve a letter of agree-ment between Hendricks and Revere allowing for the first option to buy copper in their respective home ports.[42] The continued interaction be-tween these two entrepreneurs suggests a satisfactory business relation-ship.[43]

The records of the mill note all transactions; even sales of fifty-five cents were carefully recorded. Each entry includes the date, the client's name, the client's cross-reference number, the number of pounds of sheet purchased, the price per pound, and the total cost. The majority of the entries are listed by first and last names, with a few exceptions such as the United States Navy, agents for building the new State House, and the New North Society. In a few entries a ship's name was used in lieu of a client's. The ships *Devotion* and *Boston*, and the brig *Argus* are the only such recorded instances.[44]

Each account was assigned a number in the wastebooks. The ledger books listed this reference number chronologically along with all entries for that account during the year. This two-part entry system allowed for production planning as well as simplifying periodic debit and credit tabu-lation.

Though Revere's early business dealt primarily in large transactions, there was apparently no minimum charge; sales of from 50 cents to over 4,200 dollars were recorded. All business was welcome; it was all the more warmly welcomed, however, if paid in cash on the barrel-head. An 1808 letter from Mr. Hazard to Revere reveals the former's delight at a 4.5

Sales of Copper Sheet Table 2

	Average Retail Price (cents/pound)	Transactions	Average Amount/ Transaction	Gross Sheet Revenue
1800		0		
1801		1		$ 14.00
1802		1		3,837.50
1803	51.0	10	$1,461.00	14,610.24
1804	49.2	16	549.09	8,785.57
1805	47.06	18	462.15	8,325.22
1806	52.11	26	321.15	8,350.40
1807	46.66	7	279.77	1,958.39
1808	49.60	11	136.04	1,496.51
1809	49.50	13	113.90	1,480.68
1810	53.85	26	215.11	5,592.92

percent discount for "prompt pay, which determines me now to pay the money down instead of taking the four months credit."[45] The grace period after which payment was due varied from 60 to 120 days, presumably based upon the client's importance to Revere.

The Hazard letter introduces a further point. Hazard claimed that he "can purchase English copper in Boston at forty-five cents per pound, and even cheaper in New York, *but* having a higher opinion of your copper than I have of English copper and being disposed to encourage the manufacture of our own country leads me to give a decided preference to your copper." Here is an unsolicited testimonial of the high quality of Revere's sheet copper, as well as an indication of the competitive edge that Revere's domestically produced copper enjoyed over that of English manufacture. The average retail cost of copper sheet between 1800 and 1810 was 50 cents per pound, though it varied from 23.5 cents to 59 cents (Table 2).

Entries until 15 October 1805 were always written as pounds of sheathing copper. Although bolts and spikes were denoted by lengths, no such differentiation was made for copper sheet. References are made in Revere's correspondence to sheets weighing thirty-two ounces to the "superficial foot," but in the books such nomenclature is not used until 1806.[46] The standard sheet sizes mentioned in the wastebooks were either four feet long by fourteen inches wide, or four feet long by thirteen and one-half inches wide.[47] Revere was able to manufacture a range of gauges, and in fact he lists the weights of ten different thicknesses (ounces per superficial foot) of copper sheathing.

In 1805 the entries began to include the number of sheets, the total number of pounds, and, at times, the weight per superficial foot. The change in recordkeeping was perhaps due to the demand for a greater range of thicknesses in sheet copper. Sales of thirty-two ounce weight sheet, the old standard, continued, but entries of thirty-nine, twenty-eight, twenty-six, twenty-two, and twenty ounce weights were now recorded.

The new method of bookkeeping became more prevalent in the following years, but not to the total exclusion of the earlier method. It appeared that October 1805 marked the transition to the new entry style of the wastebooks, and that subsequent periodic lapses into the former style can be attributed to force of habit.

A further change occurred in some entries during October 1807. A charge against Edward Hart listed "2 copper sheets, 24g. copper, wt. 22 lb." The "g." would indicate gauge and so must refer to the adoption of a standard unit of measurement of sheet thickness introduced to the manufacturing of copper during this period. Further research into the nature and origin of this scale would provide an interesting insight into nineteenth-century measurement standardization in manufacturing.

The sales of sheet recorded in the ledger books from January 1800 to March 1811 reveal seasonal fluctuations in Revere's business. January and February contain few recorded sales, which would be expected since ship construction and repair would have been curtailed in the dead of winter. Correspondingly, a greater number of sales during the spring and summer would corroborate an assumed increase in shipbuilding activity during the warm months. The works at Canton, though, were water-powered, and as such were subject to seasonal variations in the Neponset River's flow (Figs. 35 and 38). An 1803 description of the mill notes its inability to function in the summer when the river's height was low.[48] This problem also probably existed during those months when freezing temperatures could have slowed the river's flow.

Stockpiling would have been Revere's best solution for this variable power source. As long as the gauge of copper remained fairly constant, stockpiling would have presented few problems. However, as gauges became more diversified, the problems of maintaining a sufficient quantity of rolled copper in various sizes would have increased dramatically. So too, the capital tied up in inventory would also increase, adversely affecting profitability.

To estimate the percentage of copper sheet manufactured, as opposed to the total copper production of the mill, the sales of sheet were compared to general gross revenues for the period of 1804 to 1805 and 1806 to 1807. The figures for these years reveal that sheet sales comprised only 15.2 percent of the total revenues during 1804 to 1805, and 18.7 percent for the subsequent period. Both of these percentages are surprisingly low. Although the total volume of sales increased during the last years of the decade, the revenue generated by sheet sales dramatically declined after 1806. Not until 1810 did sales income even remotely approach the heyday of 1803 to 1806.

In the company's first years, a small number of transactions yielded large revenues. During this period sheet production may have represented a greater proportion of the gross revenue; the large contracts for sheet for the Massachusetts State House dome and the U. S. Navy would have made a significant contribution to yearly revenue. After 1806 the actual number of transactions increased, but total tonnage of copper sales dropped. Overall, copper sheet sales contributed less to the revenue of the mill. The exact cause of reduction in sheet sale income is probably due to a combination of factors. A general economic depression during this period led, as Revere mentioned in a 16 September 1809 letter, to numerous bank failures.[49] The Embargo Act of the same year also contributed to the decline. Revere wrote on 6 March 1809, "The miserable conduct of our Rulers in laying that cursed Embargo had nearly deprived us of selling coppers for ships."[50]

In the closing years of the first decade of the nineteenth century, Revere began an active and at times acrimonious correspondence lobbying for the legislation of an importation tax on English sheet copper (Fig. 40).[51]

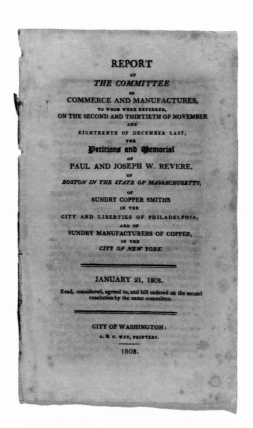

Figure 40

Report of the Committee of Commerce and Manufactures in response to petitions regarding copper duties filed by Paul Revere, Joseph Warren Revere and others. Printed by A. & G. Way, Washington, D.C., 1808 (Cat. No. 144). Courtesy, Paul Revere Memorial Association.

Copper bolts and spikes already had this protection. It would have been against his nature for Revere to have demanded a sheet tariff unless it was of extreme necessity. The lower cost of English sheet would have severely undercut Revere's market during these years of economic recession. In the years following the Revolution, England's mercantile policy included dumping merchandise—that is, artificially lowering the price of an article to eliminate competitors—on the American market. Whether or not this occurred in sheet copper, the market was closely related to general economic conditions.[52]

A portion of the 1810 increase in sheet revenues was due to a 10 percent increase in the cost per pound of sheet. More importantly, the entries in the wastebook contain a significant number of sales comprised of small quantities of extremely heavy sheet. Revere supplied the material for the steam boilers built by Robert Fulton in New York at this time. Though constructed of standard three-foot-wide by five-foot-long sheets, the metal was three to five times thicker than copper used for sheathing ships' bottoms. Further study may reveal that the Canton works specialized in sheet production of thick gauges after 1810. These gauges, requiring less manufacturing, were more profitable. The construction of steam boilers was a new industry and demand was increasing dramatically.

The Revere works began manufacturing its well-known "copper bottoms" for culinary utensils in 1807, although consistent entries for these items do not appear until 1810. In the final ledger book examined for this study, the diameters and gauges needed for various capacity pots and kettles are listed. Although "bottoms" at this point did not amount to more than 15 percent of the total sheet sales, it seems likely that this application of rolled copper increased in the following years.

A Profitable Domestic Industry

The quantity of documentation presents a unique opportunity to establish the economic gain that Revere experienced as a result of sheet production at the mill. As in any business, profit is the amount of money remaining from the gross revenues after deducting all the costs of production. In this essay the determination of profitability was based upon the examination of the company's records for the years from June 1804 to June 1805 and June 1806 to June 1807. Sales of sheet for this period amounted to an average 17 percent of the mill's gross revenue. It is assumed that the costs of production on a pound basis were equal among the different divisions of the mill.[53] Therefore 17 percent was applied to the yearly summation of production costs previously discussed. In order to simplify the results the net gain was interpreted on a per pound basis.

The average retail price for this period was 48 cents a pound. The greatest cost was found to be the raw materials, which averaged 28 cents a pound.[54] Factory-wide labor costs were 2,495 dollars; $424.15 reflects the direct cost of sheet production. Since 22,171 pounds of sheet were sold, the labor cost per pound was almost 2 cents. Energy costs averaged 300 dollars, translating to a little more than 1 cent per pound. Transportation of raw material cost about the same.[55]

There most certainly were other costs that are not stated in the ledger books. How much they contributed to the overall production costs will probably never fully be known. The costs of energy, transportation, labor, and raw materials are today the main factors in determining the profitability of a given article. The figures advanced are the best possible approximations given the raw data available. When totaled, these costs show that the sheet metal section of Revere's mill was profitable. In effect, for every pound of sheet sold, Revere would clear a little less than 16 cents or 33 percent over the cost of production. When hidden costs are considered, it is possible that the profit margin could shrink to 30 percent. Even at this lower figure, the profit from the sale of sheet during these two years would be over 2,666 dollars. This amount would represent about five times the annual wage of the highest paid worker during this same time period.

In March of 1811, Paul Revere retired from active ownership of the Canton mill. In order to execute transference to his son, an inventory of the company's assets was performed and recorded in a 1 March entry in the ledger books. Exclusive of the property and equipment at the mill, the company in ten years had amassed a worth of over 50,000 dollars.[56]

Though sheet copper production was not a large factor in the accumulated wealth of the mill, it had provided the original impetus for the creation of a company which was inextricably linked to national defense needs.

The concept of economic gain is inherently comparative. By today's standards the profitability of Revere's venture into sheet production would be considered only marginally successful. Given the newness of the industry, and the economic standards of the time it is possible that the revenues generated from sheet justified its production. Further research into the company's later years will provide the information necessary to determine the long-range viability of Revere's calculated risk. Whatever the conclusion to this question will be, Revere managed to establish the first economically sound enterprise of its type in America. His boast of 1800 was not so hollow; Revere had indeed made "himself master of this business."

Notes

1.
Revere's letter of 30 June 1783 to William Foster of London states: "as my dependence for a living will chiefly depend on the goldsmith business, which will be carried on by my son." The eighteenth-century nomenclature for a worker in silver seems to have been changing by the end of the century. His letter of 5 December 1791 to George and William Burchell, also of London, asks for "a complete plating [rolling] mill it is for a silversmith." See Letterbook, 1783–1800, RFP.

2.
John G. Glover, ed., *The Development of American Industries and Their Economic Significance* (New York, 1959), 249.

3.
See Noah A. Phelps, *A History of the Copper Mines and Newgate Prison at Granby, Connecticut* (Hartford, CT, 1845); and Henry J. Kauffman, *American Copper and Brass* (1968, reprint New York, 1977), 13–24.

4.
Kauffman, 34.

5.
Harry N. Scheiber, Harold G. Vatter, and Harold U. Faulkner, *American Economic History* (New York, 1973), 59–60.

6.
Scheiber, Vatter, and Faulkner, 70.

7.
William Ashley, *The English Brass and Copper Industries to 1800* (London, 1934), 152.

8.
Robert G. Albion, *Forests and Sea Power* (Hamden, CT, 1926), 11.

9.
Maurer Maurer, "Copper Bottoms for the United States Navy, 1794–1803," *The United States Naval Institute Proceedings* 17 (June, 1945): 693–99.

10.
Scheiber, Vatter, and Faulkner, 88.

11.
Samuel Eliot Morison, *The Maritime History of Massachusetts 1783–1860*, 6th ed. (Boston, 1961), chapters 1–3.

12.
In 1784 only 45 ships were launched in Massachusetts compared with an estimated 125 before the war. By 1785 to 1787 only 15 to 20 ships were constructed annually. See Morison, chapter 3.

13.
Ibid., chapters 1–3.

14.
Clark G. Reynolds, *Command of the Sea, the History and Strategy of Maritime Empires* (New York, 1974), 276.

15.
Maxwell Whiteman, *Copper for America - The Hendricks Family and a National Industry 1755–1939* (New Brunswick, NJ, 1971), 49.

16.
PR to Harrison Gray Otis, Letterbook, 1783–1800, RFP.

17.
Dudley Knox, ed., *Naval Documents Relating to the Quasi War Between the United States and France*, 7 vols. (Washington, 1935–1938), 4:118–19.

18.
Whiteman, 49.

19.
Knox, 3:74.

20.
Ibid., 4:118–19.

21.
Ibid., 1:27.

22.
American State Papers, Naval Affairs, 1:9 [Hereafter cited as ASPNA], and Knox, 5:129, 6:95. Also $1,215 for "woolens for sheathing."

23.
ASPNA, 1:35.

24.
PR to Benjamin Stoddard [Stoddert], 17 January 1801, Letterbook, 1801–1806, RFP.

25.
Ibid.

26.
Revere employed the period term "plating mill" when referring to the machinery used for flatting silver. Copper flatting machinery, however, was invariably called a "rolling mill" in Revere's correspondence. Although the two different terms were in use at the turn of the century, there was no fundamental difference in the apparatuses, except in the larger scale of the copper machinery.

27.
PR to Edward Edwards, 20 January 1801; and PR to Joshua Humphreys, 22 January 1801, Letterbook 1801–1806, RFP.

28.
A large portion of this debt was due undoubtedly to Revere's purchase of the buildings and land that would be transformed into the Canton copper works.

29.
This transaction was in addition to the earlier contract for 191,000 pounds of copper bolts and spikes.

30.
Although the exact date of the loan is not known, from correspondence we know that it must have occurred after 29 June 1801. See Sam Brown to PR, 7 June 1801, Letterbook, 1801–1806, RFP.

31.
PR to Joshua Humphreys, 22 January 1801, Loose Manuscripts, RFP.

32.
This type of hammer could also be operated as a power forging hammer used in thinning the copper blanks. This usage is indicated by the fact that the Canton mill used primarily refined metal.

33.
Further distortion can result if the two rolls are not in true parallel. Rippling and increased thinning along one edge of the flatted sheet is indicative that the rolls were not properly aligned as the sheet passed between them. This in fact did occur to a portion of Revere's first delivery of copper, with a deviation of one-quarter to three-quarters of an inch on one side of the sheet.

34.
PR to Nathaniel Goodwin, 31 May 1802 and 19 January 1804; PR to Thacher and Hayward, May 1804 and April 1806; and PR to W. B. Lyman, 20 August 1806, Letterbook, 1801–1806, RFP.

35.
PR to H. M. Solomon, 21 June 1810. Revere was responding to Solomon's inquiry of 30 May 1810 concerning rolls made in Boston. Letterbook, 1805–1810, RFP.

36.
The reduced number of personnel in 1808 was probably due to severe economic conditions discussed later in this essay.

37.
The rate which Willaby Dexter was charged for workmen accommodations per worker was 2 dollars per week in April 1803. See Wastebook, 1805–1811, RFP.

38.
The yearly cost of labor for the mills as entered in the wastebook reflects the entire range of factory operations. The labor rolls as given in Table 1 show a general growth trend for the company. Was this trend the result of profitable copper sheet manufacturing? If we assume that the labor expenditure is equal between the various divisions of the factory, it is possible to determine the approximate labor costs incurred by copper sheet production. These costs will be examined at length in this essay.

39.
The nails used to anchor copper sheathing to ships' hulls have an increased tendency to break or snap when the copper sheet has been cold-rolled. Revere was also acquainted with the difficulties of shaping cold-rolled sheet to conform to the contours of a ship's hull.

40.
The price per cord of hard wood varied from 10 dollars to 16 dollars, and pine was usually less than 7 dollars per cord.

41.
As with most modern concerns, the cost of transportation of the product to its destination was the client's responsibility. The cost of boxing was also included at a cost of a little more than a dollar. The only exceptions to this practice were the early government contracts.

42.
Whiteman, 55.

43.
Hendricks would eventually reclaim the Soho mines in Belleville, New Jersey, and become in 1813 Revere's direct competitor in copper smelting and sheet metal production.

44.
A 23 May 1806 entry for Joseph Lee, Jr. is amended "for the ship Cavinan."

45.
Thomas Hazard, Jr. to PR, 9 June 1808, RFP.

46.
It can be proven that the term "superficial foot" meant, in fact, square foot, and that the most common thickness of copper which Revere supplied was equivalent to the modern Brown & Sharpe gauge number 17.

47.
The weight of one sheet of each size can be calculated as nine pounds and five ounces and nine pounds, respectively.

48.
Whiteman, 63.

49.
PR to Joseph Carson, 16 September 1809, Letterbook, 1805-1810, RFP.

50.
PR to Joseph Carson, 6 March 1809, Letterbook, 1805–1810, RFP.

51.
PR to Josiah Quincy, December 1807, Loose Manuscripts, RFP; and PR to Gabriel Duvall, 20 August 1810, Letterbook, 1805–1810, RFP.

52.
The only possible expansion of the market
by exportation to England effectively was
blocked by a British embargo decree. See
Revere's letter of 29 September 1806, RFP.
53.
This assumption is strengthened by the
fact that the retail price of cannons, sheet,
bolts, and bells was the same within a
given time period. The order of the divisions given above reflects their size within
the company.
54.
A 10 percent increase was added to the actual raw material cost of 25 cents the
pound for the period. This corresponds to
the figure that Revere used when calculat-
ing the "wastage" on the first government
contracts. There are no further records of
exactly how much raw copper produces a
certain amount of sheet.
55.
The weight of raw material used for calcu-
lations included 10 percent wastage.
Twelve and one-fifth short tons would have
to be transported.
56.
Sheet copper and bottoms comprised the
second highest total of inventory after
bolts and spikes.

Figure 41

Notification for Saint Andrew's Lodge, from a copperplate engraving by Paul Revere, ca. 1767. Used to summon members to meetings, it would have been filled in with the time, date, and Master's name. Courtesy, American Antiquarian Society.

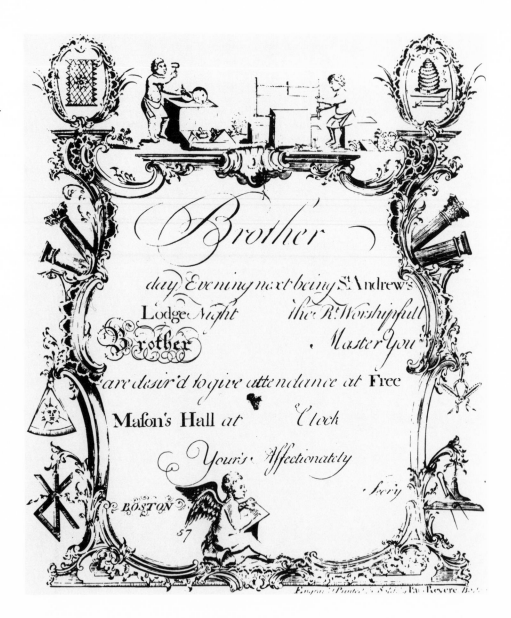

Fraternity, Philanthropy, and Revolution

Paul Revere and Freemasonry

Edith J. Steblecki

Paul Revere's life spanned a time of considerable growth, turmoil, and change in America. In its midst, Revere—craftsman, entrepreneur, and patriot—emerged as an energetic, productive leader of eighteenth-century society. While Revere's patriotic activities and business affairs are well documented, his personal affairs are less so, and with the absence of diaries and many personal letters Revere's thoughts and feelings remain even more obscure. Not surprisingly, public perception portrays him more as a man of action than of ideas. Nevertheless, it is possible to approach another side of Paul Revere through an examination of how he chose to spend his leisure time. In the postwar period, Revere contributed his time and money to numerous voluntary associations and societies as well as holding several public posts. This intensive organizational involvement clearly reflects his sense of civic responsibility.

Perhaps Paul Revere's character is best expressed through his lifelong commitment to Freemasonry. Established in North America by the early eighteenth century, this fraternal organization was very much a product of rational Enlightenment thought.[1] It was the group with which Revere was involved the longest, his participation beginning in 1760 and lasting nearly fifty years, until approximately 1810. Revere's activities with three separate masonic lodges—St. Andrew's Lodge, Rising States Lodge, and the Massachusetts Grand Lodge—suggest not only the social and financial benefits he hoped to derive from this moral society, but also his concurrence with its ideals.

The Masonic Heritage

When Revere became a Freemason, he was joining an organization that had been in existence for several hundred years. The view that Revere and his contemporaries held of Freemasonry was expressed in a volume of constitutions and rituals compiled in 1792, which contained "all things necessary for the use of the fraternity." Revere was on the committee that compiled the volume.[2] The committee described "present day" Freemasonry as "an institution for the promotion of the most extensive philanthropy, the most diffusive and disinterested benevolence and universal virtue."[3] Eighteenth-century Freemasonry had evolved a long way from its origins in the fourteenth century when masons were stoneworkers who cut, laid, and set stone. Under the direction of a master mason, masons in the middle ages constructed cathedrals, castles, and monasteries, usually in rural areas where mason's groups, or lodges, took the place of regular medieval craft guilds. After seven years of training, a mason was entered in a lodge as an "Entered Apprentice," where after seven further years of instruction he became a "Fellow of Craft." The most skilled master builders were "Master Masons." As early as 1356, a code of regulations was written in London for the craft. As in most trade guilds, the "secrets" of the craft were jealously guarded, and a ceremony of admission had already evolved by 1390. Traces of masonic symbolism and its moral precepts began to appear as early as 1425. Still, there is a large philosophical gap between the stoneworkers' lodges of the fourteenth century and the modern masonic organization devoted to benevolence and philanthropy that Paul Revere joined several centuries later.[4]

The transition to modern Freemasonry began in England in the seventeenth century. As early as 1619, the London Masons' Company established an organization for men who were not stonemasons by trade. These men became known as "Accepted" masons, and still seemed to have some knowledge of the stonemason's craft. Since the growth of architecture as a distinct profession was only beginning in the seventeenth century, the emerging gentleman's interest in architecture may also have prompted some men to join masons' lodges. Equally significant were the changes occurring in the medieval craft guilds themselves. By the seventeenth century, the worker's craft associations had been gradually transformed along with the changing economy of England, until many guilds, including the masons' lodges, were closer to being social clubs than trade organizations. The fact that masonic lodges did become more than social clubs can be credited to the individuals who took an interest in the craft by the early eighteenth century.[5]

These men, heirs of the scientific revolution, were interested in science, philosophy, and history. They saw in the traditions of Freemasonry the fraternity's potential as an agent of moral instruction. By imbuing the ancient rituals and traditions of the mason's craft with a higher moral tone, they created an organization that provided a sense of social order, encouraged stable values, and offered a hierarchy of merit within which members could attain status through instruction, while also instilling a universalism that transcended both political and religious diversity. It was a new sort of voluntary association, responsive to the anxieties created by the rapid social changes of the day. The establishment of modern Freemasonry was not without conflict, but the appealing organization persisted. By combining the conviviality of a social club and the exclusiveness of a secret society with a sense of higher purpose, Freemasonry attracted men from all walks of life.[6]

This Freemasonic organization devoted to virtue, philanthropy, and benevolence had taken nearly two hundred years to develop completely.[7] Its existence was finally formalized in 1717 with the creation of the Grand Lodge of England.[8] Equally important, in 1723, was the adoption of a volume of constitutions, history, charges, orders, regulations, and usages compiled primarily by those men interested in elevating the purposes of the organization. This publication basically laid the groundwork for the growth of Freemasonry as a moral fraternity, particularly with its significant assumption that masonic lodges were no longer responsible for regulating the building trade. The constitutions also established the authority of the Grand Lodge as the central body by which additional lodges could be chartered.[9] As early as 1735, masonic ritual, through which the customs and tools of the working stonemasons attained allegorical significance, was in full bloom in England.[10] Since most men joining the fraternity by this time were not stoneworkers, they were called "speculative" masons. They came from all professions and probably had little actual connection with, or knowledge of, architecture and geometry. In contrast, the actual working stonemasons were termed "operative." The volume of constitutions compiled in America in 1792 explained the distinction.

Formerly masonry was chiefly operative; confined to manual labor, and studied for improvement in those useful and elegant arts . . . But as morals, learning and religion advanced in the world, it became speculative, and attended to the cultivation of the mind, and the regulation of the manners.

Operative masonry referred to "the useful rules of architecture, whence a structure derives figure, strength and beauty" while speculative masons "learn to subdue the passions . . . keep a tongue of good report, maintain secrecy and practice charity." It was this sort of speculative, theoretical masonic organization that Paul Revere joined in 1760.[11]

As with many English institutions, Freemasonry transferred quickly to the American shores with its ideology virtually intact, providing colonists with a special connection to the mother country. The first legally mandated masonic organization in America was established in Massachusetts scarcely two years before Revere's birth.[12] Although interested men had been conducting informal masonic meetings in the colonies since at least 1720, it was not until 1732 that Henry Price (1697–1780), a prosperous merchant tailor, obtained the official sanction of the Grand Lodge of England to establish a legally constituted lodge in Boston. As a result, not only was a Boston lodge created on 30 July 1733, but Henry Price was appointed the "Provincial Grand Master of New England and Dominions and Territories thereunto belonging" with the power to establish additional lodges. Thus did colonial America obtain its first legal Provincial Grand Lodge, historically known as St. John's Grand Lodge.[13]

Freemasonry in America was initially an urban phenomena, appearing chiefly in seaport communities and other centers of commerce.[14] Systematic evaluations of membership for eighteenth-century lodges have been few, making it difficult to offer a comprehensive description of the typical Freemason. Yet several studies indicate that, while membership was diverse, the organization tended to attract mobile, politically active men, many with commercial interests, who often held positions of leadership in their communities.[15] The ideology itself was also a powerful attraction. The society emphasized a respect for tradition as well as enforcing the enlightened belief that men could create a better world through reason, harmony, and right conduct. Masonry fit well with the prevailing Protestant values yet represented the liberal religious attitudes of the day. As a secret society with an exclusive membership, Freemasonry appealed to men as a group set apart, thoroughly in keeping with the eighteenth-century popularity of clubs, yet it encouraged its members to strive for the highest ideals. The organization provided a ready-made social network consisting of men of similar thoughts and attitudes.[16] Revere had much to gain by joining these men. Masonic membership broadened his circle of acquaintances, brought customers to his shop, and gave him continuous opportunities for recreation, companionship, and leadership.

Despite the obvious advantages of masonic membership, it is impossible to know for certain what actually motivated Paul Revere to become a Freemason. However, it is likely that he and others recognized the society as a potential avenue of financial opportunity and social mobility. As an upwardly mobile artisan who ended his life as a successful industrialist, Revere may have noticed as a youth that Boston's First Lodge contained many of the more well-to-do members of the community such as merchants and owners of businesses.[17] It is possible that, in joining a lodge, he hoped to associate with influential men who otherwise might not have

Figure 42

Early nineteenth-century leather and brass document box with a history of ownership by Paul Revere (Cat. No. 30). Courtesy, Paul Revere Memorial Association.

been included within his immediate social circle. Revere also may have been influenced to join the fraternity by his military experiences during the French and Indian War. During the expedition to Crown Point, New York, in 1756, Revere had served as a second lieutenant of the artillery train in the regiment commanded by Richard Gridley (1711–1796).[18] An active Freemason, Gridley obtained a charter dated 13 May 1756 from St. John's Grand Lodge in order to create an army lodge for the regiment. Although it is difficult to know how much contact Revere actually had with this army lodge or its members, he did become a Freemason himself by 1760.[19]

It is revealing that when Revere made the decision to become a Freemason, he did not join the First Lodge of Boston which had been founded in 1733. Although Revere no doubt hoped to benefit from the social relationships gained through the fraternity, he may have found that he had more in common with the members of St. Andrew's Lodge, a newer lodge which had been organized in 1752. Its founding relates to a complex movement that began in England where, by 1751, a group of dissenters had split from the original 1717 Grand Lodge of England, terming themselves "Ancient" masons. Among their complaints, the dissenters were dissatisfied with the ritual currently being used and accused the English Grand Lodge of being "Modern," claiming that their rituals deviated so much from the ancient landmarks of masonry that the practices were no longer traditional. Justified or not, this rift between ancient and modern factions persisted in English Freemasonry until 1813. Although never as great an issue in America, the controversy did affect the colonies, and the founders of St. Andrew's Lodge who met informally at the Green Dragon Tavern in Boston considered themselves to be ancient masons.[20] Consequently, they applied to the Grand Lodge of Scotland for a charter, a body that was sympathetic to the ancient movement, and were granted a dispensation on St. Andrew's Day, 30 November 1756, explaining the origin of the lodge's name.[21]

Artisanry and Freemasonry

On 9 September 1760, Paul Revere was initiated as an Entered Apprentice in St. Andrew's Lodge, receiving the first of three masonic degrees which were based upon the actual stoneworker's progression from apprentice to master. Possibly before 8 January 1761, Paul Revere was "passed" to the Fellow Craft degree, earning the highest degree, that of a Master Mason, only two weeks later on 17 January 1761.[22] In the late eighteenth century, it was not uncommon for men initiated in a lodge to advance through the three degrees fairly rapidly. According to the early regulations of St. Andrew's Lodge, members were encouraged to advance, as any member who remained an Entered Apprentice for too long would "in due time be desired to withdraw unless he desires to be made a Fellow Craft."[23] Initiates were taught the basic truths and symbols of Freemasonry, which acquired deeper meanings as they advanced toward the "sublime degree of Master Mason."[24] After attaining the Master Mason degree, members might choose to gain further distinction by serving as lodge officers. As with many fraternal organizations, lodges were structured with a hierarchy of officers, the highest being that of Master of a lodge. Admission to a lodge was based upon character; advancement depended entirely upon merit. The 1792 *Constitutions* specified that "all preferment among masons is grounded upon real worth and personal merit only." Revere was quick to take advantage of an organization in which individual mobility seemed virtually limitless.

It is not surprising that Revere chose St. Andrew's Lodge in which to make his mark. Aside from its being a relatively new lodge, many of its meetings were held at the Green Dragon Tavern, a public house located close to the North End.[25] As a result, the lodge drew many of its members from among the North End's artisans, men who also shared with Paul Revere a common economic and social background. Although Revere's status had risen considerably by the end of his life, he joined St. Andrew's Lodge at the age of twenty-five, only several years after he embarked upon his career as a master goldsmith. In late December 1761, the Lodge voted "That a list of this Lodge [be] Printed with the Names & Occupation." However the list was not compiled until the lodge meeting held on the second Thursday of January 1762. Of the thirty-seven men recorded on this list only seven called themselves "Merchants." The other thirty made their livelihood at the following trades: baker (2), carver (2), chairmaker, glazier, bricklayer, auctioneer, "Gold Smith & Engraver" (Revere), sugar refiner (2), tin plate worker, cooper, gunsmith (2), stationer and bookbinder, housewright, jeweler, jappaner and painter, physician, hatmaker, and painter. The physician was Joseph Warren, a future revolutionary leader and friend of Paul Revere.[26]

An additional twenty-four members of St. Andrew's Lodge worked at various maritime trades, an important aspect of life in Boston's North End. Even Revere's own goldsmith shop was located close to the neighborhood's longest wharf. The list included eighteen ship captains, termed "Seafaring Members," as well as a ship joiner, ship chandler, shipwright, boat builder (Nathaniel Hitchborn, Paul's cousin), and two sailmakers. The total lodge membership by 1762 consisted of these fifty-three men with whom Paul Revere would have shared a common sense of community and similar point of view.

It is likely that Paul Revere and his fellow artisans also recognized in their masonic membership the potential for financial reward. This relationship between Freemasonry and business was most clearly pronounced during Revere's period as a goldsmith (1756–1799), which neatly coincides with his most active years as a Freemason (1760–1800). While many of his customers appear only once in his goldsmith accounts, others regularly

Figure 43

Seal made for Rising
States Lodge, ca. 1784,
and attributed to Paul Revere (Cat. No. 209). Courtesy, Grand Lodge of
Masons in Massachusetts,
A.F. & A.M.

patronized Revere and provided a base of loyal support for his other business ventures. A sampling of 309 customers of Revere's shop between
1761 and 1796 reveals that approximately 146 were fellow masons.[27] Unfortunately, there are no figures recording the total number of masons in
Massachusetts during Revere's goldsmith period, but it has been estimated that, in 1776, there were only one hundred lodges with no more
than five thousand masons in all the thirteen colonies combined.[28] It
seems hardly a coincidence that nearly half of Revere's customers were
Freemasons. All things considered, he was a logical choice for masonic
patronage. Not only was he a fine craftsman but his association with the
masons assured his fellow brethren that he was a man of high principles.
He also had the unique knowledge of the fraternity which enabled him to
produce items of symbolic masonic significance, unlike most Boston goldsmiths of the day.[29] Lodges were in need of many items which a goldsmith
could produce, such as jewels, seals, ladles, and medals. A goldsmith who
did engraving could also provide necessary copperplate engravings for certificates and notification of meetings. Revere made all these things and
more.

Frequently, although not exclusively, Revere worked for masons and
lodges known to him personally. It was no coincidence that Revere's earliest masonic work was for masons from St. Andrew's Lodge.[30] Nevertheless, Revere's masonic orders represent at least twenty different lodges,
no fewer than six of which were in Boston. Of these Boston lodges, Revere
was personally associated with three: St. Andrew's Lodge, Rising States
Lodge—which Revere helped to found in 1784 and for which he also engraved a silver seal, (Fig. 43)—and the Massachusetts Grand Lodge,
founded in 1769. Revere was also an officeholder in all three lodges, culminating in his election as Grand Master of the Massachusetts Grand
Lodge in 1795–1797. The other three Boston lodges for which Revere did
masonic work were the First Lodge, Massachusetts Lodge, and Columbian Lodge.[31] Revere could also include among his masonic customers
several of the lodges which he himself had chartered while Grand Master,[32] such as Columbian, Bristol, St. Paul's, and Washington Lodges.
Several orders also came from American Union Lodge and Washington
Lodge No. 10,[33] both traveling army lodges. Revere also made several
items for the Tyrian Lodge of Gloucester, Massachusetts. In 1770, the
year of its founding, Tyrian Lodge voted Revere thanks "for the zeal and
activity he has shown and extended in the establishment of this Lodge."[34]
Although the majority of Revere's masonic orders came from Massachusetts lodges, he also had business dealings with three lodges in Maine and

one in Surinam (Dutch Guiana). Despite the distance of these lodges from Boston, it is revealing that the representatives of each were all masons who had previously been associated with St. Andrew's Lodge, where they would have had the opportunity for personal contact with Revere.[35]

Revere's work as a masonic craftsman began almost simultaneously with his intitiation to the fraternity. Even before Revere had received his third masonic degree in late January 1761, he had already produced and sold his first masonic item. Not only was this Revere's first masonic sale, but it also happened to be the very first transaction recorded on the first page of the earliest known account book for the goldsmith shop. The item was a Freemason medal, purchased by James Graham, a North End chairmaker and officer in St. Andrew's Lodge, on 3 January 1761. On the facing page in the same account book, Revere's next two masonic orders are recorded. On 24 February 1762 merchant Richard Pulling, a member of St. Andrew's Lodge, purchased "a Masons Medal for a Wach," while James Jackson also bought a "Masons Medal" on 2 March. James Jackson was a member of Boston's First Lodge, not joining St. Andrew's until 1769.[36]

In addition to medals, Revere also crafted masonic "jewels," symbolic emblems worn by the lodges' officers. A complete set consisted of a jewel for each officer. Revere made no fewer than eleven sets of officer's jewels, containing anywhere from five to twelve pieces.[37] Although the number of jewels in a set was usually not specified in Revere's accounts, it seems that he did not always make complete sets. For John Jenks, in 1792, he made only "a Masons Jewel," while for Tyrian Lodge he crafted "two Stewards Jewils" in 1773.[38] The jewels were usually made of silver. Several other recorded items were almost certainly masonic officer's jewels, such as the pairs of "Cross Keys" made for both Simon Greenleaf in 1772 and the Tyrian Lodge in 1773, and the "p Silver cross pens" crafted for Samuel W. Hunt in 1787. The crossed keys and crossed pens usually signified the lodge treasurer and secretary respectively.[39] Many masonic lodges still own officers' jewels which were made by Paul Revere, including a notable set of twelve silver jewels made for Washington Lodge in 1796 (Fig. 44).[40] An original receipt for Columbian Lodge jewels, crafted in 1795, also survives. This receipt, made out from "Paul Revere and Son" lists ten lodge jewels. The notice of payment, recorded at the bottom, was signed by "Paul Revere J."[41] This receipt illustrates Paul Revere's declining involvement with his goldsmith shop by the 1790s when he increasingly left that business under the supervision of his son in favor of concentrating on his other newer business ventures. It is possible, however, that these masonic specialty items were still being made by Revere himself even as late as the 1790s, although it should be noted that his son, Paul Jr., was also a Freemason as well as a goldsmith.[42]

In addition to jewels, the masonic items mentioned most frequently in Revere's account books are copperplate engravings. As early as the St. Andrew's Lodge membership list of January 1762, Paul Revere was listed as an engraver as well as a goldsmith, soon producing trade cards, cartoons, portraits, and magazine illustrations, among other things.[43] Copperplate engraving was a logical extension of Revere's work as a goldsmith, which often involved the engraving of skillful designs and family arms upon pieces of silver. As early as March 1762, Revere received an order

Figure 44

Set of silver jewels made
for Washington Lodge by
Paul Revere in 1796. Each
jewel signifies a different
Lodge office (Cat. Nos.
222–233). Courtesy, Wash-
ington Lodge, A.F. & A.M.

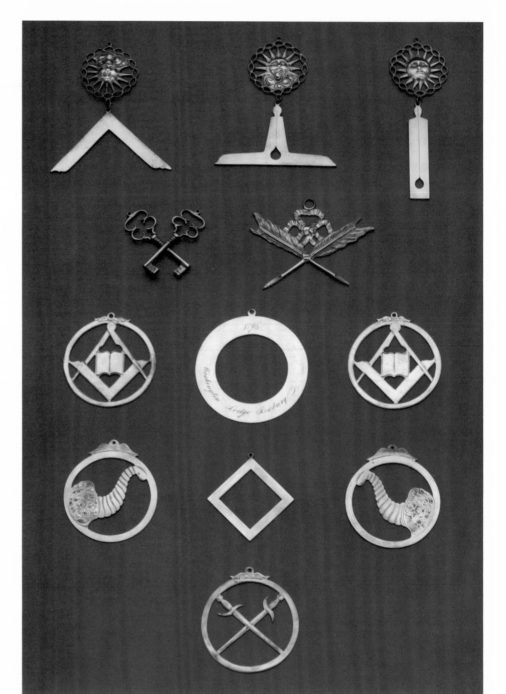

for a "Copper Plate for Notifications," which strongly suggests a masonic
use. The customer was John Pulling, Jr., a member of both St. Andrew's
Lodge and the Philanthropic Lodge in Marblehead, Massachusetts.[44]
Lodges regularly issued notifications or summonses to their members in-
forming them of the times, dates, and locations of meetings. Between 1762
and 1784, Paul Revere made at least six of these notifications for specific
lodges including one for St. Andrew's Lodge (Fig. 41).[45]

In addition, Revere also engraved masonic certificates or diplomas,
which were awarded to masons as they earned the three degrees. Most
notably, he engraved several certificates intended for general masonic use
which contained blanks for the name of the recipient, the masonic degree
being awarded, the lodge, and the date. Such a general certificate could
be purchased from Revere in quantity by any masonic lodge and filled in
for the use of its own members. This was no doubt convenient for the

lodges and profitable for Revere. A large certificate of this type has been identified as Paul Revere's, engraved in 1773 or earlier. Numerous copies of this engraved certificate exist, including two that were filled in by St. Andrew's Lodge—one issued on 3 February 1774 awarding the third degree, and another, used while Revere was lodge Master, conferred upon William Pierce for his completion of the first degree on 4 January 1779. This large plate bears the notation "Engraved Printed & Sold by Paul Revere Boston" at the bottom.[46] In 1780, Revere engraved another similar but smaller masonic plate with blanks, which was marked "Printed & Sold opposite Liberty Stump Boston," indicating the location of Revere's goldsmith shop at this time. The earliest-known impression from this plate is dated 30 May 1780, although the same certificate was also used by Rising States Lodge a decade later while Revere was lodge Master.[47]

Revere was also known to have reused masonic plates, adding or deleting various images in order to slighty change the print. For example, in 1790 after Revere had already moved his goldsmith shop to Dock Square, he deleted the outdated "Liberty Stump" marking from the bottom of a small 1780 certificate, and continued its use.[48] As was often the case with Revere's other commercial engravings, he seems to have followed English design sources for his masonic work.[49]

While Freemasons regularly engaged Paul Revere to make jewels, notifications, seals, and medals for lodge use, this business represents only a portion of Paul Revere's total masonic patronage. The real financial advantage to Revere lay in the fact that many of his masonic customers purchased gold and silver items for personal use entirely unrelated to their lodges. Even James Graham, the mason who purchased Revere's first recorded "Free Mason Medal" in January 1761, also left with a "Pair of Silver Knee Buckles." Simon Greenleaf, a mason from Newburyport, purchased a "Frame and Glass for a picture" and a "Floor Cloth" along with a masonic "plate for Notifications" in September 1772. Edward Foster and Captain Winthrop Sargent, both masons, bought silver punch ladles from Revere in 1763 and 1783 respectively.[50] It is not known whether these ladles were intended for personal or lodge use, although Samuel Barrett did purchase two ladles from Revere in 1762 which he donated, with suitable engraving, to St. Andrew's Lodge.[51] Paul Revere enjoyed similar masonic patronage for the hardware store which he opened immediately following the war in 1783. One ledger for the hardware store for the years 1783 to 1788 contained an alphabetical listing of seventy-nine customers. Of the seventy-two complete names recorded, again nearly one-half were Freemasons.[52]

Just as Freemasons patronized Paul Revere's business ventures, Revere himself also sought out fellow masons for needed goods and services. For example, Samuel Danforth, who was initiated in St. Andrew's Lodge in 1764, was Paul Revere's doctor. In 1783, Revere paid him for medicine and attendance to his family for the years 1770 through 1783.[53] Likewise, when Revere needed carpentry work done in 1768 he turned to "Bouve & Stodder," two masons from St. Andrew's Lodge. Gibbons Bouve was a housewright who became a mason in 1765, while Asa Stodder, a bricklayer, was initiated in 1764. In 1776, Revere again hired Bouve to build a small barn on his North Square property. Bouve charged Revere £3 for "Building your Cow House" and £2.16.8 for "350 feet of Board."[54] Paul Revere owned his North Square house for thirty years from 1770 to 1800. Although he lived at the house through most of the revolutionary period, his residence was sporadic after 1780, at which time he appears to have rented out the building and lived elsewhere until approximately 1790. At least two of his tenants during this ten year period were fellow Freemasons. On 27 May 1780, Revere wrote that he "lett my House at the North End to Mr. George Dᵉfrance for twenty five Spanish mill Dollars P Quarter, or as much paper as will purchase them at the time the Rent is due." This was probably the same George DeFrance who served as an officer of Friendship Lodge in 1780. He was still paying rent to Revere in August 1781.[55] On 19 April 1784, Joseph Dunkerley also leased the house for £45 per year, where he conducted "his Profession of Painting in Miniature." Dunkerley was still residing there in 1786 and probably painted the surviving miniature of Rachel Revere, Paul Revere's second wife, around this time. Dunkerley had become a member of St. Andrew's Lodge in July 1776 and was also active with Paul Revere in Rising States Lodge in the 1780s.[56]

The lifelong patronage that Paul Revere received from his fellow Freemasons, and often reciprocated, may have been partially the result of his faithful lodge attendance and his career as an active masonic officeholder. It is significant that he did not merely join the fraternity, but quickly sought positions of leadership within it. Revere held his first St. Andrew's Lodge position in 1762, not long after he earned the third masonic degree, serving his last masonic office in 1797. In the thirty-five years between 1762 and 1797, there were only four years when Paul Revere was not holding a lodge office, at times even serving as an officer in two lodges simultaneously. Elections of officers took place annually. From 1760 to 1770, Paul Revere's masonic attention was focused primarily upon St. Andrew's Lodge, for which he held offices and served regularly on the various committees that were raised to keep the lodge running smoothly. Revere's attendance at lodge meetings, which were usually held once each month, was also reliably consistent. For example, of 185 meetings held by St. Andrew's Lodge between 1761 and 1771, Revere missed only 16. He finally became Master of St. Andrew's Lodge in 1771, nearly ten years after his initiation, holding the position again in 1778, 1779, 1781, and 1782.[57]

The governing structure of a masonic lodge usually consisted of approximately ten positions, each signified by a symbolic emblem or jewel (Fig. 44). The 1756 Charter of St. Andrew's Lodge lists the following typical hierarchy of masonic offices—Master, Senior Warden, Junior Warden, Treasurer, Secretary, Senior Deacon, Junior Deacon, and Tyler. There were also two lodge Stewards. Several of the officer's jewels were based upon the actual stonemason's tools. Although a man could not be a lodge Master, the highest position, until he had held other offices, advancement was determined by merit rather than seniority. The Master presided over the lodge. His jewel consisted of a square, a tool used for measuring right angles. The ideal lodge Master was "nobly born, or a gentleman of the best fashion, or other artist, descended of honest parents and who is of singular great merit." The Senior and Junior Wardens wore jewels bearing a level and plumb respectively. The Senior Warden was essential, as he assisted the Master in lodge business and governed the lodge in the Master's absence. The Junior Warden was directed to "take care of the Reckening," a fee which each member paid at every lodge meeting, as well as being responsible for the examination of visitors and the introduction of candidates. The Secretary kept two books, one containing a copy of the charter, bylaws, and the list of members with the dates of their degrees, while the other book preserved the minutes of the meetings. The Secretary also issued summonses for meetings and appropriately wore a jewel composed of two crossed quills, while the Treasurer, whose jewel featured crossed keys, kept the lodge accounts. The Stewards attended to the lodge "refreshment" and accommodated visitors, their symbolic emblem being a horn of plenty. The Deacons were directed only "to assist in their proper office at the making or raising of any brethren," referring to the conferment of degrees, for which they would be "equipt with their proper wands." The Deacon's jewel bore the square and compass. The Tyler was the only officer of the lodge who was regularly paid for his services. He was a guardian of the lodge and wore a jewel bearing swords, which were often crossed.[58]

Leadership and Revolution

Paul Revere did not limit his masonic activities to attending meetings and holding offices. By 1769, he had participated in founding the Massachusetts Grand Lodge, through which he gained additional opportunities for leadership and social contacts. The creation of the Massachusetts Grand Lodge is tied to the ancient/modern controversy which first spawned St. Andrew's Lodge in 1752. As St. Andrew's Lodge organized and expanded, its members wanted the approval and fraternal respect of their fellow brethren in St. John's Grand Lodge, the legally sanctioned provincial representative of the English Grand Lodge established by Henry Price in 1733. However, since St. Andrew's Lodge had received its charter from Scotland as an ancient lodge, St. John's refused not only to recognize its existence but also felt that its own jurisdiction was infringed upon by this "Lodge [of] Scotch masons in Boston," a lodge which was not "regularly constituted" in the opinion of St. John's Grand Lodge.[59] The relationship between these two Boston lodges failed to improve significantly throughout the 1760s, finally prompting the ancient masons of St. Andrew's Lodge to consider "the expediency of applying to the Grand Lodge of Scotland for a Grand Master of Ancient Masons in Boston,"[60] a position which would be appointed by the Scottish Grand Master. In conjunction with three British military lodges that were in Boston at the time, the masons of St. Andrew's Lodge, notably Joseph Warren and Paul Revere, petitioned the Scottish Grand Master in 1768 for permission to found an ancient grand lodge. Under a commission dated 30 May 1769, Joseph Warren was duly appointed "Grand Master of Masons in Boston, New England and within one hundred miles of the same." Soon afterwards, Joseph Warren chose Paul Revere as his Senior Grand Deacon. Revere was a consistent officeholder in this new Massachusetts Grand Lodge, serving repeatedly in the positions of Senior Grand Deacon from 1770 to 1774, and Junior and Senior Grand Warden from 1777 to 1783. Revere was chosen as Deputy Grand Master, the position directly below Grand Master, for the years 1784–1785, 1790, and 1791, finally attaining the most prominent office of Grand Master between 1795–1797.[61]

Following the establishment of the Massachusetts Grand Lodge, the decade from 1770 to 1780 was marred by the commencement of hostilities between Great Britain and her American colonies. While the Revolutionary War had a definite impact on Massachusetts Freemasonry, the masons had an equal impact on the conflict. Although not all masons were radical sympathizers, it is worth noting that the resistance movement and the fraternity shared many participants. The North Caucus, one of Boston's three local political groups, consisted of sixty members in 1772.[62] Although incomplete lodge records often make it difficult to identify Freemasons

Figure 45

Ink and watercolor sketch of the Green Dragon Tavern drawn by John Johnson in 1773 (Cat. No. 163). Courtesy, American Antiquarian Society.

conclusively, it is clear that at least fifteen of the sixty members were masons, with the majority of the fifteen belonging to St. Andrew's Lodge. Joseph Warren and Paul Revere were part of this group, and also belonged to the "Long Room Club," an exclusive secret radical organization whose membership included such men as John Hancock, James Otis, and Samuel Adams.[63] The Sons of Liberty, upon which most of Boston's mob activity was blamed, also included Joseph Warren and Paul Revere. One contemporary account of its membership referred to Revere as an "Ambassador from the Committee of Correspondence of Boston to the Congress at Philadelphia,"[64] in reference to his considerable activity as a courier for the patriot cause. Joseph Warren was also the president of this Boston Committee of Safety.[65]

Undoubtedly, many of the Freemasons of St. Andrew's Lodge were deeply involved in radical activities. This assertion is difficult to prove since, as a rule, political sentiments were not discussed during masonic meetings and were rarely recorded in lodge minutes.[66] A striking exception to this rule relates to the Boston Tea Party of December 1773, an incident which clearly demonstrates the interrelationship between Freemasonry and radical groups. On 30 November 1773, as recorded in the St. Andrew's Lodge minutes, the meeting for the annual election of officers was adjourned "on account of the few Brethren present. (N.B. Consignees of Tea took up the Brethren's Time.)" On the night of the incident, 16 December 1773, the lodge meeting was again adjourned "on account of the few members present." Although no list was kept of the men who dumped the tea into Boston harbor, numerous masons from St. Andrew's Lodge were said to have participated, notably many of those who were also members of the North End Caucus, such as Paul Revere. A surviving sketch of the Green Dragon Tavern provides additional evidence (Fig. 45). Its legend reads "Where we met to Plan the Consignment of few Shiploads of Tea Dec 16 1773."[67] Significantly, St. Andrew's Lodge not only held its meetings at the Green Dragon Tavern but had also owned the building since 1764.

In addition to illustrating the organizational overlap between the North Caucus, the Sons of Liberty, and St. Andrew's Lodge, the tea party incident also suggests how a nonpolitical fraternity could play an organizational role in radical political activities, when its membership was so inclined. Despite the fact that St. Andrew's Lodge contained many radical sympathizers, there were also Freemasons who viewed the tea party and the revolutionary conflict with regret. While Paul Revere, in his own words, was "imployed by the Select men of the Town of Boston to carry the Account of the Destruction of the Tea to New-York," Freemason John Rowe (1715–1787) was writing, of this "Disastrous affair," that he was "sincerely sorry for the event" which he believed "might have been prevented." Rowe claimed to "know nothing of the matter nor who were concerned in it."[68]

It is hardly surprising that there were masons who shared the Tory sentiments of John Rowe, considering the English roots of Freemasonry, but the fraternity was far from being discarded as an English invention. On the contrary, its doctrines of universal brotherhood, which effectively transcended national boundaries, helped to prepare the way for its adoption as an American institution,[69] attractive to both conservatives and radicals alike. As the tension between Great Britain and her American colonies increased, the fraternity probably offered Paul Revere another opportunity to share his opinions with his fellow artisans. By 1774, Paul Revere writes that he soon became "one of upwards of thirty, chiefly mechanics, who formed our selves in to a Committee for the purpose of watching the Movements of the British Soldiers, and gaining every intelegance of the movements of the Tories." Revere adds that "we held our meetings at the Green Dragon Tavern." It is tempting to speculate how many of Revere's fellow "mechanics" might also have been members of St. Andrew's Lodge. While many of Revere's fellow patriots were Freemasons, the radical activity in which he participated also diverted his attention from the fraternity, notably interrupting his regular lodge attendance. When Paul Revere rode to New York with news of the Boston Tea Party in 1773, he missed the annual Grand Lodge election of officers held on 27 December 1773. Despite his absence he was chosen Senior Grand Deacon for the following year. In 1774, Revere was again riding as a courier for the radical cause, having been employed by the selectmen, he later wrote, "to carry their dispatches to New-York and Philadelphia for calling a Congress several times."[70] On one of these trips, Revere delivered the Suffolk Resolves which had been written by Joseph Warren. Congress approved the Resolves on 17 September 1774.[71] Possibly due to this out-of-town activity, Revere attended only one meeting of St. Andrew's Lodge between August and December 1774, while missing both meetings of the Massachusetts Grand Lodge in September and December.

The battles of Lexington and Concord on 19 April 1775 brought masonic activity in Boston to a complete halt. After the eruption of fighting, Boston became the seat of an occupying army; British troops remained until their forced evacuation nearly a year later in March 1776. Paul Revere had made his now famous midnight ride, about which he wrote "On Tuesday evening, the 18th, it was observed, that a number of Soldiers were marching towards the bottom of the Common. About 10 o'Clock, Dr. Warren Sent in great haste for me, and beged that I would imediately Set off for Lexington." About these events, the Massachusetts Grand Lodge noted that "Hostellitys Commenc'd between the Troops of G. Britain and America, in Lexington Battle. In Consequence of which the Town was blockaded and no Lodge held until December 1776."[72] The population of Boston underwent considerable dislocation during the occupation; many patriot sympathizers fled the town while Loyalists sought British protection. Paul Revere did not return to Boston after his mission to Lexington but instead stayed in Watertown, supporting himself and his family by engraving and printing money, among other things.[73] His account books record very little goldsmith work between 1775 and 1780. After the British evacuation, Revere was commissioned as a major of artillery in the regiment raised for Boston's defense and was stationed at the garrison on Castle Island in Boston harbor. There he served under Colonel Thomas Crafts, a fellow Freemason from St. Andrew's Lodge, soon receiving a promotion to lieutenant colonel.[74]

Both St. Andrew's Lodge and the Massachusetts Grand Lodge had reconvened by 1777. Although the military action had moved away from Boston by this time, the hardships of war were still apparent. Even the Green Dragon Tavern was nearly turned into a hospital by the occupying British. In the spirit of masonic charity, collections for the poor were taken and "strange brethren," even British prisoners of war, were assisted.[75] Before the war's end in 1783, Revere served as Master of St. Andrew's Lodge in 1778, 1779, 1781, and 1782. Although expressions of political sentiment are highly unusual in lodge minutes, the brethren of St. Andrew's Lodge did not bother to hide their animosity on one occasion in 1778 when they assisted a "Dutch Young Gentleman who was taken by one of Tyrant George's Frigates and had everything taken from him even to his certificate." Also while Revere was Master, the lodge aided a British prisoner of war "as a Token of the Love and friendship this Society has for one of the Fraternity tho' an Enemy."[76] Due to his military obligations, Revere missed many lodge meetings during the war years and might have found it more convenient to decrease or discontinue his active participation. That he continued to hold offices indicates his loyalty to Freemasonry and the fraternity's value to Revere as a ready source of companionship and support.[77]

Despite the fact that masonic activity was renewed in 1777, by the war's end Revere's lodges were in a state of flux. The Massachusetts Grand Lodge suffered considerable confusion when Joseph Warren, the appointed Grand Master, was killed at the battle of Bunker Hill in June 1775. Rather than wait for the Grand Lodge of Scotland to appoint a new Grand Master, the Massachusetts Grand Lodge elected its own leader in 1777, merchant Joseph Webb (1735–1787), who was repeatedly re-elected throughout the war years.[78] By 1782, the Massachusetts Grand Lodge took a bold step destined to alter Paul Revere's future as a Freemason. A committee was appointed in June 1782, which included Paul Revere, to determine and redefine the authority of the Massachusetts Grand Lodge. The committee, which delivered its report in December 1782, justified the election of Joseph Webb, undertaken independent of Scotland, on the grounds that, without a leader, the lodges "must Cease to Assemble, the Brethren be dispersed, the Pennyless go unassisted, the Craft Languish & Ancient Masonry be extinct in this Part [of the] World." Their appointment of the new Grand Master was clearly an action of self-preservation, intended to insure the continuation of masonic activity until the military situation was resolved. However, the committee went one step further to resolve that "This Grand Lodge be forever known & Called by the Name of the Massachusetts Grand Lodge of Ancient Masons, and that it is free and Independent in its Government & Official Authority of any other Grand Lodge or Grand Master in the Universe."[79] The report, including this bold resolution declaring complete independence from the

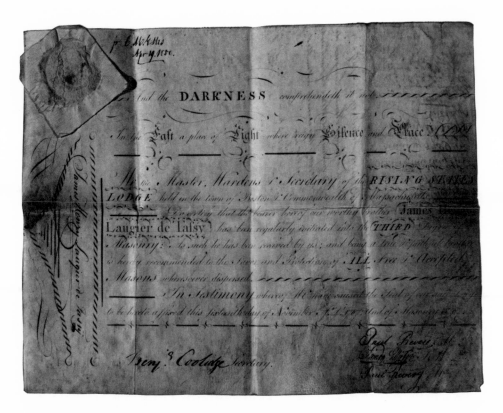

Figure 46

Handwritten third-degree diploma for Rising States Lodge, awarded to James Henry Laugier de Tassy on 16 November 1787 and signed by Lodge Master, Paul Revere (Cat. No. 213). Courtesy, New England Historic Genealogical Society.

Scottish Grand Lodge, was approved by the Massachusetts Grand Lodge in 1782.

The 1782 report, signed by Paul Revere and three other masons, posed a serious question of allegiance for all ancient masons under the jurisdiction of the Massachusetts Grand Lodge. As an ancient lodge, St. Andrew's was suddenly forced to decide whether it wished to ally itself with this newly independent Grand Lodge in Boston or remain loyal to Scotland. When a vote was finally taken in January 1784, the majority of St. Andrew's Lodge voted for the Grand Lodge of Scotland. For Paul Revere, a vote for Scotland would have meant denouncing the Grand Lodge in which he had just been chosen by Grand Master John Warren to serve as Deputy Grand Master.[80] Supporting the controversial resolution he had helped to draft, Revere voted for the Massachusetts Grand Lodge, throwing his vote with John Warren and the new republic.

Repercussions followed swiftly. Two weeks later, St. Andrew's Lodge voted that "no person shall be admitted a member of this Lodge who acknowledge the authority of the Assumed Massachusetts Grand Lodge."[81] Having voted with the minority, Paul Revere suddenly found himself ousted from the lodge which he had served as Master only two years earlier. More importantly, it was also the lodge where he had first been initiated as a Freemason, and to which he had given over two decades of active service. Although this rejection by St. Andrew's Lodge must have shocked Revere, he was not alone. By March 1784, Revere and twenty-two fellow masons founded a new lodge with a charter granted by the Massachusetts Grand Lodge. Although the new lodge was originally called St. Andrew's, it had been renamed Rising States Lodge by October 1784.[82]

Freemasons and Republicans: The Postwar Years

The postwar decade was fraught with economic and political difficulties, reflected both in Freemasonry and in the nation at large. While St.

Andrew's Lodge isolated itself by its continued loyalty to Scotland, the Massachusetts Grand Lodge endeavored to define its authority, puzzling over how to compel its constituent lodges to pay dues and send representatives to its quarterly meetings.[83] Likewise, Paul Revere struggled to pay the debts from his new hardware store business, started in 1783, at the same time that he was overseeing the output from the goldsmith shop and no doubt beginning to think about the iron and brass foundry that he would open by 1788. In the midst of this activity, Revere founded Rising States Lodge in 1784, serving as Treasurer from 1784 to 1786, and Master from 1787 to 1789, and again from 1791 to 1793[84] (Fig. 46). His fellow brethren in the lodge included numerous close relatives and acquaintances, such as his son Paul Revere, Jr. and son-in-law Amos Lincoln, his cousin Robert Hitchborn, an immediate neighbor Manasseh Marston, and Joseph Dunkerley, who was renting Revere's North Square house by 1786.[85] Revere's account book, kept while he served as Treasurer, records the procurement of lodge necessities, such as officers' jewels, ladles, candlesticks and a copperplate for summonses. Although it is not specified that Revere himself made the jewels or the copperplate, it is possible that he did. A surviving seal used by Rising States Lodge also has been attributed to him (Fig. 43).[86]

Despite Revere's concentration on Rising States Lodge in the 1780s, he continued to attend Grand Lodge meetings regularly, acting as a representative of his new lodge. In addition, Revere served as Senior Grand Warden between 1780 and 1783 and Deputy Grand Master from 1784 to 1785, and again from 1790 to 1792.[87] Due to incomplete records, Revere's additional activities and offices in Rising States Lodge cannot be determined.

The climax of Paul Revere's masonic career came in 1794 when, at the age of sixty, he was elected Grand Master of the newly created Massachusetts Grand Lodge. Revere's election to the most prominent masonic position in the state came only two years after the Massachusetts Grand Lodge finally joined with St. John's in March 1792 to create one united Grand Lodge for Massachusetts. This union brought together twenty-two constituent lodges.[88] As Grand Master, with the exclusive authority to charter new lodges, Revere added twenty-three more during his three-year term (1795–1797). At this time, the Grand Lodge met quarterly on the second Mondays of December, March, June, and September.[89] Revere attended every meeting while he was Grand Master although, ironically, he had not been the first choice of the assembled brethren in 1794. John Warren had received the most votes but declined to serve, with Revere being selected on a second ballot. Nevertheless, Revere fulfilled his office with dedication and skill. He continued the distribution of a volume of *Constitutions* which had been compiled after the 1792 union, and he also wrote the "charges" that were used in the installation of officers while he was Grand Master.[90]

The most memorable event during Paul Revere's term as Grand Master was the laying of the cornerstone of the New State House on Boston Common, 4 July 1795. Governor Samuel Adams invited the Massachusetts Grand Lodge to assist in the ceremony, which was also accompanied by a lengthy masonic procession from the Old State House to the building site. The New State House, designed by Charles Bulfinch, was erected by master builder and Freemason Amos Lincoln, Revere's son-in-law, and before long had its dome sheathed with sheet copper rolled at Revere's copper

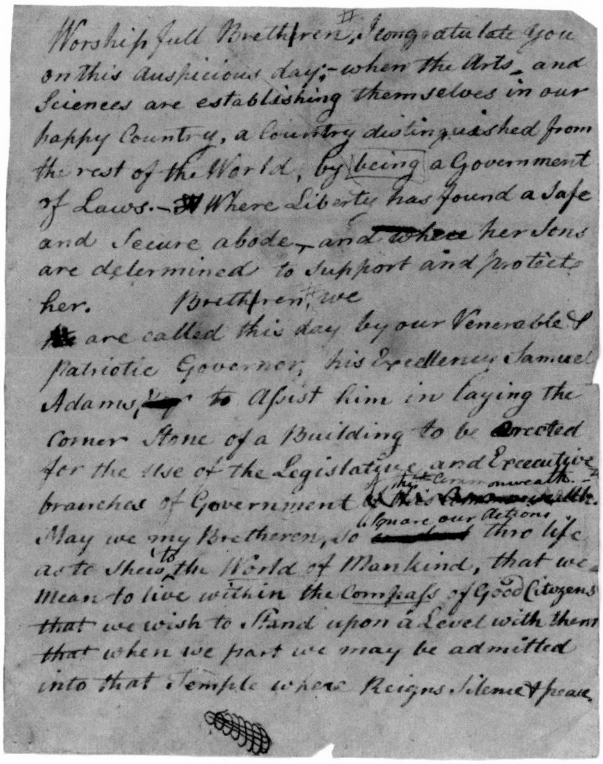

Worshipfull Brethren, I congratulate you on this auspicious day; - when the Arts and Sciences are establishing themselves in our happy Country, a Country distinguished from the rest of the World, by being a Government of Laws. - Where Liberty has found a Safe and Secure abode, and where her Sons are determined to support and protect her. Brethren, we are called this day by our Venerable & patriotic Governor, his Excellency Samuel Adams, to Assist him in laying the Corner Stone of a Building to be erected for the use of the Legislative and Executive branches of Government of this Commonwealth. May we my Bretheren, so Square our Actions thro life as to Shew to the World of Mankind, that we mean to live within the Compass of Good Citizens that we wish to Stand upon a Level with them that when we part we may be admitted into that Temple where Reigns Silence & peace

Figure 47

Handwritten speech delivered by Paul Revere during the masonic ceremony for the laying of the cornerstone for the New State House in Boston, 4 July 1795 (Cat. No. 215). Courtesy, Grand Lodge of Masons in Massachusetts, A.F. & A.M.

mill. At the cornerstone ceremony, Revere made the following speech (Fig. 47):

Worshipfull Brethren, I congratulate you on this auspicious day; - when the Arts and Sciences are establishing themselves in our happy Country, a Country distinguished from the rest of the World, by being a Government of Laws.—Where Liberty has found a Safe and Secure abode—and where her Sons are determined to support and protect her.

Brethren, we are called this day by our Venerable & patriotic Governor, his Excellency Samuel Adams, to Assist him in laying the Corner Stone of a Building to be erected for the use of the Legislative and Executive branches of Government of this Commonwealth. May we my Bretheren, so Square our Actions thro life as to Shew to the World of Mankind, that we mean to live within the Compass of Good Citizens that we wish to Stand upon a Level with them that when we part we may be admitted into that Temple where Reigns Silence & peace.[91]

By December 1797, Paul Revere had served as Grand Master for three years, making him ineligible for re-election. As new officers were chosen, Paul Revere "was then pleased to address the Grand Lodge in a fraternal manner in which his abilities in the masonic art were eminently displayed."[92]

After three years, Paul Revere's final speech reveals his contentment with the past, as well as the issues which concerned him for the future of Freemasonry. He was proud that there were "upwards of forty" lodges in the constituency which were represented and paid dues. He encouraged a "free correspondence" between masonic lodges, hoping that the Massachusetts Grand Lodge would soon have "the pleasure to Communicate with every G^d Lodge thro' the Globe." Ever concerned with the "necessity of subordination among masons," Revere urged "a carefull attention to our Constitution; that you never suffer the antient land marks to be removed; that a Strict attention be paid to every Lodge under this jurisdic-

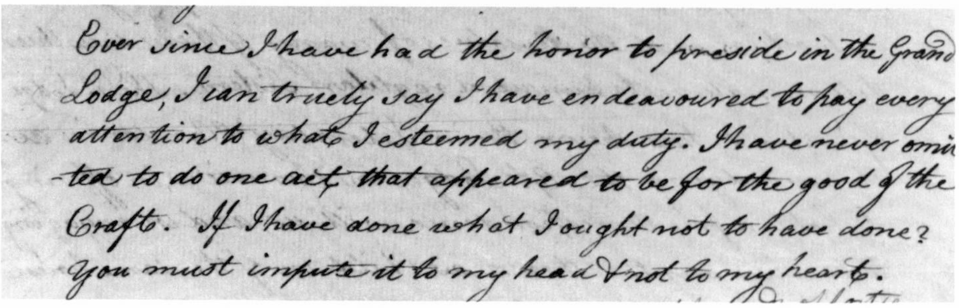

Figure 48

Detail from the handwritten address delivered by Paul Revere to the Massachusetts Grand Lodge on 11 December 1797 marking the end of his third year as Grand Master (Cat. No. 216). Courtesy, Grand Lodge of Masons in Massachusetts, A.F. & A.M.

tion" so that "they be not suffered to break thro, or, treat with neglect any of the regulations of the Grand Lodge." Revere also recommended that "a Committee be raised to form regulations for the disposal of Charity, or any other thing that will add to the happiness of Masons." He claimed that Freemasonry "is now in a more flourishing situation than it has been for Ages," adding "there is no quarter of the Globe but accknowledges its Philantrophy." He felt it was "the greatest happiness" of his life

> to have presided in the G,ᵈ Lodge at a time when Free Masonry has attained so great a heighth that its benign influence has spread its self to every part of the Globe & shines with more resplendent rays, than it hath since the days when King Solomon imployed our immortal Gᵈ Master to build the Temple.

Revere began his address with an apology, assuring his brethren that he "endeavoured to pay every attention to what I esteemed my duty," adding that "I have never omitted to do one act that appeared to be for the good of the Craft" but "if I have done what I ought not to have done? you must impute it to my head & not to my heart" (Fig. 48). In closing, Revere extended to his fellow masons "my most sincere & hearty thanks for your Candor, and assistance," since it was "owing to your kind attention and assistance that I have been enabled to do the little good which has been done." He encouraged that they "continue the same kindness to all my Successors in office."

Paul Revere's years as Grand Master (1795–1797) were also characterized by the most intensive community involvement of his life. It is no accident that this organizational activity occurred in the postwar period, when Americans were struggling to establish their new nation and fulfill the high ideals espoused through the ideology of the Revolution. The colonists had envisioned the split from England as the opportunity to realize the ideals of the Enlightenment and escape the corruption and decay of the Old World. With their independence, they attempted to establish an ideal republic, designed in the mold of the classical states of antiquity and solidly based upon a selfless, moral, and virtuous citizenry. Although Paul Revere did not deliver orations on the fragility of republican states as did fellow Freemason John Warren, he believed in the ideals of classical republicanism as much as the revolutionary theorists of his day.[93] Politically speaking Paul Revere would have been considered an ardent Federalist, yet he wrote "you know I was allways a warm Republican; I always deprecated Democracy; as much as I did Aristocracy."[94] Paul Revere and the generation of the American Revolution lived to see their new nation gradually dissolve from a moral republic led by natural aristocrats into what was perceived to be an uncontrollably materialistic popular democracy by 1820, hardly the "more perfect union" envisioned in 1776.[95] As early as 1804, Revere lamented that "our government is now completely democratic."[96]

Despite Revere's later disillusionment with the state of affairs, his republicanism found its clearest expression in his sense of civic responsibility. Revere's community service was at its height during the 1790s at a time when the influence of classicism was seen in everything from monumental government architecture to the delicate urns and swags of furniture and mantelpieces. George Washington, also a Freemason, was seen by many to embody qualities of the ideal leader for a republican state. By this time, Boston also enjoyed renewed prosperity as a seaport metropolis following the economic hardship of the 1780s. Likewise, Paul Revere's economic situation had improved and, as he neared the age of sixty, he lived the life of a respectable federalist businessman and artisan leader befitting his maturity and prosperity. Voluntary associations and societies also proliferated in the postwar years. In the spirit of a "warm Republican" Revere was never in a better position to contribute to those organizations which he considered worthy of his support.

Paul Revere's activities with local voluntary associations ranged from small financial contributions to extensive organizational involvement. In some instances Revere seems to have done little more than pay dues or an assessment, yet it indicates that he thought enough of these societies to make a contribution. The Boston Library and the Boston Humane Society fall into this category.[97] There were other organizations from which Paul Revere as well as his community could have personally benefited, such as the Massachusetts Mutual Fire Insurance Company, incorporated in 1798. Revere was the first of over eight hundred subscribers to sign the charter, dated 2 March 1798, which specified that "Funds should be raised from among its members, to be distributed among those whose houses or other buildings should be injured or consumed by fire." Only two months later, on 14 May 1798, Revere also joined the Massachusetts Charitable Fire Society, an organization which had been founded in 1794. An expression of the value which Revere placed in this society is further evidenced by a letter he wrote in 1806, six years after he purchased his property in Canton. On behalf of a neighbor whose house had recently burned, Revere appealed to "the President and Trustees of the Massachusetts Charitable Fire Society," reminding them of the principles upon which the society had been founded, "to help the unfortunate who are distressed by fire."[98]

As the successful operator of both a goldsmith shop and an iron and brass foundry by the 1790s, Revere also had an interest in any organization founded for the benefit of mechanics and tradesmen. After effectively rallying support among Boston's artisans for the ratification of the national Constitution in the 1780s, Paul Revere became an organizing member and first president of the Boston Mechanic Association, founded in 1795.[99] The history of the Massachusetts Charitable Mechanic Association, as it came to be known, with which both Revere and his son Paul Jr. were involved, is too complex to be embarked on here but Revere's inclusion in such an organization is indicative of the influence he held among the local artisans. Although it is likely that economic and political factors greatly influenced Revere's interest in this organization, his participation as a founding member suggests that he also must have shared in the association's stated benevolent purposes—to promote the public good through the encouragement of the mechanic arts and the financial support of mechanics both "ingenious" and "decayed."[100]

Revere's sense of civic responsibility can also be seen in the municipal positions he served. These public posts would have required his time and displayed a commitment to his community in keeping with the republican

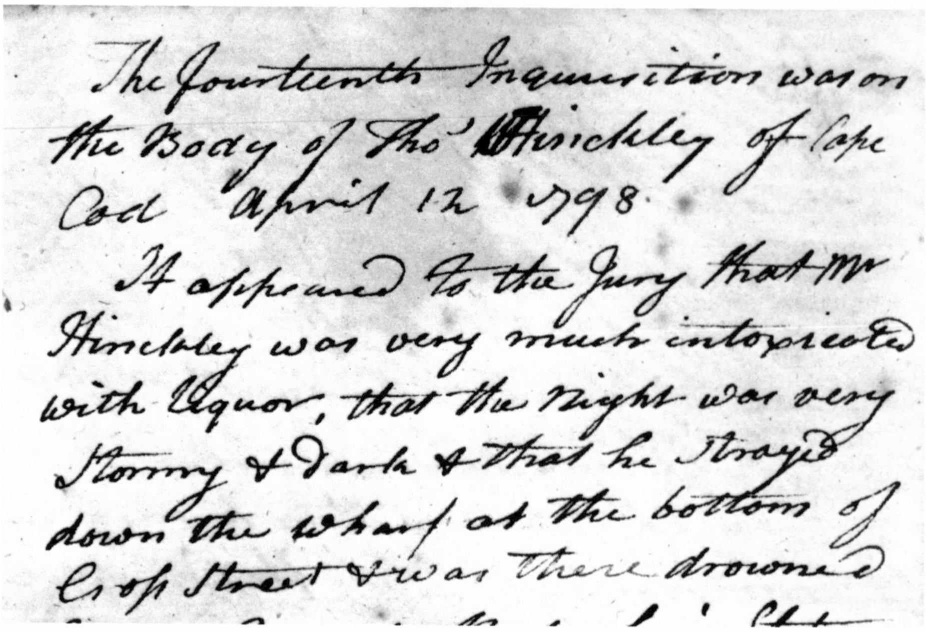

The fourteenth Inquisition was on the Body of Thos Hinckley of Cape Cod April 12 1798.
It appeared to the Jury that Mr Hinckley was very much intoxicated with Liquor, that the night was very Stormy & Dark & that he Strayed down the wharf at the bottom of Cross Street & was there drowned

Figure 49

Detail from the journal kept by Revere during his tenure as county coroner (1796–1801) recording the conclusions of the 12 April 1798 inquest regarding the drowning death of Thomas Hinckley (Cat. No. 195). Courtesy, Massachusetts Historical Society.

ideals of good citizenship. Two such positions are worthy of mention. On 11 May 1795, while serving as Grand Master, Revere was commissioned by Governor Samuel Adams as Suffolk County coroner, a post he held at least through 1800. In a memoranda book, Revere recorded the details of forty-six inquests which he conducted with a fourteen member jury, dating from February 1796 to January 1801 (Fig. 49). The deaths he investigated ranged from accidental drownings to child abuse, often involving violence, drunkenness and the use of such drugs as opium and laudanum. The coroner's office also paid for burials and making coffins.[101] Considering this exposure to issues of public health and safety, it is hardly surprising that Revere also became involved with the creation of Boston's first Board of Health, founded 13 February 1799 after an outbreak of yellow fever. In his second public office, Revere served as Board president for the years 1799 and 1800, also acting as ward representative for those two years. Two Board of Health reports signed by Revere, issued to the constituents in 1799 and 1800, outlined the problems facing the new board and the steps taken to eradicate them (Fig. 50). According to these reports, over fifteen "nuisances" were identified and declared unlawful, such as digging graves less than six feet deep, throwing animal or vegetable substances into the harbor, and keeping privy contents closer to the surface than eighteen inches. A system of garbage collection was established, whereby scavengers with carts were assigned to "receive the dirt, filth and sweepings of the inhabitants" twice each week from May through October. The board also had the power to investigate and quarantine any vessel which might carry disease. After operating for one year, the Board of Health proclaimed the success of its "system of cleanliness" which had cost the constituents a total of $4,401.28. Among other things, the board had cleaned 137 overflowing privies, "27 offensive Drains," "35 foul Cellars," "61 dirty and filthy yards," thirteen ponds of stagnant water, and two brothels. These two years as president mark Revere's only known participation with this organization.[102]

Although Revere held no additional masonic offices after 1797, he remained active with the Freemasons until at least 1800, after which time he attended lodge meetings only occasionally.[103] This sharp decrease in masonic activity coincided with, and was probably partially the result of, the

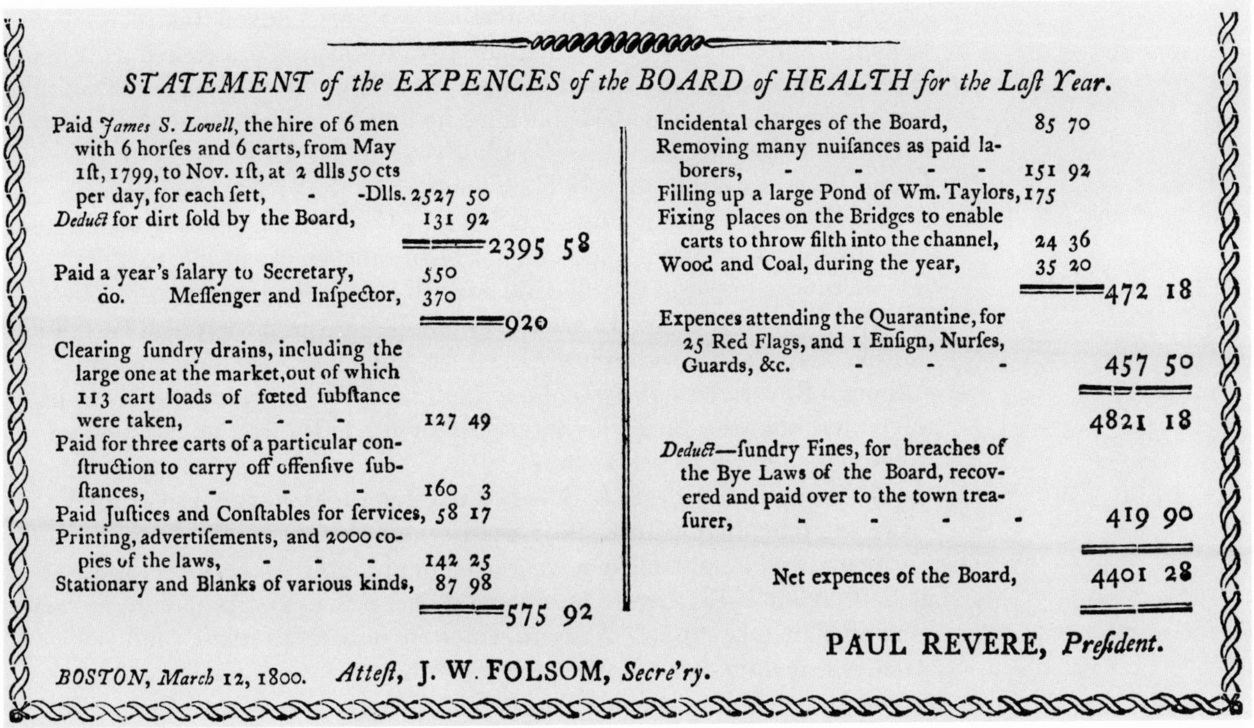

STATEMENT of the EXPENCES of the BOARD of HEALTH for the Laſt Year.

Paid *James S. Lovell*, the hire of 6 men with 6 horſes and 6 carts, from May 1ſt, 1799, to Nov. 1ſt, at 2 dlls 50 cts per day, for each ſett, - -Dlls. 2527 50
Deduct for dirt ſold by the Board, 131 92
======2395 58

Paid a year's ſalary to Secretary, 550
do. Meſſenger and Inſpector, 370
=====920

Clearing ſundry drains, including the large one at the market, out of which 113 cart loads of fœted ſubſtance were taken, - - - 127 49
Paid for three carts of a particular conſtruction to carry off offenſive ſubſtances, - - - 160 3
Paid Juſtices and Conſtables for ſervices, 58 17
Printing, advertiſements, and 2000 copies of the laws, - - - 142 25
Stationary and Blanks of various kinds, 87 98
=====575 92

Incidental charges of the Board, 85 70
Removing many nuiſances as paid laborers, - - - - 151 92
Filling up a large Pond of Wm. Taylors, 175
Fixing places on the Bridges to enable carts to throw filth into the channel, 24 36
Wood and Coal, during the year, 35 20
=====472 18

Expences attending the Quarantine, for 25 Red Flags, and 1 Enſign, Nurſes, Guards, &c. - - - 457 50
====
4821 18

Deduct—ſundry Fines, for breaches of the Bye Laws of the Board, recovered and paid over to the town treaſurer, - - - - 419 90
====
Net expences of the Board, 4401 28

PAUL REVERE, *Preſident.*

BOSTON, March 12, 1800. *Atteſt*, J. W. FOLSOM, Secre'ry.

Figure 50

Detail from a broadside issued by the Board of Health, 12 March 1800 and signed by Revere as president. It summarizes the activities of the agency during its first year (Cat. No. 197). Courtesy, Massachusetts Historical Society.

establishment of Revere's copper rolling mill in Canton. Even Revere wrote in 1804 that "I have spent the last three years most of my time in the country, where I have mills for Rolling Sheets and bolts, making spikes and every kind of copper fastenning for ships." Revere also mentioned that his son and business partner, Joseph Warren Revere, "takes care of the business in Boston," while "I take care at Canton about 16 miles from Boston."[104]

It is ironic that Paul Revere's business commitments contributed to the decrease of his masonic involvement since there had always been a happy union between business and masonry throughout Revere's life. Even Revere's last conspicuous masonic contribution related to his work as a craftsman. After the death of prominent Freemason George Washington in 1799, Paul Revere not only participated in the masonic funeral procession held in Boston in his honor, but also crafted a small gold urn (Fig. 22) in order to preserve a lock of the late president's hair.[105]

Even after Revere's masonic activity decreased, it is likely that his membership in the fraternity continued to provide social and business contacts. This is clearly evidenced by a letter written to the Reverend George Richards of Portsmouth, New Hampshire, in 1807, where Revere utilized a masonic discussion to preface a business inquiry. After complimenting the Reverend at length on his "pleasing Masonic Discourse," Revere asked if Richards would investigate why the Universal Church had not yet paid for a bell that Revere had made and delivered. Revere begged the Reverend's pardon for even mentioning the matter, adding this business request beneath his signature, as if he might not have inquired at all had it not been that the two men shared a masonic connection.[106]

A disturbing end to Paul Revere's masonic career came in 1810 when Rising States Lodge made the decision, by vote of its members, to dissolve.[107] The dissolution of a lodge was hardly a common occurrence and investigations conducted by the Grand Lodge into its causes revealed that Rising States Lodge had been suffering from internal conflicts for several years. In the absence of lodge minutes, it is difficult to determine the extent of Revere's involvement with Rising States Lodge after 1800, although it appears that his role had greatly diminished or ceased, as it had with the Massachusetts Grand Lodge. The Rising States Lodge dissolution was controversial particularly because its members had voted to divide the lodge funds among themselves, rather than deliver the money to the Grand Lodge as ought to have been done when the charter was surrendered. However, after its investigation, the Grand Lodge finally concluded that since Rising State Lodge had not been functioning properly, the members who voted to dissolve did so with honorable intentions.[108] It was also determined that the divided lodge funds, of which Revere received a portion, had been appropriately used for the relief of fellow masons. Although Revere was cleared of any fault in this matter, it must have disappointed him to witness the deterioration of a lodge that he had helped found not even thirty years earlier.[109]

Although Paul Revere had been an active Freemason for over forty years when he died in 1818, the Grand Lodge minutes make no mention of his death, and he did not receive a masonic funeral. Nevertheless, as late as September 1817, Revere found among his possessions a document written and signed by Joseph Warren, which he donated to the Grand Lodge Archives, feeling that "for the perusal of the Craft, and for the information of all men" it belonged there.[110] This last gesture summed up a lifelong dedication to a society from which Paul Revere derived many benefits. Possibly motivated by the attractions of financial reward and social mobility, Revere joined the fraternity in 1760 as a young craftsman, soon finding that many of his fellow masons shared his radical sentiments. In the postwar era, Freemasonry was embraced by many men who found its system of morality in keeping with the high ideals of the new republic. For Revere, who was relatively undistinguished as a politician or military leader, the fraternity offered him status and leadership opportunities, culminating in his term as Grand Master. The period of Revere's involvement was one of growth for Freemasonry, although with the increasing democratization of American society in the early nineteenth century, the fraternity came under suspicious scrutiny for its exclusive membership and its secrecy. Fortunately, Paul Revere did not live to experience the anti-masonic furor which began in the 1820s. Although Revere's interest in Freemasonry no doubt resulted from a combination of factors, the Reverend William Bentley, a well known Salem diarist and Freemason, offered a compellingly straightforward commentary on Revere in 1796 while he was serving as Grand Master. Bentley stated simply that "Col. Revere enters into the Spirit of it, and enjoys it."[111] Revere summed up the worth of the fraternity in equally simple terms. He chose to end his farewell speech in 1797 by reminding his listeners that "the Cause we are engaged in is the Cause of Humanity, of Masons and of Man."[112] Considering Paul Revere's lengthy masonic career, it is likely that he not only espoused the masonic rhetoric but believed it.

Notes

1.
Gordon S. Wood, ed., *The Rising Glory of America 1760–1820* (New York, 1971), 88.

2.
Freemasons, Massachusetts Grand Lodge, *The Constitutions of the Ancient and Honorable Fraternity of Free and Accepted Masons: Containing their History, Charges, Addresses etc . . . To which are added the History of Masonry in the Commonwealth of Massachusetts, and the Constitutions, Laws and Regulations of Their Grand Lodge together with a Large Collection of Songs, Epilogues, etc.* (Worcester, MA, 1792), "Sanction" page. This unnumbered page, located at the front of the volume, contains the names of the committee members who compiled it. [Hereafter cited as *Constitutions*.]

3.
Constitutions, 18.

4.
On the medieval history of Freemasonry and levels of masons see Mervyn Jones, "Freemasonry," in Norman MacKenzie, ed., *Secret Societies*, (New York, 1967), 158–59, 161. See also Harry Carr, *Six Hundred Years of Craft Ritual* (Missouri, 1977), 1–4.

5.
On the history of Freemasonry see Jones, 161–62. For references to guilds, social clubs, and lodges see Dorothy Ann Lipson, *Freemasonry in Federalist Connecticut, 1789–1832* (Princeton, 1977), 5–6, 15, 19–22. Although Lipson deals primarily with Connecticut, she begins with a chapter on "The Invention of Freemasonry," which traces the origins of the fraternity in England and describes the type of men who formulated modern Freemasonry.

6.
These ideas are condensed from Lipson's chapter on "The Invention of Freemasonry." See especially 6–7, 13–30, 37–39.

7.
William Preston Vaughn, *The Anti-Masonic Party in the United States 1826–1843* (Lexington, KY, 1983), 10.

8.
Grand Lodge of Masons in Massachusetts, *Two Hundred and Fifty Years of Massachusetts Masonry* (Boston, 1983), 1, [hereafter cited as *Two Hundred and Fifty Years*]. For a detailed discussion of the founding of the Grand Lodge of England, see Lipson, 23–33.

9.
For additional information on the 1723 Constitutions see Lipson, 29–30.

10.
See Jones, 161–62, for a brief history of masonry. He also states that masonry was in full flower by 1735.

11.
For quoted sections on operative and speculative masons, see *Constitutions*, 17–18. Vaughn (p. 10) also mentions that the distinction between operative and speculative masons was still being made in London, 1720.

12.
For a sketch of the origins of American Freemasonry, see Earl W. Taylor, *Historical Sketch of the Grand Lodge of Masons in Massachusetts From Its Beginnings in 1733 To The Present Time* (Boston, 1973), 3–4. See also Louis C. King, "The Grand Lodge of Massachusetts Birthplace of Freemasonry," *Trowel* 1 (April 1983): 6.

13.
See *Two Hundred and Fifty Years*, 2–3. According to this source (pp.iii, 16–17) the first lodge chartered in Boston under the new 1733 provincial Grand Lodge was known as "the First Lodge in Boston" or First Lodge. However, by 1783, First Lodge became known as St. John's Lodge, a name it had been referred to as early as 1772. The name First Lodge will be used in this essay.

14.
Lipson, 7.

15.

According to Lipson (p. 7), masons tended to be mobile and often leaders of political and religious dissent. For a good general explanation of Freemasonry also see Kathleen Smith Kutolowski, "Freemasonry and Community in the Early Republic: The Case for Anti-Masonic Anxieties," *American Quarterly* 34 (Winter 1982): 545–49, which discusses early masonry in Genessee County, New York, 1809–1847. According to Vaughn, so few local studies have been done that it is still difficult to "develop an accurate national profile of the typical Mason during the period between the American Revolution and the beginning of the Antimasonic crusade, 1826–1827" (p. 4). Vaughn concludes that, based on the limited studies, early nineteenth century masons tended to be prosperous and politically active men who frequently assumed leadership positions.

16.

Both Lipson and Kutolowski offer good discussions of why men were attracted to Freemasonry. See Lipson (pp. 19–20), for reference to the significance of the club to eighteenth-century life.

17.

See *Two Hundred and Fifty Years*, 4. According to this source, the membership of Boston's First Lodge consisted of "businessmen, owners of manufacturing plants, shipbuilders, merchants, physicians, writers, all well-to-do men." Forbes (p. 61), also agrees that the membership of St. John's Lodge (or First Lodge) was "slightly more elegant" than St. Andrew's Lodge, which Revere joined. Forbes also states that Revere may have been influenced by local masonic activities in his youth, given that one of Boston's first masonic parades occurred when he was fourteen (p. 60).

18.

For Revere's 1756 military experiences, see Forbes, 42–47.

19.

For reference to Richard Gridley and this army lodge, see *Two Hundred and Fifty Years*, 16–17, 31; and Henry J. Parker, *Army Lodges During the Revolution* (Boston, 1884), 2.

20.

On the founding of St. Andrew's Lodge, see Taylor, 6–7; King, 6; *Constitutions*, 134, Section 2, and Lodge of St. Andrew, *Centennial Memorial of the Lodge of St. Andrew* (Boston, 1870), 160–73 [Hereafter cited as *Centennial Memorial*]. On the ancient vs. modern controversy, see Jones, 162–63. Jones attributes the ancient/modern split to disagreements over ritual, dating from the *Book of Constitutions* of 1722–1723. King explains the formation of St.

Andrew's Lodge along class lines, attributing the split in England to a clash between Irish workmen and the gentlemen's lodges of London and claiming that similar class conflict may have caused the formation of St. Andrew's Lodge (p. 6). *Two Hundred and Fifty Years* (p. 4) also holds this view. Taylor (pp. 6–7) suggests simply that St. Andrew's Lodge was formed in response to the ancient/modern split in England.

21.

Two Hundred and Fifty Years, 5.

22.

See *Commemoration of the One Hundred and Fiftieth Anniversary of the Lodge of St. Andrew 1756–1906* (Boston, 1907), 294. For the dates of Revere's three degrees, see "Initiates and Members," 273–301. It is uncertain when Revere actually earned the second degree. [Hereafter cited as *Commemoration of Lodge of St. Andrew.*]

23.

See *Charter and By Laws of the Lodge of St. Andrew held in Boston, New-England Constituted in the year 1756*, Item 21 in the Bylaws. This source is available on microfilm in the Library of the Grand Lodge of Masons in Massachusetts, A.F.& A.M. [hereafter cited as GLMM]. The 1756 Charter quoted here is the first one on the reel. This source hereafter cited as "St. Andrew's Lodge Charters." The original charters and bylaws are owned by the Lodge of St. Andrew, Boston.

24.

For a good explanation of the symbolism, moral rhetoric, and ceremonies involved with earning the three degrees, see Allen E. Roberts, *The Craft and Its Symbols: Opening the Door to Masonic Symbolism* (Richmond, VA, 1974).

25.

The Green Dragon Tavern was located on the left side of Union Street, then Green Dragon Lane, near the corner of Hanover Street. It was demolished October 1828 for the widening of Green Dragon Lane. For the use of the Tavern by St. Andrew's Lodge, see *Centennial Memorial*, 160, 167–69.

26.

For quote, see Minutes of late December 1761 meeting (no exact date given), Lodge of St. Andrew's Meeting Minutes, Microfilm 1756–1778, owned by the Lodge of St. Andrew, Boston. Additional St. Andrew's Lodge minutes for the years 1778–1854 can be found on microfilm at the GLMM Library. The original minutes are owned by the Lodge of St. Andrew, Boston. The St. Andrew's Lodge membership list of 1762 is reproduced in *Centennial Memorial*, 241–42.

27.
A sampling of Revere's customers was compiled from the two goldsmith shop Wastebooks 1761–1797, recording every customer for the years 1761–1762, 1765, 1770–1771, 1780, 1783, 1787, 1790, 1793 and 1796. Several sources have been used to identify Freemasons. The GLMM Library contains information on members of St. John's and St. Andrew's Lodges. See *History of St. John's Lodge of Boston* (Boston, 1917), 199–232, 245–62, and *Commemoration of Lodge of St. Andrew*, 273–301. Also in the GLMM Library, see Henry J. Parker, Index 1733–1800, a handwritten volume with entries on early masons in Massachusetts, arranged alphabetically. Another source of information is the membership file at the Grand Secretary's office, GLMM. This office keeps cards on all Freemasons in the state, both active and inactive. Unfortunately, many of the early records were destroyed by fire, so that these files were largely reconstructed. They are very helpful, although not complete. *Two Hundred and Fifty Years* also contains a listing with biographical information on prominent masons.
28.
See Vaughn, 11. He estimates masonic membership in America at between fifteen hundred and five thousand from a total population of 2.5 million in 1776.
29.
See Flynt and Fales (pp. 143–364) for a listing of silversmiths who were working in Boston during Revere's day. Notable exceptions are the Hurd brothers, Benjamin and Nathaniel, who were both Freemasons and well-known goldsmiths and engravers.
30.
See Wastebooks, 3 January 1761, 24 February, 22 March, and 19 November 1762, RFP.
31.
For a listing of masonic items made by Revere, see Steblecki, Appendix 5, 108–19.
32.
Revere chartered twenty-three lodges while he was Grand Master of the Massachusetts Grand Lodge. For a listing of these lodges, see *Two Hundred and Fifty Years*, 21.
33.
See Wastebooks, 28 July 1781, RFP, for the notation that Colonel John Brooks ordered "a Sett of silver Jewels for Washington Lodge." John Brooks was associated as of 2 March 1781 with Washington Lodge No. 10 chartered 6 October 1779, and with the American Union Lodge chartered 15 February 1776 as of 28 August 1779. See *Two Hundred and Fifty Years* for charter dates (pp. 16–19), and a short biography of John Brooks (p. 24). See Wastebooks, 27 April 1782, RFP, for reference to John Blanchard purchasing "a Copper Plate for Certificates." He was also initiated in Washington Lodge No. 10.
34.
For information quoted concerning Revere's involvement with Tyrian Lodge, see Earle J.T. Merchant, Secy., Tyrian Lodge to Librarian, GLMM, 22 April 1967, in the folder "Paul Revere Project," located in the vertical files of the GLMM Library. According to this letter, Revere was present at the first meeting of Tyrian Lodge, 9 March 1770, where a bill was read from Revere charging the Lodge for one box, two candlesticks, painted flooring, a balloting box, truncheons and gildings, jewels, ribbon, a Book, and twelve aprons. According to Wastebooks, 15 June 1773, RFP, Tyrian Lodge also paid Revere for "Engraving a Plate for Summons," in addition to several masonic officers jewels. Tyrian Lodge was chartered in Gloucester, Massachusetts, on 2 March 1770.
35.
See Wastebooks, 26 June 1784, 1 June 1792, and 18 May 1796, RFP (Revere's orders from three lodges in Maine), and 14 November 1766 (reference to the Lodge in Surinam). Captain Caleb Hopkins, who became associated with St. Andrew's Lodge on 13 May 1762, paid Revere for "Engraving a Copper Plate for Notifications for a Masons Lodge in Surinam" on 14 November 1766. James Avery purchased "5 Masons Jewls for Warren Lodge" and "5 Certificates" from Revere on 26 June 1784. Warren Lodge had been chartered in Machais, Maine, 4 September 1778, with Avery serving as Master in 1784. Avery had also been initiated in St. Andrew's Lodge on 27 February 1778. James Eveleth, also an initiate of St. Andrew's Lodge (31 December 1777), paid Revere for "printing 12 paper & 12 parchment Certificates" on 1 June 1792. This was the same day that Lincoln Lodge was chartered in Wiscasset, Maine, of which Eveleth was the first Master. David Howe, who purchased certificates from Revere 18 May 1796 was also initiated into St. Andrew's Lodge, as well as being active with Revere in Rising States Lodge. In 1796, when he ordered the twelve certificates, he was also Master of Hancock Lodge, located in Penobscot, Maine.

36.
See Wastebooks, 3 January 1761, 24 February and 2 March 1762, RFP. James Graham was initiated into St. Andrew's Lodge before 10 April 1756 and was chosen Senior Deacon on 19 December 1760. According to the St. Andrew's Lodge 1762 members list, he was a chairmaker, living at the head of Clark's Wharf. Richard Pulling was a merchant from Fish Street who was initiated in St. Andrew's Lodge on 13 June 1761. James Jackson appears as a member of St. Andrew's Lodge 12 October 1769.

37.
See Wastebooks, 28 July 1781, 9 January 1782, 18 March and 26 June 1784, and 7 and 25 July 1797, RFP. For references to incomplete sets see Ibid., 1 June 1792, 15 June 1773, 15 September 1772, and 4 April 1787.

38.
Ibid., 1 June 1792, 17 June 1773.

39.
Ibid., 15 September 1772, 15 June 1773, and 4 April 1787. Simon Greenleaf joined St. Peter's Lodge, Newburyport, 23 March 1772. Samuel W. Hunt could be either Samuel Willis Hunt who was voted "to be made a Mason" in Rising States Lodge 25 October 1784, or Samuel Wells Hunt, who was associated with both the First Lodge (1790) and the Massachusetts Grand Lodge (1789).

40.
Washington Lodge was chartered by Revere while he was Grand Master on 17 March 1796. The lodge, originally located in Roxbury, is now in Lexington, Massachusetts. These jewels are still owned by the lodge.

41.
The Columbian Lodge of Boston was chartered by Revere on 9 June 1796 while he was Grand Master of the Massachusetts Grand Lodge. According to the *Proceedings of the Most Worshipful Grand Lodge of Ancient Free and Accepted Masons of the Commonwealth of Massachusetts for the Year 1967* (Boston, 1967), 526, Revere made a set of ten jewels for Columbian Lodge which were melted down in 1810. This receipt is owned by the Museum of Our National Heritage, Lexington, MA. An illustration of it can be found in Steblecki, Section XI.

42.
Paul Revere, Jr. was proposed to be made a mason in Rising States Lodge on 27 December 1784. See Rising States Lodge, Minutes of Lodge Meetings, 27 December

1784, GLMM Archives, hereafter cited as "Rising States Lodge Minutes." The Grand Lodge Archives has the original minutes only from 29 March 1784 to 28 February 1785.

43.
For the most thorough discussion of Revere's masonic engravings see Brigham, 180–97.

44.
Wastebooks, 22 March 1762, RFP. See *Two Hundred and Fifty Years* (p.40), for a brief masonic biography of Pulling.

45.
References to four copperplate notifications or summonses can be found in Revere's Wastebooks, 22 March 1762, John Pulling, Jr. (St. Andrew's and Philanthropic Lodges); 14 November 1766, Capt. Caleb Hopkins (Lodge at Surinam); 15 September 1772, Simon Greenleaf, Newburyport (St. Peter's Lodge); 15 June 1773, Tyrian Lodge. According to Brigham (p. 185), Revere also did a notification for Lodge No. 169 Ancient York Masons of Boston, probably in the 1760s. See Brigham, Plate 60a for illustration. See St. Andrew's Lodge Minutes, 12 December 1783, when it was "Voted that the Secy' supply the Lodge with blank summonses as many as he shall think necessary for the two following years." The St. Andrew's Lodge notification (Fig. 41) was originally thought to date from 1784. See Brigham, 129. However, the discovery of an earlier example, filled out in 1767 and signed by Revere as Treasurer, changes this date. See Whitehill, 211.

46.
Brigham, 188. For an illustration of this certificate, see Plate 61 in this source.

47.
Ibid., Plate 62 (for illustration of the "Liberty Stump" plate), 189, 191–92.

48.
Ibid., 188, 195. Likewise, Revere also altered his larger certificate by adding a few symbols to the plate in 1796. See Brigham, Plate 65, for an illustration of this certificate.

49.
Brigham, 180.

50.
Wastebooks, 3 January 1761, 1 February 1763, 17 September 1772, and 4 April 1783, RFP.

51.
See Ibid., 19 November 1762, for reference to "two Silver Punch Ladles" with "Wooding Handles." Samuel Barrett is listed as a member of St. Andrew's Lodge, 10 July 1760. Although these ladles are not listed specifically as masonic items in Revere's accounts, Barrett did donate ladles to St. Andrew's Lodge. See St. Andrew's Lodge Minutes, 30 November 1762, where the Lodge thanked Brother Barrett "for donation of two Genteel Silver Ladles." Numbered "Nᵒ1" and "Nᵒ2," the ladles were engraved "The Gift of/Bʳ Samˡ Barrett to/ Sᵗ Andrew's Lodge/ Nᵒ82/ 1762." See Whitehill, 212, for a photograph of the ladles, still owned by the Lodge of St. Andrew.
52.
According to Forbes (pp. 371–72, 376–77), Revere opened his hardware store by 1783 and operated the business until approximately 1789. The Revere Family Papers contain letterbooks in which Revere recorded copies of his business letters. There are many letters dealing with the hardware store, such as PR to Frederick William Geyer, 5 September 1783, Letterbook 1783–1800, Vol. 53, in which Revere writes "I have already opened a large Store of hard ware directly opposite where Liberty Tree stood." Also see Account Ledger for the Workshop at Boston 1761–1788, Vol.13, RFP. Most of this volume contains accounts kept for the hardware store. The names in this ledger were also checked against the sources listed in note 27 for possible masonic membership.
53.
See PR to Samuel Danforth, 17 January 1783, Loose Manuscripts, RFP.
54.
See Ibid., for the following receipts: "August 22 1768 Mr. Paul Revere to Bouve and Stodder" and "April 23 1776 Cor.ᵉˡ Paul Revere to Gibb Bouve."
55.
See Forbes, 360–61, 416. See also Wastebooks, 27 May and 27–28 August 1780, and 28 August 1781, RFP. For references to DeFrance and Friendship Lodge see *Proceedings in Masonry, St. John's Grand Lodge 1733–1792: Massachusetts Grand Lodge 1769–1792* (Boston, 1895) 280, 282–83, 293. [Hereafter cited as *Proceedings in Masonry*.] Although by 1 September 1780, DeFrance had been expelled from Friendship Lodge for "malconduct," by 7 September 1781, the Grand Lodge dismissed the charges. A man by this name was also made a mason in St. Andrew's Lodge, January 1782.

56.
For information about Dunkerley, see Forbes, 416, 473. Depending upon the source consulted, the spelling of his name varies. Revere called him "Dunkerley" in his Wastebooks, while the Rising States Lodge Minutes list him most frequently as "Dunckerly" or "Dunckerley." Forbes refers to him as "Dunkerly." For quote about Dunkerley, see his notice in the December 1784 *Independent Chronicle*. For references to Dunkerley in the Wastebooks, see 19 April 1784; 19 January, 19 July, and 19 October 1785; 19 January 1786, RFP.
57.
For a listing of Revere's masonic offices see Steblecki, 102–4. This list, which includes St. Andrew's Lodge, Rising States Lodge, and the Massachusetts Grand Lodge, was compiled primarily from lodge minutes and contains the dates of Revere's elections, where available, and the length of service.
58.
See St. Andrew's Lodge Charters 1756 for a list of officers and the description of their duties. See *Constitutions* (p. 167), for quote about Master and additional information about offices in the section "of Masters, Wardens, Fellows and Apprentices." The description of officers given here was compiled from both of these sources, representing the Massachusetts Grand Lodge and St. Andrew's Lodge, although there is some discrepancy in the description of duties. The tasks of some officers are not described fully in either source. The symbols of the jewels are relatively standard. See Roberts for a discussion of masonic symbolism, which also touches upon the symbolism of the jewels.
59.
See *Constitutions*, 134; and Lipson, 49–50. See *Centennial Memorial*, 268–71. These pages are part of a chronology of St. Andrew's Lodge history, compiled primarily from their minutes. The quote about Scotch masons, listed under the date 8 April 1761, is from a vote passed by St. John's Lodge in reference to St. Andrew's. Exactly where the compiler of this chronology found this information is unknown. This quote does not appear in the St. Andrew's Lodge Minutes. For a detailed account of the controversy see *Centennial Memorial* (pp. 22–31), a section by Charles W. Moore entitled "Address: The Massachusetts Grand Lodge and Its Relations With St. Andrew's Lodge," given 23 December 1869.

60.
See St. Andrew's Lodge Minutes, 12 June
and 10 July 1766 (references to letters written to Scotland about the poor relationship
between St. John's and St. Andrew's
Lodges), and 30 November 1768 (for quote).
61.
See St. Andrew's Lodge Minutes, 30 November and 8 December 1768, and 14 May
1769 for references to founding the new
Grand Lodge. See *Centennial Memorial*
(194–95 and 31–32) for Warren's appointment and the extent of his jurisdiction. See
Proceedings in Masonry (pp. 456–57) for
the text of a document from 3 March 1772
which extended Warren's authority, making him "Provincial Grand Master over all
the Lodges on the Continent of North
America, which now are or hereafter shall
be Erected and taken to hold of the Grand
Lodge of Scotland." The British military
lodges were No. 106 Registry of Scotland,
the Duke of York's Lodge from the Sixty-
fourth Regiment, the Lodge No. 58 Registry of England from the Fourteenth Regiment, and Lodge No. 322 Registry of
Ireland with the Twenty-ninth Regiment.
62.
Minutes of the North Caucus, including a
list of members, are printed in Goss,
2:635–44. See Forbes (pp. 119–22) for a
discussion of the North End Caucus.
63.
For information on the Long Room Club,
see Forbes, 122–25.
64.
Ibid., 125–27.
65.
Ibid., 275.
66.
The *Constitutions*, 170, specifically for-
bade "quarrels about religion, or nations,
or state policy."
67.
St. Andrew's Lodge Minutes, 30 November and 16 December 1773. For an account
of the Tea Party, including a discussion of
its participants, see *Centennial Memorial*,
169–70.
68.
For Paul Revere's quote about his ride to
New York, see PR to Jeremy Belknap in
*Paul Revere's Three Accounts of His Fa-
mous Ride* (Portland, ME, 1968), n.p.,
hereafter cited as *Three Accounts*. For
Rowe's remarks, see "Excerpts from Diary
of John Rowe," *Proceedings in Masonry*,
428. According to *Two Hundred and Fifty
Years* (p. 42), Rowe was Grand Master of
St. John's Grand Lodge from 1768 until
1787.

69.
Lipson, 55.
70.
For Revere quotes, see PR to Jeremy
Belknap, *Three Accounts*, n.p. Revere's
lodge attendance can be determined by
reading the minutes, which usually list at
least the officers who attended, if not
everyone present.
71.
For attribution of Warren as the author,
see Forbes, 216. For additional information
see David Ammerman, *In the Common
Cause: American Response to the Coercive
Acts of 1774* (New York, 1974), 74, 75, 130,
131. The Resolves, which were written by
Warren for a Suffolk County gathering
held at Milton, Massachusetts, declared
that the Coercive Acts should not be
obeyed and also recommended a sever-
ance of trade with Great Britain.
72.
For Revere's quote on his famous ride, see
PR to Jeremy Belknap, *Three Accounts*,
n.p. See St. Andrew's Lodge Minutes for
lapse of meetings between April 1775 and
April 1776. For Grand Lodge quote, see
Proceedings in Masonry, 258.
73.
For a thorough section on Revere printing
money, see Brigham, 213–41. Forbes (pp.
282–89) also includes information on this
period.
74.
See Forbes (pp. 317–20) for Revere's
positions on Castle Island. See also the
following two documents: Paul Revere,
Commission as major of artillery, 9 May
1776, and Paul Revere, Commission as
lieutenant colonel of artillery, 27 November 1776, in Loose Manuscripts, RFP.
75.
See *Centennial Memorial*, 180, and 111–12
(for a description of St. Andrew's Lodge
during the war years, including reference
to a collection for the poor in which £250
was donated to the Boston Overseers of
the Poor in 1777); and St. Andrew's Lodge
Minutes, 12 February 1778. The Massachusetts Grand Lodge also collected
money for the poor. See *Proceedings in
Masonry*, 267, 269–70, 286–87, 300, and
379. For aid to British masons, see *Proceedings in Masonry*, 275. See also St. Andrew's Lodge Minutes, 17 February 1778,
15 January 1779 and 14 March 1782 for reference to "distressed strange brethren."

76.
For quotation, see St. Andrew's Lodge Minutes, 12 and 17 February 1778.
77.
For Revere offices, see *Proceedings in Masonry*, 261–63, 267, 277, 285, and 297.
78.
For information on Webb, see *Two Hundred and Fifty Years*, 45. For death of Warren and revival of masonic activity see *Constitutions*, 137–40. See also *Proceedings in Masonry* (pp. 259–60, 462) for information regarding Webb's election. Taylor (pp. 9–10) also gives an account of Webb's election.
79.
For the complete text of the committee report of 1782 see *Constitutions*, 143–46, and *Proceedings in Masonry*, 298–99, 301–3.
80.
St. Andrew's Lodge Minutes, 22 January 1784. A listing of how the lodge members voted can be found in *Centennial Memorial*, 244 or Steblecki, 105. St. Andrew's Lodge had taken a vote on this question earlier in 1782 but chose to wait until the war was over to make a final decision. See St. Andrew's Lodge Minutes, 16 December 1782, 23 January 1783. See also *Proceedings in Masonry*, 304–5.

John Warren was elected Grand Master 7 March 1783 and was still Grand Master in January 1784 when St. Andrew's Lodge took its vote. For Revere's appointment as Deputy Grand Master see *Proceedings in Masonry*, 310–11, and *Constitutions*, 46. John Warren (1735–1815) was a brother of Joseph Warren and also a physician. See *Two Hundred and Fifty Years* (p. 45) for a brief masonic biography.
81.
St. Andrew's Lodge Minutes, 5 February 1784.
82.
For the founding of Rising States Lodge, see *Constitutions*, 147–48; *Two Hundred and Fifty Years*, 19; Taylor, 11–12; and *Centennial Memorial*, 40, 106. For references to the name change see Rising States Lodge Minutes, 26 July, 30 August, 27 September, and 25 October 1784.
83.
See Steblecki, 47–49.
84.
For Revere's positions, see Rising States Lodge Minutes, 28 June, 27 September, and 29 November 1784, and 28 February 1785. Since there are no surviving minutes for Rising States Lodge after February 1785, information about Revere's offices after 1785 has been gathered from references in the Grand Lodge *Proceedings*. For election to officer see *Proceedings in Masonry*, 322, 460 (Master); 324–25 (Treasurer); 359–60 (office in 1789); and 378

(1791 election). See *Proceedings of the Most Worshipful Grand Lodge of Ancient Free and Accepted Masons of the Commonwealth of Massachusetts In Union with the Most ancient and Honorable Grand Lodge in Europe and America, According to the Old Constitutions. 1792–1815* (Cambridge, 1905), 29 (1792 election). [Hereafter cited as *Proceedings, 1792–1815*.] For Revere's offices in 1787–1788, see two documents located at the GLMM Archives: "Rising States Lodge Return of Officers," 1787–5–28 and 1788–5–26.
85.
For references to members, see Rising States Lodge Minutes, 29 March 1784–28 February 1785. See Forbes (p. 199) for mention of Amos Lincoln. Both Lincoln and Paul Jr. are also listed as officers on the "Rising States Lodge Return of Officers," 1787–5-28 and 1788–5–26.
86.
See Paul Revere Account Book, 1784–1793, GLMM Archives [hereafter cited as "Rising States Lodge Account Book"]. Although most of this volume contains Revere's foundry and other business accounts, the first few pages contain the records he kept while Treasurer of Rising States Lodge from March 1784 to April 1786. This seal is owned by the GLMM Archives.
87.
For Revere's elections as an officer, see *Proceedings in Masonry*, 278, 285, 297, 301–4, 310, 325, 367–68, and 377–79. Paul Revere was not present at this 1790 meeting when officers were chosen, and the only office not mentioned is that of Deputy Grand Master. Since Revere is listed with this office for every other meeting afterwards in 1790, it is likely that he was chosen for the position. He was re-elected in 1792.
88.
See *Two Hundred and Fifty Years* (p. 7) for an account of the union of the two Grand Lodges. Also see *Proceedings in Masonry*, 340–41, and 380–81. For Revere's election, see *Proceedings, 1792–1815*, 60–61, 64–65.
89.
For a list of lodges chartered while Revere was Grand Master, see *Two Hundred and Fifty Years*, 21.
90.
For Revere's election, see *Proceedings, 1792–1815*, 60–61, 64–65. For references to this volume of constitutions, see Ibid., 28–29, 82, 88, 108–9. The GLMM Archives owns the manuscript, handwritten by Revere, entitled "The Manner of Constituting a New Lodge," n.d.

91.
See Goss (2:479–85) for an account of the cornerstone ceremony; see *Proceedings, 1792–1815* (pp. 74–76), for the order of procession, stone inscription, and short description of the event; and Forbes (p. 425) for construction of the dome.

For Revere's speech see Goss, 2:483–84, or Forbes, 398–99. Revere's original handritten copy of this cornerstone speech is in the GLMM Archives.

92.
For quote, see *Proceedings, 1792–1815*, 111. For the complete text, see Paul Revere, "Address to the Grand Lodge by R. W. Paul Revere, Esq. at the Meeting on the Evening of 11 December 1797," GLMM Archives, hereafter cited as "Address to the Grand Lodge."

93.
See John Warren, "An Oration, Delivered July 4th, 1783," reprinted in Wood, 55–69. For a good brief discussion of the ideology behind the American Revolution, see Wood "Introduction," particularly, 1–8.

94.
See PR to Capt. Thomas Ramsden, 4 August 1804, Loose Manuscripts, RFP. Also see Forbes, 427.

95.
Wood, 1–2, 6–8.

96.
PR to Capt. Thomas Ramsden, 4 August 1804, RFP.

97.
Receipt, Nathaniel Davies to Paul Revere for payment of an assessment by the Boston Library, 9 December 1797, and Receipt, S. Howard to PR for payment for membership subscription to the Boston Humane Society, 11 March [1796], Loose Manuscripts, RFP.

98.
See Goss (p. 590) for a discussion of the Massachusetts Mutual Fire Insurance Company and charter quote. Forbes (p. 482) refers to Revere as a founding member. For the Massachusetts Charitable Fire Society, see Paul Revere, Certificate of Membership in Massachusetts Charitable Fire Society, 14 May 1794, Loose Manuscripts, RFP, and PR to Arnold Wells, Esq., 15 November 1806, PRMA.

99.
Forbes, 368. For a thorough discussion of Boston's artisan support for the Constitution, see Kornblith, *From Artisans to Businessmen*, 71–77. Goss (2:451–62) also discusses the adoption of the Constitution.

100.
Kornblith, 79–81, 86, 89–90, 93.

101.
See Paul Revere, Commission as coroner of Suffolk County, 11 May 1795, Loose Manuscripts, RFP. In the same source also see Paul Revere, Order from members of coroner's jury investigating the drowning of Joshua Barton, 5 November 1796; Receipt and account of burials by George Clark for Suffolk County Coroner's Office, April 1796–May 1797, 21 January 1797; Bill and Receipt, 21 July 1798, from John French to the coroner's office for making coffins November 1796–May 1797. For coroner inquests and juries recorded by Revere, see Memoranda Book, 1797–1798, Vol. 51–X, RFP.

102.
Forbes, 482. The two Boston Board of Health reports are owned by the Massachusetts Historical Society, dated 30 March 1799 and 12 March 1800 (Broadside Collection). The library of the Bostonian Society, Boston, also owns a broadside issued by the Boston Board of Health in the nineteenth-century (n.d.) which lists the board members and officers from 1799–1821, also including which ward each member represented.

103.
For Revere's activities in the Grand Lodge after 1797, see *Proceedings, 1792–1815*, 36, 112–13, 124–27, 142, 145–46, 151, 239, 244–45, 295, 299. The extent of Revere's masonic involvement is difficult to determine after 1800. However, as his name appears infrequently in the minutes after that date, it seems that Revere greatly diminished his activities.

104.
PR to Capt. Thomas Ramsden, 4 August 1804, RFP. See also Forbes, 424–27.

105.
See *Proceedings, 1792–1815*, 156–60.

106.
PR to Rev. George Richards, GLMM Archives. Paul Revere began making bells at his Boston foundry in 1792. For a listing of Revere's bells, see Stickney and Stickney, passim.

107.
See *Proceedings, 1792–1815*, 436, 438–39, 450–51. Since there are no minutes for Rising States Lodge in existence after 1785, the information about the dissolution has been obtained from the account of the matter and the investigations recorded in the Grand Lodge minutes.

108.
See *Proceedings, 1792–1815*, 492–98.
109.
For references regarding the investigations
into how the divided funds were used, see
Ibid., 498, 531, and 533–35 (Revere's testi-
mony).
110.
PR to Francis Oliver, 1 September 1817,
GLMM Archives.
111.
William Bentley, *The Diary of William
Bentley, D.D. Pastor of the East Church,
Salem, Massachusetts*, 4 vols. (Salem, MA,
1905–14), 2:190.
112.
Paul Revere, "Address to the Grand
Lodge."

The Exhibition

Ancestry and Family Life

1

Bible
(Deborah Hitchborn Revere)
Leather binding, 1719
Printed by James Watson, Edinburgh,
Scotland
H. 5½ in., W. 2⅞ in.
Old North Church
(Fig. 5)

2

Bookplate for Paul Rivoire
Line engraving, 1720s
Attributed to Paul Revere Sr. (1702–1754)
H. 4 in., W. 3³⁄₁₆ in.
Massachusetts Historical Society
(Fig. 1)

3

Copperplate for Revere Bookplate
Engraved copper, ca. 1758
Paul Revere (1734–1818)
H. 3⅞ in., W. 2⅞ in.
Massachusetts Historical Society

4

Bookplate for Paul Revere
Line engraving, restrike, ca. 1900–1925
H. 3⅜ in. W. 2⅜ in.
Massachusetts Historical Society
(Fig. 2)

5

Covered Sugar Dish
Silver, ca. 1752–1754
Paul Revere Sr. (1702–1754)
Marked "P•REVERE" in rectangle
H. 4¾ in., Diam. (rim) 5⅛ in.
Historic Deerfield, Inc. (67–452)
(Fig. 14)

6-7

Sleeve Buttons
Gold, ca. 1725–1735
Paul Revere Sr. (1702–1754)
Marked "PR" in rectangle
Diam. ⁷⁄₁₆ in.
William Inglis Morse Collection
Gift of Mrs. Frederick W. Hilles
Yale University Art Gallery (1959.17.2)
(Fig. 12)

8

Tankard
Silver, ca. 1740–1754
Paul Revere Sr. (1702–1754)
Marked "PR" in crowned shield
Engraved "JᶜN"
H. 8¼ in., Diam. (base) 5⅛ in.
Gift of Henry F. du Pont
Henry Francis du Pont Winterthur
Museum (61.616)
(Fig. 13)

9

Large Spoon
Silver, ca. 1725–1730
Paul Revere Sr. (1702–1754)
Marked "PR" in crowned shield
Engraved "SB"
L. 7½ in.
Gift of Mr. and Mrs. Alfred E. Bissell
Henry Francis du Pont Winterthur
Museum (62.240.1400)

10

Wedding Ring
Gold, ca. 1773
Attributed to Paul Revere (1734–1818)
Made for his second wife,
Rachel Walker Revere
Engraved "[L]IVE *Co[n]tented*"
Diam. ¹¹⁄₁₆ in.
Gift of Mrs. Henry B. Chapin
and Edward H.R. Revere
Museum of Fine Arts, Boston (56.585)
(Fig. 7)

11

Bible
(Rachel Walker Revere)
Bound paper, 1730
England
H. 12 in., W. 10 in.
Massachusetts Historical Society

12

Letter
Rachel Revere to Paul Revere
Boston, 2 May 1775
Gage Papers
William L. Clements Library, University
of Michigan

We the Subscribers Do agree To the following
Articles Vizt

That if we Can have Liberty From the wardens
of Doctors Cuttlers church we will Attend there once
a week on Evenings To Ring the Bells for two hours
Each Time from the date here of For one year

That we will Choose a Moderator Every three Months
whose Business shall be To give out the Changes
and other Business as shall be Agreed by a Majority
of Voices then Present

That None shall Be admitted a Member of this Society
without a Unanimous Vote of the Members then Present
and that No member Shall begg Money of any Person
In the Tower on Penalty of being Excluded the Society
and that we will Attend To Ring at any Time when the Wardens
of the Church Aforesaid shall desire it on Penalty of Paying
three Shillings for the good of the Society (Provided we Can
have the whole Care of the Bells)

That the Members of this Society Shall nott Exceed
Eight Persons

and all Differences To be desided By a Majority of Voices

John Dyer
Paul Revere
Josiah Flagg
Barthw Ballard
Jonathan Law
Jona Brown junr
Joseph Snelling

13
Bell Ringing Agreement
Drawn up between the Wardens of Christ
Church and John Dyer, Paul Revere,
Josiah Flagg, Bartholomew Ballard,
Jonathan Law, Jonathan Brown, Jr.,
and Joseph Snelling
Boston, ca. 1750
Old North Church

14
Letter
Mathias Rivoire to Paul Revere
Ste. Foye, France, March 1782
Revere Family Papers
Massachusetts Historical Society

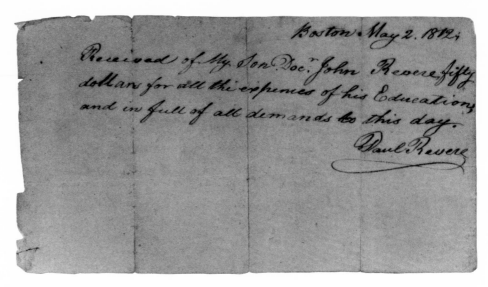

15

Receipt
Paul Revere to Dr. John Revere for
repayment of education expenses
Boston, 2 May 1812
Paul Revere Memorial Association (75.144)

16

Letter
Joshua Revere to Paul Revere
Portland, Maine, 9 July 1795
Revere Family Papers
Massachusetts Historical Society

17

Receipted Account
Mr. Wm. Turner to Paul Revere for
education expenses for Harriet and
Maria Revere
1 April 1798
Revere Family Papers
Massachusetts Historical Society

18

Thimble
Gold, ca. 1805
Attributed to Paul Revere (1734-1818)
Engraved *"Maria Revere Balestier,"*
at a later date
H. 1¼ in., Diam. (base) ⅝ in.
Gift of Mrs. Henry B. Chapin and
Edward H.R. Revere
Museum of Fine Arts, Boston (56.113)

19

Letter
Maria Revere to Rachel Revere from
boarding school
Woburn, MA, 25 May 1801
Revere Family Papers
Massachusetts Historical Society

20

Portrait of Paul Revere
Oil on panel, 1813
Gilbert Stuart (1755–1828)
28½ x 23¾ in.
Gift of Joseph W., William B.,
and Edward H.R. Revere
Museum of Fine Arts, Boston (30.782)
(Fig. 8)

21

Portrait of Rachel Revere
Oil on panel, 1813
Gilbert Stuart (1755–1828)
Signed on back "Painted by G. Stuart
Esqr. For Joseph W. Revere In The Spring
of 1813."
28½ x 23¾ in.
Gift of Joseph W., William B.,
and Edward H.R. Revere
Museum of Fine Arts, Boston (30.783)
(Fig. 9)

22

Pole Screen
Pole and frame, mahogany and pine
Embroidered panel, wool, silk and paint
on linen, 1760–1790
H. 64½ in. (screen), H. 27¾ in., W. 22½ in.
Bequest of Mrs. Pauline Revere Thayer
Museum of Fine Arts, Boston (35.1845)

23

Bowfront Chest of Drawers
Mahogany with mahogany veneer and
white pine, ca. 1780–1800
H. 32¼ in., W. 41¼ in., Depth 21⅝ in.
Bequest of Mrs. Pauline Revere Thayer
Museum of Fine Arts, Boston (35.1844)

24-25

Pair of Windsor Chairs
Hardwood and pine with black paint, early
19th century
Labeled "Charter St. Chairs"
H. 33 in., W. (seat) 16½ in., Depth 16½ in.
Gift of Miss Anna Revere
Paul Revere Memorial Association
(75.314-315)

26

Eyeglasses with Case
Steel with glass and leather case, early
19th century
W. 4½ in., L. (bows) 6½ in.
Gift of Charles W. Corbett
Paul Revere Memorial Association (75.5)

27

Letter
Edward Edwards to Paul Revere
Philadelphia, 20 January 1801
Revere Family Papers
Massachusetts Historical Society

28

Drawing of Paul Revere
Chalk on paper, ca. 1800
Charles Balthazar Julien Fevret
de Saint-Memin (1770–1852) Philadelphia
20¼ x 14¼ in.
Gift of Mrs. Walter Knight
Museum of Fine Arts, Boston (47.1055)
(Fig. 36)

29

Mezzotint of Paul Revere
Engraved by Saint-Memin
From chalk drawing by Saint-Memin
Ca. 1800
Diam. 2⅝ in.
Gift of Miss Marion Cole
Paul Revere Memorial Association (78.1)

30

Document Box
Leather with brass binding and fastenings,
early 19th century
H. 4¾ in., W. 10½ in., Depth 4¾ in.
Paul Revere Memorial Association (75.306)
(Fig. 42)

31

Watch Chain Pendant
Gold and topaz, early 19th century
H. ⅞ in.
Pauline Revere Thayer Collection
Museum of Fine Arts, Boston (35.1847)

32

Seal
Gold and sardonyx, early 19th century
Engraved *"PR"* on stone
H. 1 in., W. ¾ in.
Grand Lodge of Masons in Massachusetts,
A.F. & A.M.

34

Pitcher
Silver, ca. 1800
Paul Revere (1734–1818)
Marked "REVERE" in rectangle
Engraved "*Paul and Rachel Revere./Charter Street.*" and "*R*" all in 19th century lettering
H. 7¹⁄₁₆ in., Diam. (base) 4¼ in.
*Gift of Joseph W.R. Rogers and
Mary C. Rogers
Museum of Fine Arts, Boston (42.462)*

35

Plate
Hard-paste porcelain with blue, red, and gold Imari pattern
China, ca. 1750–1770
Diam. 9⅛ in.
*Bequest of Mrs. Pauline Revere Thayer
Museum of Fine Arts, Boston (35.1849)*

33

Sugar Urn
Silver, ca. 1790
Attributed to Paul Revere (1734–1818)
H. 10⅛ in., W. (base) 3¼ in.
*Pauline Revere Thayer Collection
Museum of Fine Arts, Boston (35.1759)*

Revere's Residences

36

Bill
Gibbs Bouve to Paul Revere for carpentering and lumber for building a "Cow House."
Boston, 23 April 1776
*Revere Family Papers
Massachusetts Historical Society*

37

Receipt
Samuel Savage to Paul Revere for payment of rent on house on Charter Street
Boston, 28 October 1788
*Revere Family Papers
Massachusetts Historical Society*

38

Sketch of Canton Dale
Pen and ink on paper, undated
Attributed to Paul Revere (1734–1818)
5½ x 11⅜ in.
Massachusetts Historical Society
(Fig. 35)

39

Canton Dale Poem
Paul Revere (1734–1818)
Canton, MA, ca. 1810
*Revere Family Papers
Massachusetts Historical Society*

Business Life
Paul Revere, Goldsmith

40

Creampot
Silver, ca. 1755–1775
Paul Revere (1734–1818)
Marked "•REVERE" in rectangle
H. 4 in.
Gift of Mrs. Emerson G. Morse
Worcester Art Museum (1974.39)

41

Creampot
Silver, ca. 1740–1754
Paul Revere Sr. (1702–1754)
Marked "PR" in rectangle
Engraved "MH" and added later
"*SEB/from/EMG/1889*"
H. 4⅛ in., W. 3¾ in.
Gift of Mrs. Warren R. Gilman
Worcester Art Museum (1933.43)
(Fig. 11)

42

Porringer
Silver, ca. 1780
Paul Revere (1734–1818)
Marked "•REVERE" in rectangle
Engraved "RGS/to RGSW"
L. 7¾ in., Diam. (lip) 5 in.
Sterling and Francine Clark Art Institute
(1963.2)

43

Caster
Silver, ca. 1755–1760
Paul Revere (1734–1818)
Marked "P•REVERE" in rectangle
Engraved "AⁿA"
H. 5⅜ in., Diam. (base) 1¾ in.
Pauline Revere Thayer Collection
Museum of Fine Arts, Boston (35.1767)
(Fig. 24)

44

Teapot
Silver, 1782
Paul Revere (1734–1818)
Marked "•REVERE" in rectangle
Engraved "SIB"
H. 6½ in., L. including spout and handle
9⅝ in.
Gift of Miss Frances Arnold, 1969
Metropolitan Museum of Art (69.147)
(Fig. 19)

45

Beaker (Originally from a set of six)
Silver, ca. 1800
Paul Revere (1734–1818)
Marked "REVERE" in rectangle with
clipped corner
H. 3⁷⁄₁₆ in., Diam. (base) 2¼ in.
Engraved "G"
*Bequest of William P. Goodwin
Museum of Art, Rhode Island School
of Design (39.064)*

46

Balance, Weights, and Case
Brass, with wooden case, 18th century
English
Balance, H. 11½ in., W. 8 in., Diam.
(pans) 3½ in.
11 weights
*Paul Revere Memorial Association
(75.313a–1)*

47

Teapot and Stand
Silver, 1787
Paul Revere (1734–1818)
Teapot marked "•REVERE" in rectangle
with "J•AUSTIN" overstruck
H. 5½ in., L. including spout and handle
10¾ in.
Engraved "HC"
Stand marked "•REVERE" in rectangle
H. 1 in., W. 6¾
Gift of the Estates of the Misses Eunice
McLellan and Frances Cordis Cruft
Museum of Fine Arts, Boston (42.377–378)

48

Waste and Memoranda Book,
Workshop at Boston
Bound volume, 1783–1797
Kept by Paul Revere
Revere Family Papers
Massachusetts Historical Society

49-50

Teaspoons
(Two from original set of twelve)
Silver, 1787
Paul Revere (1734–1818), maker;
Nathaniel Austin (1734–1818), retailer
Marked "J•AUSTIN" in rectangle
Engraved "HC"
L. 5⅜ in.
Gift of Josephine Setze in memory of John
Marshall Phillips
Yale University Art Gallery (1965.26a-b)

51

Teapot
Silver, 1789
Paul Revere (1734–1818)
Marked "•REVERE" in rectangle
Engraved "*MB*"
H. 4⅛ in., L. including spout and
handle 11⅛ in.
Pauline Revere Thayer Collection
Museum of Fine Arts, Boston (35.1777)

53

Bill
Paul Revere and Son to Moses Brown
for teapot
Boston, 1789
Pauline Thayer Revere Collection
Museum of Fine Arts, Boston (35.1777a)

52

Teapot and Stand
Silver, ca. 1790–1800
Teapot attributed to Paul Revere
(1734–1818)
H. 6⅛ in., L. of base 5¹³⁄₁₆ in.
Engraved "*A*"
Stand, Joseph Loring (1743–1815)
Marked "*J-Loring*" in cartouche
H. ¹⁵⁄₁₆ in., L. 7⅛ in.
M. and M. Karolik Collection
Museum of Fine Arts, Boston (39.200–201)

54

Cann
(One of a Pair)
Silver, 1773
Paul Revere (1734–1818)
Marked "•REVERE" in rectangle
Engraved "LO" and with Orne coat of arms
H. 5 in., Diam. (base) 3½ in.
Gift of Frances Thomas and Eliza Sturgis
Paine in memory of Frederick
William Paine
Worcester Art Museum (1937.59)

55

Butter Boat
(One of a Pair)
Silver, 1773
Paul Revere (1734–1818)
Marked "•REVERE" in rectangle
Engraved with Orne coat of arms and crest
H. 4⁵⁄₁₆ in., L. 7½ in.
Gift of Frances Thomas and Eliza Sturgis
Paine in memory of Frederick
William Paine
Worcester Art Museum (1937.57)

56-57

Large Spoons
(Two from original set of twelve)
Silver, 1773
Paul Revere (1734–1818)
Marked "•REVERE" in rectangle
Engraved with Orne crest
L. 8¾ in.
Gift of Frances Thomas and Eliza Sturgis
Paine in memory of Frederick
William Paine
Worcester Art Museum (1937.56a-b)

58-59

Teaspoons
(Two from original set of eighteen)
Silver, 1773
Paul Revere (1734–1818)
Marked "PR" in rectangle
Engraved with Orne crest
L. 5³⁄₁₆ in.
Gift of Paine Charitable Trust
Worcester Art Museum (1965.337a-b)

60

Quart Cann
(One of a pair)
Silver, 1783
Paul Revere (1734–1818)
Marked "REVERE"
in rectangle
Engraved "EHED" and "E.H.E" with D above
H. 6⁹⁄₁₆ in.
Purchase, Sansbury Mills Fund, 1958
Metropolitan Museum of Art (58.3.5)

61

Beaker
(One of four known)
Silver, 1789
Denis Colombier
(active in Paris 1776–1809)
Marked with maker's mark and French
hallmarks
H. 2⅞ in., Diam. (rim) 2¾ in.
Mr. and Mrs. Marshall P. Blankard
Gift, 1967
Metropolitan Museum of Art (67.94)
(Fig. 33)

62-63

Beakers
(Two of eight known)
Silver, 1795 or 1797
Paul Revere (1734–1818)
Marked "REVERE"
H. 2¾ in., Diam. (rim) 2¹³⁄₁₆ in.
Mrs. Russell Sage Gift, 1958
Metropolitan Museum of Art (58.3.1–2)
(Fig. 34)

64

Sugar Dish
Silver, 1761–1762
Paul Revere (1734–1818)
Marked "•REVERE" in rectangle and "PR"
in rectangle
Engraved with Chandler coat of arms and
"B. Greene to L. Chandler"
H. 6½ in., Diam. (base) 3¼ in.
Pauline Revere Thayer Collection.
Museum of Fine Arts, Boston (35.1781)
(Fig. 16)

65

Creampot
Silver, ca. 1761
Paul Revere (1734–1818)
Marked "•REVERE" in rectangle and "PR"
in rectangle
Engraved with Chandler coat of arms
H. 4⅜ in.
Pauline Revere Thayer Collection
Museum of Fine Arts, Boston (35.1782)
(Fig. 16)

66

Tankard
Silver, ca. 1760–1770
Paul Revere (1734–1818)
Marked "•REVERE" in rectangle
Engraved with Jackson coat of arms and
"J^J_A"
H. 9¼ in.
Mary B. Jackson Fund
Museum of Art, Rhode Island School
of Design (32.193)

67

Salver
Silver, 1761
Paul Revere (1734–1818)
Marked "•REVERE" in rectangle
Engraved with Tyng coat of arms and *"The*
Gift of James Tyng to his/Sister Sarah Tyng
1761."
H. 2 in., Diam. 12¾ in.
Gift of John P. Marquand to Harvard
University
The Harvard University Art Museums
Fogg Art Museum (1.1961)
(Fig. 15)

68

Coffeepot
Silver, 1772
Paul Revere (1734–1818)
Marked "•REVERE" in rectangle
Engraved "I^D_E" and added later
"FCS TO FBT/1863"
H. 12 in.
Anonymous loan
(Fig. 18)

69

Teapot
Silver, 1797
Paul Revere (1734–1818)
Marked "REVERE" in rectangle
Engraved "*Presented by the Proprietors/of*
BOSTON NECK *to Mr. William Dall/for ser-*
vices render'd them 1797"
H. 6 in., L. including handle and spout
10¾ in.
Gift of Mr. Charles Whitney Dall, Jr.
Museum of Fine Arts, Boston (1981.39)

70-79

Teaspoons
(Ten from original set of thirty-six)
Silver, 1796
Paul Revere (1734–1818)
Marked "*PR*" in rectangle
Engraved "*AA*"
L. 5⅞ in.
Gift of Amory Goddard in loving memory of
his father and mother
Paul Revere Memorial Association
(87.31 a-k)

80

Tureen Ladle
(Originally one of a pair)
Silver, 1796
Paul Revere (1734–1818)
Marked "REVERE" in rectangle with
clipped corner
Engraved "*AA*"
L. 12 in.
Gift of Amory Goddard in loving memory of
his father and mother
Paul Revere Memorial Association (87.32)

81-82

Salt Spoons
(Two from original set of eight)
Silver, 1796
Paul Revere (1734–1818)
Marked "*PR*" in rectangle
Engraved "*AA*"
L. 4¼ in.
Gift of Amory Goddard in loving memory of
his mother and father
Paul Revere Memorial Association
(87.30 a-b)

83

Creampot
Silver, ca. 1790–1800
Paul Revere (1734–1818)
Marked "*PR*" and "•REVERE"
Engraved with unidentified crest, and
"RW to LW" and added later "*H*"
H. 5⅞ in.
Gift of Mrs. Ernest G. Stillman
The Harvard University Art Museums
Fogg Art Museum (1927.3)

84-85

Pair of Casters
Silver, ca. 1790–1800
Paul Revere (1734–1818)
Marked "*PR*" in rectangle
Engraved with unidentified crest, and "IW
to LW" (1927.1) and "EW to LW" (1927.2)
Both also have "*H*" added later.
H. 6 in.
Gift of Mrs. Ernest G. Stillman
The Harvard University Art Museums
Fogg Art Museum (1927.1–2)

86

Coffeepot
Silver, 1781
Paul Revere (1734–1818)
Marked "•REVERE" in rectangle
Engraved with Sargent coat of arms
H. 12⅞ in., Diam. (base) 4⁷/₁₆ in.
Gift of Mrs. Nathaniel Thayer
Museum of Fine Arts, Boston (31.139)

87

Copperplate for Sargent Bookplate
Engraved copper, 1764
Paul Revere (1734–1818)
Engraved "P•Revere Sculp"
H. 3½ in., W. 2¾ in.
Annie A. Hawley Bequest Fund
Museum of Fine Arts, Boston (59.517)

88

Sargent Bookplate
Line engraving, restrike, 1970s
Paul Revere (1734–1818)
Signed, "P•Revere Sculp"
3½ x 2¾ in.
Museum of Fine Arts, Boston

89

Large Spoon
Silver, 1781
Paul Revere (1734–1818)
Marked "•REVERE" in rectangle
Engraved with Sargent crest
L. 9 in.
Gift of Mr. and Mrs. Alfred E. Bissell
Henry Francis du Pont Winterthur
Museum (62.240.1403)

90

Teaspoon
Silver, 1781
Paul Revere (1734–1818)
Marked "*PR*" in rectangle
Engraved with Sargent crest
L. 5⅜ in.
Gift of Mr. and Mrs. Alfred E. Bissell
Henry Francis du Pont Winterthur
Museum (62.240.561)

91

Waste and Memoranda Book,
Workshop at Boston
Bound volume, 1761–1783
Kept by Paul Revere
Revere Family Papers
Massachusetts Historical Society

92

Seal of the Massachusetts Medical Society
Silver and wood, ca. 1782–1783
Attributed to Paul Revere (1734–1818)
H. 1¾ in., L. 2 in.
Massachusetts Medical Society

93

Tankard
(One of a set of six)
Silver, 1772
Paul Revere (1734–1818)
Marked "•REVERE" in rectangle
Engraved *"The Gift of /Mary Bartlett
Widow of Eph^m Bartlett/to the third Church
in Brookfield/1768"*
H. 8⁵/₁₆ in.
*Gift of Henry F. du Pont
Henry Francis du Pont Winterthur
Museum (57.859.1)*

94

Tankard
Silver, 1768
Paul Revere (1734–1818)
Marked "REVERE" in rectangle
Engraved *"Stephano Scales,/*HARVARDI-
NATES/A.D. MDCCLXVIII./*Conferipti,/Biennio
fub ejus Tutelâ peracto,/Hoc Poculum,/
Grati Animi Monimentum,* DONANT."
H. 9 in.
*Gift of Edward N. Lamson and Barbara T.
Lamson, Edward F. Lamson, Howard J.
Lamson and Susan L. Strickler
Museum of Fine Arts, Boston (1986.678)*
(Fig. 17)

95

Urn
Silver, ca. 1800
Paul Revere (1734–1818)
Marked "REVERE" in rectangle
Engraved "TO/PERPETUATE/*The Gallant de-
fence*/Made by/Capt GAMALIEL BRADFORD./*in
the Ship Industry on the 8th of July 1800/
when Attacked by four French Privateers/in
the Streights of Gibralter./This* URN *is Pre-
sented to him*/by/SAMUEL PARKMAN."
H. 19 in., W. 10¼ in.
Massachusetts Historical Society

Commercial Engraving

96

*A Westerly View of the Colledges
in Cambridge New England*
Hand-colored line engraving, 1767
Paul Revere (1734–1818)
Drawn by Joseph Chadwick
(ca. 1721–1783)
Signed "P Revere Sculp"
Signed "Josʰ Chadwick, del-"
9¼ x 15¼ in.
Essex Institute (116, 273)

97

Copperplate for North Battery Certificate
Engraved copperplate, ca. 1762
Paul Revere (1734–1818)
Signed "P Revere Sculp"
6¼ x 8¼ in.
*Revere Collection
Massachusetts Historical Society*

98

Partial North Battery Certificate
Line engraving, restrike, 20th century
Paul Revere (1734–1818)
5 x 8¾ in.
Paul Revere Memorial Association (75.304)

99

Collection of the Best Psalm Tunes
Music book, 1764
Josiah Flagg (1737–1794)
Engraved by Paul Revere (1734–1818)
Signed "Paul Revere"
5¼ x 8 ⅝ in.
Massachusetts Historical Society

100

Bookplate for Gardiner Chandler
Line engraving, ca. 1760–1770
Paul Revere (1734–1818)
Signed "P Revere Sculp."
3⁷⁄₁₆ x 2¾ in.
Paul Revere Memorial Association (83.5)
(Fig. 26)

101

Certificate of Attendance at Anatomical
Lectures
Line engraving, ca. 1780
Paul Revere (1734–1818)
Signed "PR"
Issued to Israel Keith
Signed by "John Warren, FMS, March 28,
1782," American Hospital, Boston
7⅝ x 6 in.
Warren Papers
Massachusetts Historical Society

102

The Gerbua or Yerboa
Line engraving, 1774
Paul Revere (1734–1818)
Signed "P Revere Sc."
For the *Royal American Magazine*
9 x 5¾ in.
Paul Revere Memorial Association (75.138)
(Fig. 6)

103

Billhead for Cromwell's Head Inn
Line engraving ca. 1768–1771
Paul Revere (1734–1818)
Signed "P Revere Sc"
6¼ x 3¾ in.
Revere Collection
Massachusetts Historical Society

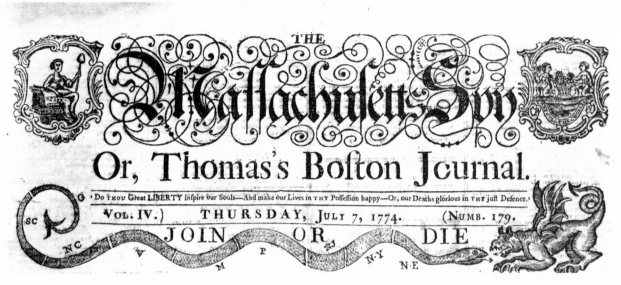

104
_____

Masthead of the Massachusetts Spy
Lead metal cut, 1774
Paul Revere (1734–1818)
4 x 10 in.
Massachusetts Historical Society

105
_____

Gunner's Calipers
Brass, ca. 1770
Paul Revere (1734–1818)
Engraved "P, Revere, Boston," and "Lieuᵗ
Williamson of Royˡ Artillery"
Paul Revere Memorial Association (78.4)

106
_____

Bill
Paul Revere to Samuel Hewes
for engraving, prints and fastening teeth
Boston, 15 April 1771
Revere Family Papers
Massachusetts Historical Society

Hardware Store

107

Letterbook (1783–1800)
Copy of letter from Paul Revere
to Frederick William Geyer
Boston, 5 September 1783
Revere Family Papers
Massachusetts Historical Society

108

Receipted Account
Paul Revere's account for goods
purchased at Enoch Brown's Store,
Faneuil Hall Market
7 November 1783
Revere Family Papers
Massachusetts Historical Society

109

Receipted Account
Joseph Spear's account with Paul Revere
for purchase of hardware items
Boston, 12 April 1786–6 October 1787
Revere Family Papers
Massachusetts Historical Society

110

Draft of Letter
Paul Revere to John Sampson
Boston, 20 May 1786
Revere Family Papers
Massachusetts Historical Society

111

Invoice Book
1783–1791
Revere Family Papers
Massachusetts Historical Society

112

Stock Book
Hardware Store Inventory
50 Cornhill Boston, 15 February 1785
Revere Family Papers
Massachusetts Historical Society

Representative items to illustrate above
inventory
— Sheep shears
— 1 Dutch looking glass
— Green handled knife and fork
— Bellows
— Spectacles
— Pair of buckles
— Iron door lock
— Bench vise
— Brass handle
— Japanned tray
Old Sturbridge Village

Foundry

113

Letter
Paul Revere to Brown and Benson
Boston, 3 September 1789
Revere Family Papers
Massachusetts Historical Society

114

Book of Receipts
Receipt book with sketches of a bell
and a cannon
1780–1805
Revere Family Papers
Massachusetts Historical Society

115

Steel Plate for Paul Revere and Son
Trade Card
Engraved steel, ca. 1796–1803
Thomas Clarke
Signed, "T. Clarke Sc."
3 ⅜ x 5 in.
Massachusetts Historical Society

116

Trade Card of Paul Revere and Son
Line engraving, restrike, 1944
3¼ x 4¾ in.
Paul Revere Memorial Association (75.151)
(Fig. 37)

117

Account Book
Foundry Accounts, 1783–1803
Revere Family Papers
Massachusetts Historical Society

118

Coehorn Mortar and Carriage
Brass mortar, reproduction carriage
(red oak with iron fittings), ca. 1788–1818
Attributed to the Revere Foundry
Mortar, L. 13½ in., bore 6⅜ in., carriage,
H. 7½ in., W. 15½ in., Depth 26 in.
Paul Revere Memorial Association (75.293)

119

Receipted Account
Amasa Davis's account with Paul Revere
for casting cannon
30 August 1798 to 21 December 1799
Receipted 17 January 1800
Revere Family Papers
Massachusetts Historical Society

120

Letter
Tench Coxe to Paul Revere regarding
production of howitzers
Washington D.C., 16 June 1794
Revere Family Papers
Massachusetts Historical Society

121

Receipt
Capt. William Sutherland to Paul Revere
for brass cannon shipped to South Caro-
lina on the *Mohawk*
26 February 1799
Revere Family Papers
Massachusetts Historical Society

122

Wooden Pattern for Mold for a Mortar
(Two-piece)
Wood and black paint, ca. 1788–1818
Probably used at the Revere Foundry
L. 22 in., W. 6½ in.
Paul Revere Memorial Association
(75.294 a-b)

123

Ship Fittings (Spikes and Nails)
Copper, ca. 1819
Attributed to Revere and Son,
Canton, MA
Used to build *U.S.S. New Hampshire*
Gift of Boston Cup Foundation
Paul Revere Memorial Association
(76.4–12)
(Fig. 39)

124

Bill
Paul Revere to the shipyard's agent
for materials for the
U.S.S. Constitution
28 October 1797
Revere Family Papers
Massachusetts Historical Society

125

Letter
Committee building frigate at Hartt shipyard to Paul Revere requesting estimate
for fittings (Revere's reply is at bottom of
page)
31 August 1798
Revere Family Papers
Massachusetts Historical Society

126

Courthouse Bell (Dedham)
Brass, 1798
Revere Foundry
Marked "Revere Boston 1798"
Dedham Historical Society

127

Account Book (1793–1810)
List of bells sold
Paul Revere and Son
Revere Family Papers
Massachusetts Historical Society

128

Letter
Copy of letter from Paul Revere and Son
to Samuel Flagg, Benjamin Heywood, and
Abel Stowell regarding delivery of
bell to First Congregational Church in
Worcester, MA
Boston, 24 May 1802
Revere Family Papers
Massachusetts Historical Society

129

Letterbook (1801–1806)
Copy of letter from Paul Revere to Samuel
Flagg, Benjamin Heywood, and Abel
Stowell regarding complaint about quality
of bell
Boston, 5 July 1802
Revere Family Papers
Massachusetts Historical Society

130

Letter
Thomas Webb to Paul Revere and Son
ordering a bell for the Hope Cotton
Manufacturing Company
Providence, R.I., 28 September 1807
Revere Family Papers
Massachusetts Historical Society

Mill at Canton

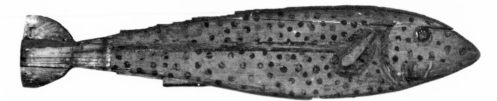

131

Weathervane from a Canton Mill Building
Painted cedar with a lead disk eye, early
19th Century
L. 31 in., W. 6½ in.
Paul Revere Memorial Association (75.35)

132

Map of Revere Copper Mill, Canton, MA
Ink and watercolor on linen, ca. 1801–1818
Attributed to Paul Revere (1734–1818)
44 x 18¾ in.
*Gift of Charles B. Dunn (Revere Copper
Company)*
Paul Revere Memorial Association (81.4)
(Fig. 38)

133

Letterbook (1810–1811)
Copy of letter from Paul Revere to Josiah
Snelling describing copper rolling mill
26 October 1810
Revere Family Papers
Massachusetts Historical Society

135

Account Book
(Recording payment of wages and cus-
tomer accounts)
Canton, MA, December 1802–1806
Revere Family Papers
Massachusetts Historical Society

136

Letter
Thacher and Hayward to Paul Revere and
Son concerning the fabrication of rollers
Plymouth, 14 June 1812
Revere Family Papers
Massachusetts Historical Society

134

Saddlebags (Owned by Paul Revere)
Leather with metal buckles, mid-18th
century
H. 13 in., W. 12 in. (each bag)
Gift of Mrs. M. W. Boyden
Paul Revere Memorial Association (75.303)

137

Windsor Arm Chair
Wood painted black, early 19th Century
(Probably used in Canton mill office, rockers added later)
H. 31 in., W. 14 in., Depth 17½ in.
Gift of Miss Anna Revere
Paul Revere Memorial Association (76.1)

138

Partnership Agreement
Between Paul Revere and Joseph
Warren Revere
7 June 1804
Revere Family Papers
Massachusetts Historical Society

139

Letter
Letter of introduction by Paul Revere
for his son Joseph Warren Revere
Boston, 20 October 1804
Revere Family Papers
Massachusetts Historical Society

140

Passport
(Joseph Warren Revere)
Sealed document, 15 March 1805
Revere Family Papers
Massachusetts Historical Society

141

Letter
Paul Revere to Joseph Warren Revere
concerning Seth Boyden
25 March 1810
Paul Revere Memorial Association (83.1)

142

Petition
Draft of petition to Congress
from Paul Revere and Son
Boston, 12 February 1807
Revere Family Papers
Massachusetts Historical Society

143

Letter
Copy of letter from Paul Revere to Josiah
Quincy regarding petition to Congress
about copper duties
Boston, 10 December 1807
Revere Family Papers
Massachusetts Historical Society

144

Pamphlet
Report of the Committee of Commerce
and Manufactures
Printed by A. & C. Way Printers,
City of Washington
21 January 1808
Paul Revere Memorial Association (80.1)
(Fig. 40)

145

Letter
Gabriel Duvall to Paul Revere and Son
regarding copper duties
Washington, D.C., 4 September 1810
Revere Family Papers
Massachusetts Historical Society

146

Wastebook with Accounts for Canton
and Boston Businesses
1 May 1799–31 May 1804
Paul Revere and Son
Revere Family Papers
Massachusetts Historical Society

147

Piece of Copper Roofing from St.
Stephen's Church, Boston
Sheet copper, ca. 1803
Revere and Son, Canton, MA
15 x 20 in.
St. Stephen's Church, Boston

148

Letter
Thomas Hazard Jr. to Paul Revere
and Son ordering copper sheathing
New Bedford, MA, 9 June 1808
Revere Family Papers
Massachusetts Historical Society

149

Sketches of Copper Boiler Plates
Drawn by Robert Fulton
New York, 22 November 1808
Revere Family Papers
Massachusetts Historical Society

150

Letter
Robert Fulton to Paul Revere and Son
about poor quality plates
New York, 29 May 1811
Revere Family Papers
Massachusetts Historical Society

151

Letter
Robert Fulton to Paul Revere and Son
regarding terms for ordering copper boiler
plates for steam warship
New York, 28 July 1814
Revere Family Papers
Massachusetts Historical Society

152

Account Ledger
1799–1804
Revere Family Papers
Massachusetts Historical Society

Public Life
Crown Point

153

Commission
Commission as second lieutenant
issued to Paul Revere
Signed by Governor Shirley,
18 February 1756
Morristown National Historical Park

154

Deposition
Regarding Crown Point Expedition
Written by Paul Revere, 1816
Revere Family Papers
Massachusetts Historical Society

A High Son of Liberty

155

A View of the Year 1765
Line engraving, ca. 1765
Paul Revere (1734–1818)
Signed "Engrav'd Printed & Sold by
P*Revere BOSTON"
6 x 7⅝ in.
Massachusetts Historical Society

156

A Warm Place—Hell
Line engraving, 1768
Paul Revere (1734–1818)
3⅜ x 5 in.
*John Carter Brown Library,
Brown University*

157

A View of Part of the Town of Boston in New England and British Ships of War Landing Their Troops, 1768
Hand-colored line engraving, 1770
Paul Revere (1734–1818)
Drawn, designed, and colored by Christian Remick (1726–1773)
Signed "Engraved, Printed & Sold by Paul Revere, Boston"
9¾ x 15½ in.
Boston Athenaeum

158

Salt
Silver, ca. 1768–70
Paul Revere (1734–1818)
Marked "*PR*" in rectangle
Engraved "*The Illustrous* NINETY-TWO" and added later (?) "wᴴᴱ"
H. 1⁷⁄₁₆ in., Diam. (rim) 2 in.
Mabel Brady Garvan Collection
Yale University Art Gallery (1930.961)

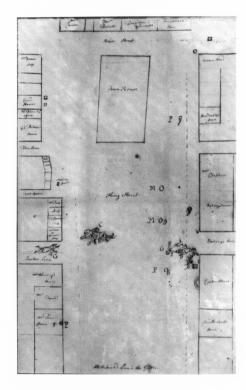

159

Diagram of the Massacre Scene
Pen and ink on paper, 1770
Paul Revere (1734–1818)
Boston Public Library

160

The Bloody Massacre
Hand-colored line engraving, 1770
Paul Revere (1734–1818)
Colored by Christian Remick (1726–1773)
Signed "Engrav'd Printed & Sold by Paul
Revere Boston" and "Col^d by Christ^n
Remick."
9⅝ x 8⅝ in.
*Gift of Miss Margaret A. Revere, Miss
Anna P. Revere, Mr. Paul Revere, and Mr.
John Revere Chapin.*
Museum of Fine Arts, Boston (62.506)

161

Copperplate for Boston Massacre
and Currency
Engraved copper, 1770
Paul Revere (1734–1818)
Signed "Engrav'd, Printed, & Sold by
Paul Revere, BOSTON"
8¼ x 9¼ in.
*Commonwealth of Massachusetts,
Archives Division*

162

Newspaper Report of Memorial
"Illumination"
Boston Gazette, 11 March 1771
Paul Revere Memorial Association (75.248)

163

Sketch of the Green Dragon Tavern
Ink and watercolor wash on paper, 1773
John Johnson (1753–1818)
Signed "John Johnson"
8⅛ x 12¼ in.
American Antiquarian Society
(Fig. 45)

164

*The Able Doctor, or America Swallowing
the Bitter Draught*
Line engraving, 1774
Paul Revere (1734–1818)
Signed "P Revere Sculp"
7 x 4⅞ in.
Massachusetts Historical Society

Many Rides of Paul Revere

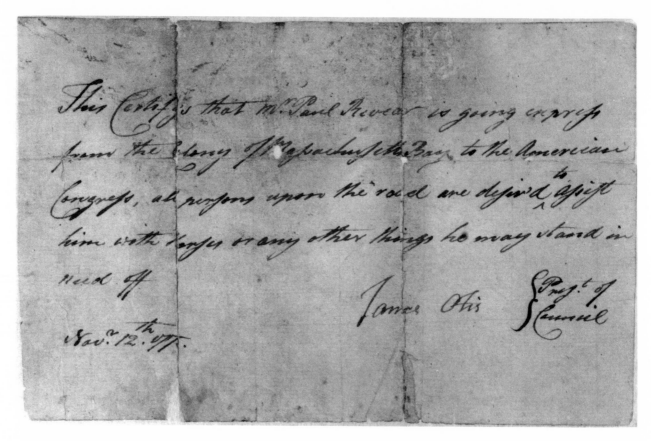

165

Pass
For Paul Revere to ride express
to Continental Congress
Signed by James Otis, 12 November 1775
Paul Revere Memorial Association (75.140)

167

Receipt
David Wood to Paul Revere
for payment of travel expenses for ride to
Kings Bridge, NY
28 May 1774
Revere Family Papers
Massachusetts Historical Society

166

Trunk (Belonged to John Hancock)
Leather bound with brass fastenings,
mid-18th century
H. 2½ ft., W. 4 ft., Depth 2½ ft.
Worcester Historical Museum

168

Letter
Paul Revere to Jeremy Belknap recording
the story of the "Ride"
Boston, 1 January 1798
Revere Family Papers
Massachusetts Historical Society

169

The Battle of Lexington, April 19th, 1775
Hand-colored line engraving, 1775,
New Haven, CT
Amos Doolittle (1754–1832)
Signed "A. Doolittle, Sculp'"
13 x 17½
The Connecticut Historical Society

170

Poem
"Paul Revere's Ride"
Atlantic Monthly, January 1861
Henry Wadsworth Longfellow (1807–1882)
Published by Ticknor and Fields, Boston
Paul Revere Memorial Association (75.330)

171

Book
Tales of a Wayside Inn
Poem, "Paul Revere's Ride"
Henry Wadsworth Longfellow (1807–1882)
Ticknor and Fields, Boston, 1863
Paul Revere Memorial Association, (87.26)

172

Sheet Music
"Paul Revere's Ride March Two-Step"
Published by E.T. Paull Music Company
New York, 1905
Paul Revere Memorial Association (87.23)

Revolutionary War Service

173

Agreement to Print Currency
Between Paul Revere and House
of Representatives
Watertown, MA, 8 December 1775
Commonwealth of Massachusetts,
Archives Division

174

Copperplate for Printing Massachusetts
Currency
Engraved copper, 1775 (Dec. 7 issue)
7⅞ x 12½ in.
Commonwealth of Massachusetts,
Archives Division

175

Massachusetts Currency
7 December 1775 issue
Massachusetts Historical Society

1778 State of Massachusetts Bay to Paul Revere Dr

To Engraving a Copper plate for a State Note £ 20 " 00 " 0

Nov 16 To Engraving a Copper plate over again for 12 small Bills — 72 " 00 " 0

To Printing 8000 impressions at 6 pence 200 " 00 " 0

1779 May 20 To Engraving a Copper Plate for 12 small Bills of the emission of 16 Octr and the plate 108 " 00 " 0

To Printing 9400 impressions at 8 pence 355 " 00 " 0

£755 " 00 " 0

Errors Excepted Paul Revere

Received the above in the full, by an Order On Mr Benjamin Sumner one of the Collectors for the Town of Boston

Deduct for Error 41.13.4

£713..6..8

Paul Revere

Boston Octr 7 1779

Thos Dawes

Jon Brown

Richard Cranch

RW 663

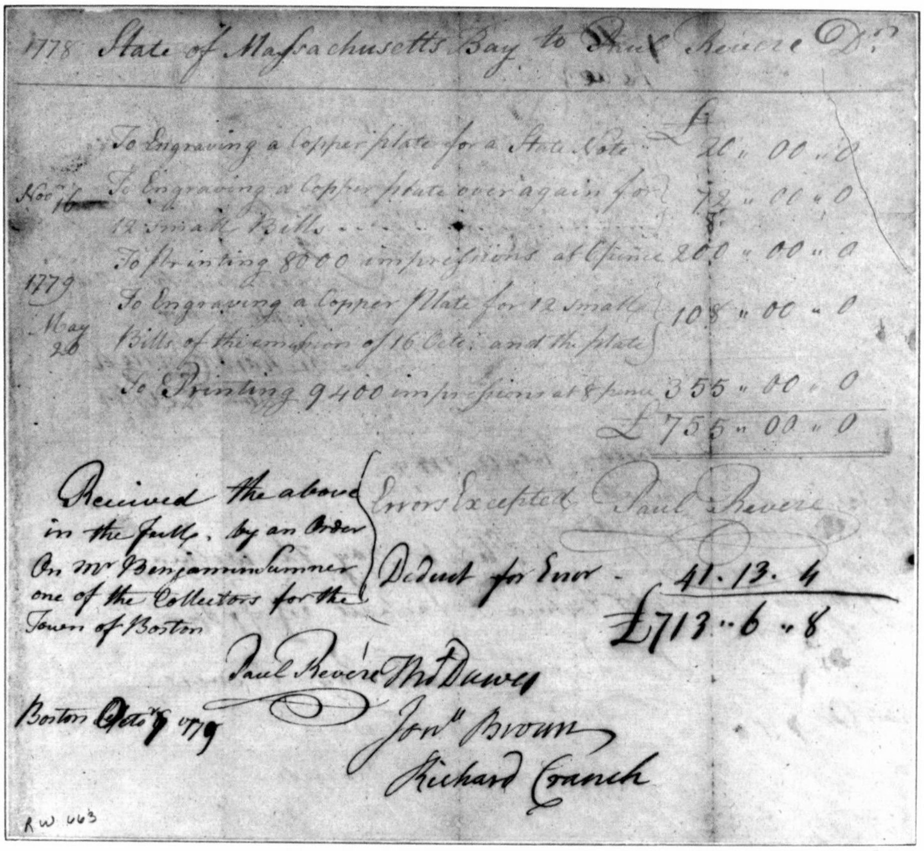

176

Receipted Bill
Paul Revere to State of Massachusetts Bay for engraving plates and printing currency 1778 issue
Dated 16 November 1778, 20 May 1779, and 7 October 1779
Manuscript Collection
Boston Public Library

177

Minutes of War Office
Order from J. Swan to Thompson for casting of cannon by Col. Revere
28 December 1776
Revere Family Papers
Massachusetts Historical Society

178

Order from the Board of War
Samuel Otis to Col. Revere to procure ordnance from State Furnace
28 February 1777
Revere Family Papers
Massachusetts Historical Society

179

Receipt
To Thomas Crane for delivery of gunpowder to Castle Island
20 October 1777
Bostonian Society

180

Commission
Commission as lieutenant-colonel
of artillery issued to Paul Revere
Signed by John Avery, 27 November 1776
Revere Family Papers
Massachusetts Historical Society

181

Plan of the Island Castle William
Ink with watercolor wash on paper,
ca. 1775
Henry Deberniere (Ensign in the British
10th Regiment)
Signed "Henry Deberniere Fecit"
28½ x 41½ in.
Anonymous Loan

182

Letter
Jonathan Pollard to Lt. Col. Paul Revere,
with instructions for deploying troops at
Castle William
Boston, 10 March 1778
Revere Family Papers
Massachusetts Historical Society

183

Council Order
Copy of orders from John Avery to Paul
Revere regarding the firing of cannon
upon arrival of French Frigate
Boston, 13 May 1778
Revere Family Papers
Massachusetts Historical Society

184

Orderly Book
For the Rhode Island Expedition kept
by Paul Revere
Rhode Island, August 1778
Revere Family Papers
Massachusetts Historical Society

185

Council Orders
Orders from Jer. Powell
to Lt. Col. Paul Revere to ready the
garrison at Castle Island
3 April 1779
Revere Family Papers
Massachusetts Historical Society

186

Council Orders
Orders from John Avery to Col. Paul
Revere to prepare to embark on
Penobscot Expedition
26 June 1779
Revere Family Papers
Massachusetts Historical Society

187

Orders
John Marston to Lt. Col. Paul Revere to
send flatboats to Boston from Castle Island
8 July 1779
Revere Family Papers
Massachusetts Historical Society

188

Receipt
Peleg Hunt to Paul Revere for flatboats
and oars for Penobscot Expedition
9 July 1779
Revere Family Papers
Massachusetts Historical Society

189

Letter
Lt. Col. Paul Revere to the General Court
requesting a military hearing
9 September 1779
Commonwealth of Massachusetts,
Archives Division

Paul Revere and the New Nation

190

Letter
Samuel Otis to Paul Revere regarding
political appointment
7 May 1789
Revere Family Papers
Massachusetts Historical Society

191

Poem
Section of a poem by Paul Revere
regarding leadership of Jefferson and
Madison, ca. 1811
Revere Family Papers
Massachusetts Historical Society

192

Letter
Bishop Cheverus to Paul Revere and Son
thanking them for loan of employees to
work on harbor fortifications
28 September 1814
Revere Family Papers
Massachusetts Historical Society

193

Commission as Suffolk County Coroner
Issued by John Avery to Paul Revere
Boston, 11 May 1795
Revere Family Papers
Massachusetts Historical Society

194

Account
Burials performed by George Clark as
ordered by Paul Revere, County Coroner
April 1796–May 1797
Revere Family Papers
Massachusetts Historical Society

195

Journal (1777–1810)
Coroner's Inquests written by
Paul Revere, 1796–1801
Revere Family Papers
Massachusetts Historical Society

196

Board of Health Broadside
30 March 1799
Signed by Paul Revere, President
Broadside Collection
Massachusetts Historical Society

197

Board of Health Broadside
12 March 1800
Signed by Paul Revere, President
Broadside Collection
Massachusetts Historical Society
(Fig. 50)

198

Board of Health Broadside
Listing Members and Presidents 1799-1821
Bostonian Society

Voluntary Associations and Societies

199

Membership Certificate
Certificate made out to Paul Revere for
Massachusetts Charitable Fire Society
Boston, 14 May 1798
Revere Family Papers
Massachusetts Historical Society

200

Letter
Paul Revere to the President and Trustees
of the Massachusetts Charitable Fire
Society
Boston, 15 November 1806
Paul Revere Memorial Association
(75.142)

201

Meeting Notice
Quarterly Meeting of the Boston Mechanic
Association
John W. Folsom to Paul Revere Esq.
Boston, 7 September 1795
Revere Family Papers
Massachusetts Historical Society

202

Minutes of the Massachusetts Charitable
Mechanic Association
Bound volume, 1795–1813
Paul Revere, President 1795–1798
Massachusetts Charitable Mechanic
Association

203

Snuff Box
Silver, ca. 1799–1807
Attributed to Paul Revere (1734–1818)
Engraved "*BR*"
H. ⅞ in., W. 2⅞ in., Depth 2 in.
Massachusetts Charitable Mechanic
Association

204

Receipt
Nathan Davies to Paul Revere for payment
of one year's assessment for use of the
Boston Library
Boston, 9 December 1797
Revere Family Papers
Massachusetts Historical Society

205

Receipt
John Eliot to Paul Revere for payment of
dues in the Boston Humane Society
Boston, July 1811
Revere Family Papers
Massachusetts Historical Society

206

Letter
Deborah Gannett to Paul Revere
asking for money
22 February 1806
Revere Family Papers
Massachusetts Historical Society

Freemasonry

207

Masonic Certificate
Line engraving, ca. 1773
Paul Revere (1734–1818)
Signed "Engraved Printed & Sold by
Paul Revere BOSTON"
Inscribed for St. Andrew's Lodge, Capt.
Shuball Downes, 3 February 1774
12¼ x 9⅝ in.
*Grand Lodge of Masons in Massachusetts,
A.F. & A.M.*

208

Ladle (One of a pair)
Silver, 1762
Paul Revere (1734-1818)
Marked "REVERE" in rectangle
Engraved "Nᵒ 2/The Gift of/Bʳ Samˡ Barrett
to/Sᵗ ANDREW.s Lodge/Nᵒ 82/1762"
L. 14⅛ in.
Lodge of St. Andrew, A.F. & A.M.

209

Seal for Rising States Lodge
Silver, ca. 1784
Attributed to Paul Revere (1734-1818)
H. 1 in., Surface 1⅛ x 1½ in.
Grand Lodge of Masons
in Massachusetts, A.F. & A.M.
(Fig. 43)

210

Minutes
Meeting of Rising States Lodge
Boston, 26 July 1784
Grand Lodge of Masons
in Massachusetts, A.F. & A.M.

211

Account Book for Rising States Lodge
Bound volume, 1784-1793
Kept by Paul Revere, Treasurer
Grand Lodge of Masons
in Massachusetts, A.F. & A.M.

212

Return of Officers
Rising States Lodge
Boston, 2 May 1787
Grand Lodge of Masons
in Massachusetts, A.F. & A.M.

213

Third-Degree Diploma for
Rising States Lodge
Black and red ink on parchment, 1787
Inscribed to James Henry Laugier de
Tassy, 16 November 1787
Signed by Paul Revere
9¼ x 12 in.
New England Historic
Genealogical Society
(Fig. 46)

214

Commission
Commission as Deputy Grand Master
Conferred by Jos. Webb,
GM to Paul Revere
Boston, 24 June 1784
Grand Lodge of Masons
in Massachusetts, A.F. & A.M.

215

Speech
Delivered at the laying of the cornerstone
for the New State House, 4 July 1795
Paul Revere
Grand Lodge of Masons
in Massachusetts, A.F. & A.M.
(Fig. 47)

216

Speech
Address to the Grand Lodge
Paul Revere, 11 December 1797
Grand Lodge of Masons
in Massachusetts, A.F. & A.M.
(Fig. 48)

217

Memorial Urn
Gold, 1800-1801
Attributed to Paul Revere (1734-1818)
Engraved "This URN incloses a Lock of
HAIR/of the Immortal WASHINGTON/PRE-
SENTED JANUARY 27, 1800/to the Massachu-
setts GRAND LODGE/by HIS amiable WIDOW./
Born Feb: 11ᵗʰ 1732/Ob: Dec: 14. 1799"
H. 3¾ in., Diam (base) 1½ in.
Grand Lodge of Masons
in Massachusetts, A.F. & A.M.
(Fig. 22)

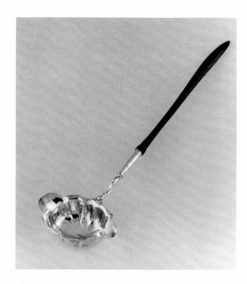

218

Ladle
Silver, 1797
Paul Revere (1734-1818)
Marked "REVERE" in rectangle
Engraved "*The Gift of/Brother* John Soley"
L. 14¾ in.
Anonymous Loan to the Sterling and
Francine Clark Art Institute (TR499/75)

219
___
St. Peter's Lodge Notification
Line engraving, 1772
Paul Revere (1734-1818)
Signed "Paul Revere Scp"
Inscribed for J. Lock 24 February 1797
Essex Institute, Salem, MA
(BR 366.1 S14)

220
___
Receipted Account
Paul Revere to the Columbian Lodge,
Boston
Boston, 25 June 1795, 30 June 1795
Museum of Our National Heritage,
Lexington

221
___
Past Master Jewel
Silver, ca. 1805
Attributed to Paul Revere (1734-1818)
Engraved "Presented/by/King Hiram's
Lodge/to Jon. Cook."
Gift of John F. Snow
Museum of Our National Heritage,
Lexington (86.34.1)

222-233
___
Washington Lodge Jewels (Set of twelve)
Silver, 1796
Paul Revere (1734-1818)
Washington Lodge, A.F. & A.M.
(Fig. 44)

Last Years

234

Cane
Wood, silver and brass, early 19th century
L. 34 in., Diam. (head) 1 in.
Engraved "Paul Revere, 1818"
Gift of Mrs. John Philip Reynolds
Paul Revere Memorial Association (75.302)

235

Draft of Will (Paul Revere)
15 November 1816
Revere Family Papers
Massachusetts Historical Society

236

Will with Codicil (Paul Revere)
14 March 1818
Revere Family Papers
Massachusetts Historical Society

Bibliography

Primary Sources from Manuscript/Archival Collections

Boston Public Library

Newspaper Collection (Microfilm)
Boston News-Letter, 21 May 1730
Independant Chronicle, December 1784
Massachusetts Centinel, 10 December 1785

Suffolk County Probate Records
(Microfilm)
Estate Inventory, John Coney,
15 October 1722
Will, Francis Pattishall Hitchborn,
26 December 1749

The Boston Directory Boston: John Norman, 1789

Grand Lodge of Masons in Massachusetts, Boston, MA

Miscellaneous Masonic Documents and Speeches
Paul Revere Account Book, 1784–1793
Parker Index, 1733–1800
Rising States Lodge, Minutes of Meetings, 29 March 1784 to 28 February 1785

Lodge of Saint Andrew, Boston, MA

Minutes of Meetings, 1756–1778
Minutes of Meetings, 1778–1854 (Microfilm at GLMM)
Charters and Bylaws, 1760–1778 (Microfilm at GLMM)

Massachusetts Historical Society, Boston, MA

Benjamin Bangs Diary, 10 September 1747
Benjamin Greene Ledger, 1734–1758

Revere Family Papers
Account Ledger for the Workshop at Boston, 1761–1788, Vol. 13
Book of Invoices, 1783–1791, Vol. 37
Letterbook, 1783–1800, Paul Revere,
Vol. 53
Letterbook, 1801–1806, Paul Revere,
Vol. 53
Letterbook, 1805–1810, Paul Revere and Son, Vol. 53
Loose Manuscripts, 1746–1818
Memoranda and Journal for the Workshop at Boston, 1788–1795, Vol. 51
Memoranda and Journal for the Workshop at Boston, 1793–1796, Vol. 51
Orderly Book for the Second Rhode Island Expedition, 1788, Vol. 55
Waste and Memoranda Book for the Workshop at Boston, 1761–1783, Vol. 1 [sometimes referred to as daybook]
Waste and Memoranda Book for the Workshop at Boston, 1783–1797, Vol. 2 [sometimes referred to as daybook]
Wastebook for Canton, 1805–1812, Vol. 20

Yale University Library, New Haven, CT

Brigden Papers
Daybook for Zachariah Brigden,
1765–1775

Published Sources

Albion, Robert G. *Forests and Sea Power*. Hamden, CT: Archon Books, 1926.

American Silver and Pressed Glass: A Collection in the R.W. Norton Art Gallery. Shreveport, LA: R.W. Norton Foundation, 1967.

American State Papers, Naval Affairs, Washington: Gales and Seaton, 1832–1861.

Ammerman, David. *In the Common Cause: American Response to the Coercive Acts of 1774*. New York: W. W. Norton & Co. Inc., 1974.

Andrews, William Loring. *Paul Revere and His Engraving*. New York: Scribner's Sons, 1901.

Ashley, William. *The English Brass and Copper Industries to 1800*. London: Frank Cass and Company, 1934.

Avery, C. Louise. *Early American Silver*. New York: The Century Company, 1930.

———. *American Silver of the XVII and XVIII Centuries*. New York: The Metropolitan Museum of Art, 1920.

Baird, Charles W. *History of the Huguenot Emigration to America*. 2 vols. New York: Dodd, Mead and Company, 1885; reprint, Baltimore, 1966.

Bentley, William. *The Diary of William Bentley, D.D. Pastor of the East Church, Salem, MA*. 4 vols. Salem, MA: Essex Institute, 1905–1914.

Bigelow, Francis Hill. *Historic Silver of the Colonies and Its Makers*. 1917; reprint, New York: The MacMillan Company, 1941.

Bohan, Peter J. *American Gold, 1700–1860*. New Haven, CT: Yale University Art Gallery, 1963.

Bolton, Kenyon C. et al. *American Art at Harvard*. Catalogue for an exhibition at Harvard University from April, 1972–June, 1972. Boston: Harvard College, 1972.

Bortman, Mark. "Paul Revere and Son and Their Jewish Correspondents." *Publications of the American Jewish Historical Society* 43 (1953–1954): 199–229.

———. *Simon Willard's Letters to Paul Revere 1782–1786*. 1952.

Boston Board of Assessors. "Assessors 'Taking Books' of the Town of Boston, 1780," *The Bostonian Society Publications* 9 (1912), 9–59.

Bourne, Russell. "The Penobscot Fiasco." *American Heritage* (October 1974): 28–33, 100–101.

A Brief Sketch of the Business Life of Paul Revere. Taunton, MA: New Bedford Copper Co., 1928.

Brigham, Clarence S. *Paul Revere's Engravings*. Rev. ed., New York: Atheneum, 1969.

Buck, J.H. *Old Plate, Ecclesiastical, Decorative, and Domestic: Its Makers & Marks*. New York: The Gorham Manufacturing Company, 1888.

Buhler, Kathryn C. *American Silver*. Cleveland, OH: World Publishing Company, 1950.

———. *American Silver, 1655–1825, in the Museum of Fine Arts*. 2 vols. Boston: The Museum of Fine Arts, 1972.

———. *American Silver from the Colonial Period through the Early Republic in the Worcester Art Museum*. Worcester, MA: Worcester Art Museum, 1979.

———. "The Ledgers of Paul Revere." *Museum of Fine Arts Bulletin* (June 1936): 38–45.

———. "Master and Apprentice: some relationships in New England Silversmithing." *Antiques* 68 (November 1955): 456–60.

———. *Masterpieces of American Silver*. Richmond, VA: The Virginia Museum of Fine Arts, 1960.

———. *Paul Revere, Goldsmith 1735–1818*. Boston: Museum of Fine Arts, 1956.

———. "Paul Revere, Patriot and Silversmith." *Discovering Antiques* 57 (1971): 1350–1354.

———. "Three Teapots with Some Accessories." *Museum of Fine Arts Bulletin* 61 (1963): 52–64.

——— & Hood, Graham. *American Silver, Garvan, and Other Collections in the Yale University Art Gallery*. 2 vols. New Haven, CT: Yale University Press, 1970.

Butler, Jon. *The Huguenots in America: A Refugee People in New World Society*. Cambridge, MA: Harvard University Press, 1983.

Cadman, Paul. *Boston and Some Noted Emigres*. Boston: State Street Bank and Trust Company, 1938.

Carr, Harry. *Six Hundred Years of Craft Ritual*. Grand Lodge of Missouri, 1977.

Chamberlain, Georgina S. "Morits Fürst, Diesinker and Artist." *The Numismatist* (June 1954).

Clayton, Michael. *The Collector's Dictionary of the Silver and Gold of Great Britain and North America*. 2nd ed., Suffolk, England: Baron Publishing for the Antique Collector's Club, Ltd., 1985.

The Constitutions of the Ancient and Honorable Fraternity of Free and Accepted Masons Containing their History, Charges, Addresses and Collected and Digested from their Old

Records, Faithful Traditions and Lodge Books. For the Use of Masons to which are added the History of Masonry in the Commonwealth of Massachusetts, and the Constitution, Laws and Regulations of their Grand Lodge together with a Large Collection of Songs, Epilogues, etc. Worcester, MA: Massachusetts Grand Lodge, 1792.

Cooper, Wendy A. In Praise of America. New York: Alfred A. Knopf, 1980.

_____. "Paul Revere's Boston." Antiques 108 (July 1975): 80–93.

Diderot Encyclopedia. The Complete Illustrations, 1763–1777. 4 vols. New York: Harry N. Abrams, Inc. Publishers, 1978.

Dow, George Francis. The Arts and Crafts in New England 1764–1775. Topsfield, MA: The Wayside Press, 1927.

Dresser, Louisa. "American and English Silver Given in Memory of Frederick William Paine, 1866–1935." Worcester Art Museum Annual 2 (1936–1937): 89–98.

Fales, Martha Gandy. Early American Silver. Rev. ed., New York: Excalibur Books, 1970.

_____. Joseph Richardson and Family, Philadelphia Silversmiths. Middletown, CT: Wesleyan University Press, 1974.

Federhen, Deborah. "Revere Re-examined." Winterthur Newsletter (Summer, 1985).

Fennimore, Donald L. "Elegant Patterns of Uncommon Good Taste: Domestic Silver by Thomas Fletcher and Sidney Gardiner," Unpublished master's thesis. University of Delaware, June 1972.

Flynt, Henry N. and Fales, Martha Gandy. The Heritage Foundation Collection of Silver With Biographical Sketches of New England Silversmiths, 1625–1825. Deerfield, MA: The Heritage Foundation, 1968.

Forbes, Esther. Paul Revere and the World He Lived In. Boston: Houghton Mifflin Company, 1942.

Fowler, William M., Jr. "Disaster in Penobscot Bay." Harvard Magazine (July–August 1979): 26–31.

Friedman, Ruth L. "Artisan to Entrepreneur: The Business Life of Paul Revere." Unpublished research paper, Paul Revere Memorial Association Library, 1978.

Gillingham, Harrold E. "Cesar Chiselin, Philadelphia's First Gold and Silversmith, 1693–1733." The Pennsylvania Magazine of History and Biography 57 (1933): 244–59.

Glover, John G., ed. The Development of American Industries and Their Economic Significance. New York, 1959.

Goler, Robert I. The Healing Arts in Early America. New York: Fraunces Tavern Museum, 1985.

Gordon, Ed. "Pierce-Hitchborn House Owners and Occupants 1781-1951." Unpublished research paper, PRMA Library.

Goss, Elbridge Henry. The Life of Colonel Paul Revere. 2 vols. Boston: Joseph George Cupples, 1891.

Grundy, Elizabeth and Triber, Jane. "Paul Revere's Children: Coming of Age in the New Nation." Unpublished research paper, PRMA Library.

Guillim, John. A Display of Heraldry. 6th ed, London: Printed by T.W. for R. and J. Bronwicke and R. Wilkin, and J. Walthoe and Thos. Ward, 1724.

Henretta, James. "Economic Development and Social Structure in Colonial Boston." William and Mary Quarterly 22 (January 1965): 75–92.

Hipkiss, Edwin J. "The Paul Revere Liberty Bowl." Museum of Fine Arts Bulletin 47 (1949).

_____. "The Paul Revere Room." Museum of Fine Arts Bulletin 29 (October 1931): 84–88.

History of St. John's Lodge of Boston. Boston, 1917.

Hood, Graham. American Silver. New York: Praeger Publishers, 1971.

Hoopes, Penrose R. Shop Records of Daniel Burnap, Clockmaker. Hartford, CT: The Connecticut Historical Society, 1979.

Jones, E. Alfred. The Old Silver of American Churches. Letchworth, England: National Society of the Colonial Dames of America, 1913.

Jones, Mervyn. "Freemasonry" in Norman MacKenzie, ed. Secret Societies. New York: Crescent Books, Inc., 1967.

Kauffman, Henry J. American Copper and Brass. Camden, NJ: T. Nelson, 1968, Reprint, New York: Bonanza Books, 1977.

_____. The Colonial Silversmith: His Techniques & His Products. New York: Galahad Books, 1969.

Kevitt, Chester B. Solomon Lovell and the Penobscot Expedition 1779. Weymouth, MA: Weymouth Historical Commission, 1976.

King, Louis C. "The Grand Lodge of Massachusetts, Birthplace of Freemasonry." Trowel 1 (April 1983): 4–7.

Kimball, James. "Orderly Book for the Regiment of Artillery Raised for the Defense of the Town of Boston 1776." Essex Institute Historical Collections, 13 (1876), 14 (1877).

Knox, Dudley, ed. *Naval Documents Relating to the Quasi War Between the United States and France.* 7 vols. Washington, D.C.: United States Government Printing Office, 1935–1938.

Koenig, David T. "A New Look at the Essex 'French' Ethnic Frictions in Seventeenth Century Essex County, Massachusetts." *Essex Institute Historical Collections* 10 (July 1974): 167–80.

Kornblith, Gary John. *From Artisans to Businessmen: Master Mechanics in New England, 1789–1850.* Ph.D. diss. Princeton University, June 1983.

Kutolowski, Kathleen Smith. "Freemasonry and Community in the Early Republic: The Case for Anti-Masonic Anxieties." *American Quarterly* 34 (Winter 1982): 543–61.

Labatut, Andre J. "Paul Revere, hero of the American Revolution (1735–1818) and his cousins of Sainte Foye en Agenais in France." Unpublished manuscript, New England Historic Genealogical Society, Boston and PRMA, Boston.

Levin, Alexandra Lee. "John Revere, M.D." *Maryland Magazine* (Autumn 1976): 10–13.

Lipson, Dorothy Ann. *Freemasonry in Federalist Connecticut 1789–1832.* Princeton: Princeton University Press, 1977.

The Lodge of Saint Andrew. *Centennial Memorial of the Lodge of St. Andrew.* Boston: The Lodge of St. Andrew, 1870.

The Lodge of Saint Andrew. *Commemoration of the One Hundred and Fiftieth Anniversary of the Lodge of St. Andrew 1756–1906.* Boston: The Lodge of St. Andrew, 1907.

Luddington, John. *Starting to Collect Silver.* Suffolk, England: Baron Publishing for the Antique Collectors' Club, Ltd., 1984.

Maier, Pauline. *From Resistance to Revolution.* New York: Vintage Books, A Division of Random House, 1974.

Maurer, Maurer. "Copper Bottoms for the United States Navy, 1794–1803." *The United States Naval Institute Proceedings*, 17 (June 1945).

The Metropolitan Museum of Art. *Paul Revere, A picture book.* Essay by Louise Condit. New York: The Metropolitan Museum of Art, 1944.

Montgomery, Charles F. & Patricia E. Kane, ed. *American Art: 1750–1800, Towards Independence.* Boston: The New York Graphic Society, 1976.

Morison, Samuel Eliot. *The Maritime History of Massachusetts, 1783–1860.* 6th ed. Boston: Houghton-Mifflin Co., 1961.

Mulholland, James A. *A History of Metals in Colonial America.* Birmingham, AL: University of Alabama Press, 1981.

———. *The Work of Seventeenth and Eighteenth Century Silversmiths.* Boston: Museum of Fine Arts, 1906.

Nichols, Arthur H. "The Early Bells of Paul Revere." *The New England Historical and Genealogical Register* 48 (April 1904): 151–57.

Parker, Henry J. *Army Lodges During the Revolution.* Boston, 1884.

"Paul Revere Project." Vertical File. Grand Lodge of Masons in Massachusetts.

Paul Revere's Three Accounts of His Famous Ride. Introduction by Edmund S. Morgan. Boston: Massachusetts Historical Society, 1968.

Phelps, Noah A. *A History of the Copper Mines and Newgate Prison at Granby, Connecticut.* Hartford, CT: Press of Case, Tiffany and Burnham, 1845.

Phillips, John Marshall. *American Silver.* New York: Chanticleer Press, 1949.

———. "Masterpieces in American Silver Part III: Ecclesiastical Silver." *Antiques* 55 (April 1949): 281–85.

———. "Masterpieces in American Silver Part IV: Rococco and Federal Periods." *Antiques* 55 (April and July 1949): 41–45.

———. *Masterpieces in New England Silver, 1650–1800.* Cambridge, MA: Printed at the Harvard University Press for the Associates in Fine Arts at Yale University, 1939.

Proceedings in Masonry, St. John's Grand Lodge 1733–1792: Massachusetts Grand Lodge 1769–1792. Boston: Grand Lodge of Masons in Massachusetts, 1895.

Proceedings of the Most Worshipful Grand Lodge of Ancient Free and Accepted Masons of the Commonwealth of Massachusetts in Union with the Most Ancient and Honorable Grand Lodge in Europe and America, According to the Old Constitutions, 1792–1815. Cambridge, MA: Press of Caustic-Claflin Co., 1905.

Report of the Committee of Commerce and Manufactures, To Whom Were Referred, On the Second and Thirteenth of November, and the Eighteenth of December Last, the Petitions and Memorial of Paul and Joseph W. Revere, of Boston in the State of Massachusetts, of Sundry Coppersmiths in the City and Liberties of Philadelphia, and of Sundry Manufacturers of Copper in the City of New York. Washington, 1808.

191

Revere, Herbert Eugene and Rodgers, Robert. *A Record of Ancestors and Descendents of Paul Revere*. Unpublished manuscript NEHGS and PRMA.

Reynolds, Clark G. *Command of the Sea, the History and Strategy of Maritime Empires*. New York: William Morrow and Company, 1974.

Roberts, Allen E. *The Craft and Its Symbols: Opening the Door to Masonic Symbols*. Richmond, VA: Macoy Publishing and Masonic Supply Company, Inc., 1974.

Roelker, Nancy L. *The French Huguenots: An Embattled Minority*. St. Louis, 1977.

Ross, Jane. "Paul Revere—Patriot Engraver." *Early American Life* 6 (April 1975): 36–37.

Roth, Rodris. "Tea Drinking in Eighteenth-Century America: Its Etiquette and Equipage." *U.S. National Museum Bulletin* 225, Contributions from the Museum of History and Technology. Washington, D.C.: Smithsonian Institution, 1961.

Safford, Frances Gruber. "Colonial Silver in the American Wing." *The Metropolitan Museum of Art Bulletin* 41 (Summer 1983).

Scheiber, Henry N., Vatter, Harold G., and Faulkner, Harold U. *American Economic History*. New York: Harper and Row, 1973.

Schelling, Graham. "Paul Revere's Boston." *Americana* 3 (May 1975): 2–7.

Shipton, Clifford K. *Sibley's Harvard Graduates*. 17 vols. Boston: Massachusetts Historical Society, 1975.

Skerry, Janine E. "Regionalism in American Neoclassical Silver." *The 1987 Washington Antiques Show Catalogue*. Washington, D.C.: The Thrift Shop Charities, 1987.

Steblecki, Edith J. *Paul Revere and Freemasonry*. Boston: Paul Revere Memorial Association, 1985.

Stevens, Benjamin F. *The Silver Punch Bowl Made By Paul Revere*. Boston, 1895.

Stickney, Edward and Stickney, Evelyn. *The Bells of Paul Revere, his sons and grandsons*. Bedford, MA, 1976.

Taylor, Earl W. *Historical Sketch of the Grand Lodge of Masons in Massachusetts From Its Beginnings in 1733 to the Present Time*. Boston: Grand Lodge of Masons in Massachusetts, 1973.

Thomas, M. Halsey, ed. *The Diary of Samuel Sewell 1674–1729*. New York: Farrar, Strauss and Giroux, 1973.

Tourtellot, Arthur B. *Lexington and Concord*. New York: W.W. Norton Co., 1959.

Two Hundred and Fifty Years of Massachusetts Masonry. Grand Lodge of Masons in Massachusetts. Boston: Rapid Service Press, 1983.

Vaughn, William Preston. *The Anti-Masonic Party in the United States, 1826-1843*. Lexington, KY: The University of Kentucky Press, 1983.

Volborth, Carl-Alexander von. *Heraldry Customs, Roles, and Styles*. Poole, Dorset England: Blanford Press, 1983.

Ward, Barbara McLean. "Boston Goldsmiths, 1690–1730" in Ian M.G. Quimby, ed. *The Craftsman in Early America*. Winterthur, DE: Henry Francis du Pont Winterthur Museum, 1984.

_____ and Gerald W.R. Ward. *Silver in American Life*. New Haven, CT: Yale University Art Gallery, 1979.

Weisberger, Barnard A. "Paul Revere, the man, the myth, and the midnight ride." *American Heritage* 28 (April 1977): 24–37.

Whitehill, Walter Muir et al. *Paul Revere's Boston 1735–1818*. Boston: Museum of Fine Arts, 1975.

Whiteman, Maxwell. *Copper for America, The Hendricks Family and a National Industry, 1755–1939*. New Brunswick, NJ: Rutgers University Press, 1971.

Wood, Gordon S., ed. *The Rising Glory of America 1760–1820*. New York: George Braziller, 1971.

Worcester Art Museum. *Paul Revere 1735–1818: The events of his life painted by A. Cassell Ripley and some examples of his silver and prints*. Worcester, Mass.: Worcester Art Museum, 1965.

Wyman, Thomas, Jr., ed. "Records of the New Brick Church." *New England Historical and Genealogical Register* 18 (1864); 19 (1865).

Younge, Greaves and Hoyland, *Trade Catalogue*. Sheffield, England, ca. 1790.

Zieber, Eugene. *Heraldry in America*. Reprint, New York: Greenwich House, 1985.

Zimmer, Ed. "Early History of the Pierce-Hitchborn House Property and Residents." Unpublished research paper, PRMA.